ORGANIZATIONS FOR PEOPLE

ORGANIZATIONS FOR PEOPLE

CARING CULTURES, BASIC NEEDS, AND BETTER LIVES

MICHAEL O'MALLEY

AND

WILLIAM F. BAKER

STANFORD BUSINESS BOOKS
AN IMPRINT OF STANFORD UNIVERSITY PRESS
STANFORD, CALIFORNIA

Stanford University Press
Stanford, California

Special discounts for bulk quantities of Stanford Business Books are available to corporations, professional associations, and other organizations. For details and discount information, contact the special sales department of Stanford University Press. Tel: (650) 725-0820, Fax: (650) 725-3457

Printed in the United States of America on acid-free, archival-quality paper

Library of Congress Cataloging-in-Publication Data

Names: O'Malley, Michael, date- author. | Baker, William F., date- author.
Title: Organizations for people : caring cultures, basic needs, and better lives / Michael O'Malley and William F. Baker.
Description: Stanford, California : Stanford Business Books, an imprint of Stanford University Press, 2020. | Includes bibliographical references and index. Identifiers: LCCN 2019010218 (print) | LCCN 2019011675 (ebook) | ISBN 9781503611054 (electronic) | ISBN 9781503602540 (cloth; alk. paper)
Subjects: LCSH: Personnel management. | Personnel management—Psychological aspects. | Quality of work life. | Psychology, Industrial.
Classification: LCC HF5549 (ebook) | LCC HF5549 .O515 2019 (print) | DDC 658.3/14—dc23
LC record available at https://lccn.loc.gov/2019010218

Cover design: Rob Ehle

Typeset by Classic Typography in 10/14 Minion

To the 21 companies who created humane workplaces and opened their doors to us to reveal what good businesses can look like, and in memory of James Berger who led with vision and respect

CONTENTS

FOREWORD

Rachel S. Moore
President and CEO
The Music Center
Los Angeles, California

I can still see their faces as I walk up to the podium. Written all over them is the question, "What could she possibly have to say about running a business? A former professional ballet dancer and philosophy major . . . how is she even employed?" Yes, it is an unusual combination. Yet when I describe my background, I push back on the stereotypes. I argue that my past as a performing artist and my background in ethics and political philosophy inform my work as a CEO numerous times every day. In fact, it is *because* of these experiences that I believe values-based leadership is critical to the development of high-functioning teams in the 21st century.

For many the notion of being a professional ballet dancer is glamorous. One imagines performing on stages around the world and not having to deal with the day-to-day challenges of a "regular" job. The reality is, being a professional dancer is extremely difficult, highly stressful work, where one is compelled to perform at a very high level at all times, even through injury and illness, because "the show must go on." For me, dancing with the American Ballet Theatre in the 1980s was both a great honor and an emotional journey. At that time the dancers were treated not as respected, highly trained professionals, but as cogs in a much larger mechanism, a ballet production. We were told to be silent and obedient. Dancers were often punished—by not getting opportunities to perform certain roles—for speaking out, for asking questions, and for trying to demonstrate some personal efficacy or wanting to have some control over their professional lives. Repeatedly, we were told to "shut up and do as you are told."

This daily marginalization was corrosive to the spirit. It created an inordinate level of low morale among the artistic talent, the company's greatest asset, and compelled many of its gifted employees to look for other professional opportunities or, even worse, leave the field altogether. Consider the fact that one must train like an Olympic athlete, seven days per week for years on end, to become a professional dancer, and you can see how this loss of expertise would be a considerable drain on the productivity of the institution.

While I recognized something was wrong with this treatment and that my colleagues and I would perform better and longer if we were treated with dignity and support, I was not able at that time to articulate my misgivings. It seemed this was the way ballet companies were supposed to function, and there were no options to change that.

After dancing professionally for seven years, I succumbed to a foot injury. As a result, I left my burgeoning ballet career to attend a university. Pursuing a college degree was a revelation for me. When I arrived, my self-esteem was so low I could barely speak in public, which is notable since as a child I was quite outspoken. My experience as a dancer had crushed my self-confidence and silenced my "voice." Luckily, I ended up at a university with a supportive culture and found a subject to study, Ethics and Political Philosophy, that proved not only revelatory but also restorative.

My major was extraordinary, but it was one book, *A Theory of Justice* by John Rawls, that proved foundational in the development of my management style. In short, Rawls was seeking to answer the question, "What constitutes a just society?" and his answer was rooted in justice as fairness. I modified this question to be, "What constitutes a just workplace?" and, similarly, I have come to believe that fairness is required for a just workplace. This is the kind of workplace that O'Malley and Baker passionately and convincingly portray in their wonderful book, *Organizations for People*. I knew what a workplace lacking in justice or fairness looked like (and how unproductive that can be). What I wanted to understand were the characteristics of a workplace managed with a sense of fairness and dignity. From this question I framed the notion of leadership around a simple premise: *While an employer cannot treat everyone equally, a true leader should treat every employee as a moral equal.*

Throughout my years working in the nonprofit sector, I have sought to operationalize this foundational value. Whether it was increasing the flexibility in work hours for young parents or those with aging or ill family members, eliminating numerical scoring methodologies in the annual review process, holding authentic discussions of employee goals and accomplishments, or introducing new professional development opportunities for artists and staff, I tried to support "the whole person" rather than see employees as means to an organizational end.

Now, as president and CEO of The Music Center, one of the largest performing arts centers in the country, which is home to thousands of employees, I am seeking to further institutionalize the notion of treating every staff member as a moral equal. I believe this approach not only creates a more productive workplace, but also makes sound business sense. By treating every patron, employee, and constituent in this fashion, the Music Center team is positioning both our organization and the performing arts more generally for relevancy in the 21st century.

The first steps we took to reframe our organization included transforming our work to be both top-down and bottom-up and rooting every interaction in the idea of service: service to one another, service to our mission, and service to the public. We believe we must work from a moral center, guided by our commitment to compassion and social justice. Each day we seek to make the Music Center a welcoming place for all in Los Angeles County, regardless of background, and as Music Center employees we seek to treat one another with the same respect and care that we extend to those who visit us as tourists, audiences, or creators.

Through these efforts the Music Center has evolved into a much more inclusive and diverse organization, one that is truly representative of the people of Los Angeles County. Not surprisingly, our programmatic offerings have also been transformed and have become increasingly successful, both financially and in terms of social relevancy.

An example is our highly popular *Sleepless: The Music Center After Hours* program. With an eye to increasing the diversity of our audiences, we created a low-cost program that runs from 11:30 p.m. to 3:00 a.m. We transform our theaters from palaces of high art to comfortable and deeply creative spaces with participatory programs, DJs, live bands, dance, visual art, craft projects, performance art, and more in a setting of beanbag chairs, cocktails, and general conviviality. This program draws in audiences of all races and ages, and it typically sells out in hours, with people waiting in long lines, hoping to be let in.

Our *Sleepless* program would never have been developed in an atmosphere that did not value diversity, relish inclusion, and deeply respect those from all walks of life. This type of work can happen only when these values are embraced across the organization.

Because I believe values-based management is the best way to develop and support an organization, I was thrilled when I learned that Bill Baker and Michael O'Malley were writing *Organizations for People*. Their efforts to raise awareness of the importance of this leadership approach and to provide successful examples across industries is very welcome in our world. My hope is that this approach, which highlights the power of working from a moral center and the importance of human dignity, will be adopted broadly and embraced deeply. To quote Desmond Tutu, "My humanity is bound up in yours, for we can only be human together." And only together can we achieve greatness in the workplace and in our community.

ACKNOWLEDGMENTS

We are grateful to many people who either endured our preoccupation with this book, such as family members, or who directly nurtured its completion through material support or comments on drafts of the manuscript. Specifically, we are thankful for tolerant spouses, Stephanie and Jeanmarie. The incisive edits and suggestions made by Madeleine Broder, Julie Adams, Christine Porath, Rick Boyatzis, and anonymous reviewers helped to shape and substantiate the final product. Each invigorated our efforts to bring to light a new, meaningful way to manage and conduct business. Additionally, we are indebted to Barbara Slifka and Bernard Schwartz for their continuing support of our research, and to Dan Ritchie for his ever-present benevolence and guidance. Finally, we are grateful to Stanford University Press who saw the promise of this project and provided expert editorial assistance in the forms of Steve Catalano, Sunna Juhn, and Jeffrey Wyneken.

ORGANIZATIONS FOR PEOPLE

INTRODUCTION

This book features the stories of 21 companies that have been cited as best places to work. We made visits to each, and it is clear why they have earned their reputations. Most of the organizations began their existence in the past 25 years. They range in size from roughly 100 employees to 5,000, and from $50 million in revenues to $5 billion. All of the people-related practices used in these organizations can be adopted by much-larger companies. For example, Costco with 250,000 employees and astounding net profit margins of 27 percent is a practitioner of the people-centric ethic we espouse in this book. If a barrier to implementation exists, it likely is self-imposed. Large size is not an inevitable confinement; everything discussed in this book can be scaled up or down to suit the needs of organizations of any size. (The companies are described in the Appendix.)

With a few exceptions the companies in our sample are privately held. However, a private structure is not a necessary condition to earn a place among the most admired companies. Many exceptions, including companies in our sample, exist. The usual assumption is that publicly traded companies must satisfy their investors first and foremost and, of necessity, sacrifice the welfare of the workforce when the needs of shareholders and employees conflict. A moral argument that elevates the interests of some over others based on investment dollars, however, is flimsy and appalling. This claim is like saying that paying customers to a theatrical venue must be evacuated first in case of fire; those who received free tickets or snuck in through the back door have to wait until the moneyed patrons have safely exited. Of course, customers may say that the only way they will buy tickets to a venue is if they get to exit first from a burning building. But then we would have to question what kind of venue would acquiesce to such a demand, and the kind of people who would make it.

Although we do not consider the practices of 21 companies to constitute a conclusive study, these companies provide a robust set of practices that make sense. None of the organizations we visited would say that they are perfect—good companies never would—but they are very good at creating congenial and stimulating work environments and have forced us to rethink where true organizational value lies and about what really matters.

Our plan is to intersperse the stories of these organizations, and others, with information from the social sciences to reveal the principles any company can adapt and follow in its unique ways. Our stories and examples are thus illustrative of concepts that can be modified to suit the inclinations of any organization. The book contains many examples. If we do not associate a company with a particular practice or offering, it does not mean it does not have it. Rather than overwhelm with redundancy, we pick and choose the best examples for given issues or ideas. What's more, the companies in our sample are continuously refreshing or replacing their programs. Therefore, between the times of our visits and the appearance of this book, there is a good chance that a program described herein will have changed.

The companies we selected for inclusion appeared on one of several of the "best companies to work for" lists over the past three years, either on consecutive years or on more than one list in a given year. The companies we selected also had to be geographically dispersed and represent various industries. Thus, the companies are located in different regions of the United States and span financial services, pharmaceuticals, hospitality, manufacturing, retail, consulting, distribution, consumer goods, and technology. And, naturally, the companies had to agree to meet with us and be willing to dedicate six to eight hours of one day to our visit. These visits included interviews with executives, discussions with members of the human resources department, focus groups with cross-functional samples of employees, and tours of facilities.

With regard to nomenclature in the book, we use the familiar references to "human resources" and "employees" throughout, duly acknowledging that many departments are not named "human resources" nor are staff called "employees." Commonly, for example, human resources appropriately is seen as a "people" department and employees are referred to as associates, members, or by some demonym. Employees at Patagonia are Patagoniacs and employees at The Motley Fool are Fools. In general, the companies in our sample are loathe to use the word "employee" since it denotes a contractual and subservient relationship versus organizations' preferred way of thinking about people as "owners," "associates," or "members" of a team.

Finally, until someone comes up with inclusive terminology for gender, we alternate between "she" and "he" by chapter.

Licensure

This book is partially argument and partially practical application. The argument is that in business's unidimensional pursuit of financial success it has cordoned off a vast segment of life and exempted it from the kinds of civil behaviors we expect in other areas of our lives. Businesses falsely function with their own social conventions that are far too accepting of behaviors on the outskirts of collegial, kind, or good.

Indeed, when describing managers, we are far too loose and permissive with what it means to be good. We generally equate technical skill with "good." A good carpenter is one who can flawlessly execute a repair or build a sturdy structure that is true to specifications using the right materials. Similarly, fulfilling the objectives of the job is interpreted as good and, often, as good enough. The better the results, presumably the more "good" one is. However, it is easy to think of examples in which getting results is not good enough. Dr. Larry Nasser is an osteopath who was the lead doctor for the United States' gymnastics team. He was the go-to physician for sports injuries for many of the elite female gymnasts. Today he sits in prison for having sexually abused 332 of them—for restoring the physical health of the athletes while inflicting permanent lifetime wounds. No matter how competent he may have been in his profession, he was not a good doctor.

Most activities in which we can cause harm to others require a license or certification before we can practice. The certification applies to the ability to practice as well as to the implicit or explicit agreement to perform one's duties with due care and for the right motives. Chauffeurs, lifeguards, and physicians must meet qualifying criteria before undertaking their chosen occupations. We place no such demands on managers. Instead, we entrust lives to people who may be unsuited for their positions and who in fact may cause significant psychological and physical damage. To continue the analogy, placing people into jobs as managers is often like letting people who are good at working on cars drive, or people who can swim lifeguard. That is, we accept people who show mechanical proficiency even though that knowledge does not translate into the ability to drive or save lives; nor does it ensure that a person has the right attitude toward his chosen line of work. A lifeguard who cannot place another's life above his own—who fears for his own safety in an emergency—is not a good lifeguard.

Attitudes are paramount. We do not know of anything in the capitalist's manifesto that prohibits managers from treating employees kindly, and vice versa, as part of a bundle of leadership capabilities. If the presumption is that capable, profit-making management should be cool to the way people are treated, then our vision of business is terribly flawed. The flaws are due not necessarily to a failed exegesis of how markets work, but to gross misconceptions of how people work. People have reasonable expectations of being treated in ways that are conducive to their well-being. We cannot possibly promise people a good life through work and then rob them of the very nutrients they need to live well within the workplace.

In the first part of the book, then, we look at the status of *people* within organizations and question those aspects of business that cripple the abilities of people to live healthier and more creative, productive, and satisfying lives. Our argument is not that treating people well is good for business—although it is—but that it is good for people.[1] Hand-wringers who worry that this may be a diversion from the primary aim of business, namely profit, miss the ultimate point of business, which is to improve quality of life. Regarding employees as impartial bystanders on the road to a better life is counterproductive to that aim.

Human Needs

This book is not a sermon on the mischief making of shortsighted profit taking, although we can say how that sermon ends: not well for mankind, who in just a fragment of planetary time has achieved what no other earthly inhabitant has done before (we will leave that as a cliffhanger). Perhaps by simply directing an ethical focus on what people are owed by virtue of their humanness, we will spur deeper moral deliberations in other spheres of our lives that suffer at the hands of self-interest. For now, our purpose is to demand better leadership from our leaders, which is the explanatory mission of the first part of the book.

When we ask managers merely to perform their duties and to be an instrument within a money-making apparatus, we are asking them to do far too little. This formulation only asks managers to follow a simpleton financial script that frees them from the ethical quandaries that defy easy solution. This brute doctrine requires little finesse. We are not asking ourselves tough questions about what is most important in life. Instead, we seize upon economic alchemy to escape the civic responsibilities we have toward one another, erroneously believing that through agnostic business dealings the good life will trickle down. We can be much more direct by insisting that leaders foster human potential and support human flourishing as obligations of their role. If we do not have any deeper aims for business, then for whom and for what do we go through all the trouble?

Those who may worry that we risk losing our competitive advantage by taking our eye off the profit motive can rest assured that the eyes of those whose needs are given up at the altar of money are not following the corporate news very carefully anyway. They have more important concerns. There is debate about exactly what those concerns are, but we believe that academic psychologist Carol Ryff has it about right in her articulation of universal needs.[2,3] Ryff originally developed her ideas of well-being—what people need to flourish—by synthesizing accounts of quality of life from philosophy, the humanities, and social sciences. The set of needs she proposes substantially overlaps with, or subsumes, those laid out in other need theories.[4,5] We are therefore confident that her list covers needs that are generally agreed upon as essential for individuals' happiness and personal welfare. The way companies meet these needs is the subject of Part 2 of the book.

The results of Ryff's work yield six needs. Below, where two terms are listed for an individual need, the first is the nomenclature used by Ryff and the second is the one we use in the chapter headings.

Positive relations / Belonging: Has warm, pleasurable, and trusting relationships with others; feels connected and accepted by others

Purpose in life / Meaning: Believes that one has important aims in life and a clear sense of direction

Autonomy: Freely acts according to one's standards, values, and beliefs

Self-Acceptance: Holds a positive evaluation of oneself, accepting of who one is inclusive of strengths and imperfections

Environmental mastery / Confidence: Competently manages one's life, maintaining personal composure, control, and efficacy in problematic and emotion-infused situations

Personal growth: Progressively develops expertise and continuously
   advances toward personal potential

There is an abundance of proof that employees whose needs are fulfilled
are more satisfied with their lives as well as more creative and productive at
work.[6] In general, people who are thriving fare better in all domains of their
lives: physical, psychological, social, familial, occupational, economic, and
spiritual. However, as Maslow famously argued, it is difficult for people to
aspire to personal fulfillment when their most basic needs for safety and security are unmet.[7] Only monastics can find fulfillment through deprivation; the
rest of us, those devoted to finding our way in this earthly realm, need help.
Consequently, we discuss the need for minimum material welfare as a precur-
sor to our treatment of the other needs covered in Part 2.

PART 1

KINDNESS IN THE WORKPLACE

CHAPTER 1

M O

Create a culture of respect

James was driving along a dark stretch of highway. There is not much more he remembers. He remembers being lifted into the emergency vehicle. He remembers the lights. He wrested his phone from his pocket and managed to hit the right keys. "Len, I think I've been in an accident."

Len is not a family member. Len Schleifer is the president and CEO of Regeneron, a progressive, growing biotechnology company located in Tarrytown, New York. James is a senior manager. He thought of calling Len first because Len would know what to do.

Roland was fishing off the coast of Key West, Florida. When he had not returned by dusk, his family became alarmed. They called Paul. Paul is the CEO of a transportation company in Key West and Roland is one of his employees. Paul also is a licensed pilot and as soon as he heard the news that Roland was missing, he notified authorities and joined the search by air. They found Roland on one of the deserted islands that dot the area. He had abandoned his capsized boat and swum two hours through choppy waters to land.

These are not typical people to call in emergencies. Yet these calls from employees and their families to company executives illustrate the types of relationships we observed within premier organizations. These calls and the quick reactions of executives are typical of people who trust and care deeply for one another.

Most of us have gone through half our working lives believing that close relationships of the sort depicted in these accounts are impossible within organizations; we think it best to keep work relationships, especially those that traverse grade levels, businesslike or at arm's length. We refrain from revealing too much that is personal, or counting on one another beyond basic courtesies. Our impulses tell us not to get too close for fear our social and business affairs will become enmeshed and complicate our lives. We worry that our feelings may interfere with the icy reasoning that is presumed needed for effective decision-making.

All of this is a business fable that promotes an untruth. Yes, close relationships sometimes crumble, badly. However, relationships that embody loving concern and compassion are more pleasurable, mutually beneficial, and durable than those that are missing warm bonds and fellow feeling. Healthy, close relationships make productive social living easier, not harder.

We have no doubts about the kind of organizations employees prefer. Employees will take their chances on companies like Regeneron where people have genuine affection for one another and are able to grow while doing their best work. They prefer organizations where friendly relations and trust prevail. They prefer to be free from the interpersonal turmoil and political intrigue of combative workplaces. Employees, in fact, want to work in companies whose operational premise is kindness.

Do Employees Matter?

Bill and I are on a mission. We want to change the way organizations are managed. Given the preponderance of evidence and stockpile of human experiences that indicate what good and bad management look like, we would expect to see more of the former and less of the latter. We do not. In practice, many organizations seem stuck on worn-out theories and antiquated notions of management, and are hesitant to embrace truer, more invigorating forms of organization. Companies remain too accommodating of managerial abominations who take them perilously close to new-age sweatshops. Without changes in our attitudes toward the way people should conduct themselves and relate to others in the workplace, our fear is that institutions will linger in an aged form, and on the wrong side of history, longer.

When it comes to people, companies seem out of step. Despite the known value of leadership in improving employee welfare and productivity, most of the glory for gains in corporate productivity are attributed to capital improvements, financial maneuvers, and technological advances. We credit the efficiencies of new machines, the facility of intelligent systems, the advances of momentous innovations, and the accretion of smart investments for corporate progressiveness. In contrast, we attend too little to our management practices, which, sans soot and grime, remain archaically mired in an age of "dark satanic mills" (as decried by William Blake).

Unvarnished capitalism seems well past its prime. But we do not need a new economic system; we need a variation on a theme that is more just and responsive to the human condition. We need more talk about quality of life alongside GDP, productivity, cost containment, and jobs, for better financial results do not ensure better lives.[1] To enhance human welfare, we will need institutions that are prepared to refute an ethos of selfishness and survival and boldly embrace corporate communities that are more receptive to human virtues.

As we were writing this book, many people wanted to know the secret of exemplary companies that perform and grow while creating humanizing cultures. Although each company contains mystery ingredients particular to its success, all companies have one ingredient in common that rises above the others. Every reader of this book can wager a guess as to what that is—and win. It is perceptive, inspirational leadership. This revelation may disappoint since it is a cliché; however, it also should comfort since it confirms what is known to be true: companies absorb and personify the values and attitudes of their leaders.[2] We need great leaders to show the way.

The corporate founders we spoke with built their companies with people in mind. They coupled a market idea with a workplace where people could thrive. They created places where a healthy culture is as important as a healthy balance sheet.[3] These founders' goals are to provide the organizational nutrients analogous to soil, air, water, and sun that allow people to develop their capabilities and to flourish.[4] Their goal is to fulfill human potential.

If the goal of organizations is to keep employees psychologically well nourished, the prognosis is not good. Only 20 percent of the adult population describe themselves as flourishing, defined as mentally healthy. The World Health Organization describes mental health as a state where people are able to realize their capabilities, tolerate normal daily stresses, work productively and beneficially, and contribute to their communities.[5] Business has plenty of opportunity to transform the workplace and contribute to the well-being of millions of people.

People-centric Companies

The companies we visited are built on uncompromising ethical foundations and strong cultures. These cultures unobtrusively establish ideological boundaries that operate to produce close, trusting communities of motivated actors. The chief executive establishes the culture on which the institution rests. Human resources is charged with strengthening, modifying, and sustaining the culture. In this regard, human resources functions as the chief cultural (or, as we prefer, behavioral) officer of the company as well as the chief advocate for employees. The latter role is tantamount to policy prescription. Do what is best for employees provided it is not conspicuously harmful to the organization. Doing the right thing for people does not require an irrefutable business rationale to be enacted. If a decision makes business sense and is good for employees, that is reason enough.

The human resource role of chief cultural officer puts human resources at the epicenter of all organizational activity. This is not the human resources lampooned in magazines and derided as unnecessary.[6] This human resources is strikingly operationally efficient and the primary arbiter of the few prickly employee relations problems it encounters. Most importantly, this human resources spends the majority of its time perfecting the culture and upgrading the human experience.

Accordingly, human resources does not have to fight for its place at the table and prove its worth by demonstrating that its function is as analytical as finance or as business savvy as strategic planning. The chief executive pulls up a chair for human resources to sit among equals, realizing the importance of a function that creates the environment where people can do their best work and, on Sunday night, look forward to Monday morning.

The reversal of human resources from corporate acolyte to employee advocate is described by Health Catalyst, a leader in data warehousing, analytics, and outcomes improvements in the healthcare industry, as "the harder path." The path is harder because Health Catalyst prefers to operate with a minimal handbook and to resolve employee dilemmas as they come. The company acknowledges the many gray areas in life and understands that ambiguous situations cannot be unraveled formulaically. It is the harder path because it forces organizations to stray from the reflexive application of rules, to think through the issues, and to arrive at solutions that work. Most importantly, this path reframes the employer-employee relationship as collaborative versus dogmatic. One member of human resources told us about his relief in coming to Health Catalyst: "At my old company, my job was to make sure people weren't doing what they wanted to do. Now my job is to figure out ways to make team members happier, more effective, and more productive." When organizations create inflexible sets of rules, a large part of the human resource mission becomes one of compliance: correcting people when they have strayed from standards. As a result, human resources frequently is designed as the "Office of No."

Health Catalyst believes that people can be counted on to conduct themselves in principled ways: in ways that policies may guide but seldom determine. It is a risk that Health Catalyst is willing to take. It trusts in the decisions that people will make on behalf of the company, rather than orchestrating human activity and condensing it into controllable, bite-size pieces at the cost of disenfranchising the majority and locking up a large quantity of human potential. Besides, what really is the alternative when the health and welfare of a team member's child, say, conflicts with a corporate policy? The response should be a given; it is at Health Catalyst. The only thing that remains to be done is to think of a workable solution for the family: to navigate the gray area between cold policy and sumptuous overkill.

Much of the work of human resources is subtle. Since culture is the product of accumulated experiences, it cannot be issued on demand by clever slogans and edicts and magically spread through the company like a vapor moving through ventilation ducts. Rather, it is up to human resources to engineer a setting that provides the right incentives and experiences, and incites proper employee conduct each day of the year.

The ancient Chinese text *Xunzi* has a word, *mo*, that means to "rub up against." The word is a reference to the social power of constructed environments, to the ways we brush up against each other daily and the effects these many minute encounters cumulatively have on our attitudes and the quality of our relationships. These brushes convey the feel and effect of many social pleasures or, by contrast, many small harms that, like repeat abrasions, subtly erode our confidence that others are well meaning and that we are people of worth.[7,8]

Concord Hospitality, a preeminent developer, management company, and hotelier, gets this and strives to make interactions mutually rewarding. Debra, the senior vice president of human resources at Concord Hospitality, told us: "Culture cannot be implemented; it has to be lived and breathed." Culture is built one person at a time. One principled and kind person forms a relationship with other like-minded people who form relations with others of similar persuasion to create a network of actors who share a common set of beliefs and worldviews. The system coheres through values and mutual concern; it cannot be methodically assembled and bolted together like an IKEA table. It is a system built on the foundation of attachments. To prevent fissures from developing, executives work hard to ensure that everything that is said, signified, and done comports with a kind regard for every individual and with the values of the organization. For example, Concord communicates about culture *every day* ("Culture Item of the Day") as part of the huddles that take place each morning among staff (conducted at each site). The Ritz-Carlton does the same during their daily line-ups, in which a portion of the meeting is reserved for "wow" stories where service staff describe how they turned a guest's problem into a magical experience.[9,10]

Like Concord, the other companies we met with are masters at *mo*, shaping and guiding behavior through incisive cues and norms as opposed to formal rules and policies. Through the aegis of human resources, companies guide employees by deftly structured influences that bring out their better selves. In fact, Health Catalyst is not the only company among our group that has chosen to rely less upon the employee handbook in favor of less invasive regulatory tactics. At The Motley Fool—the go-to source for honest investment advice for the masses—policy prescriptions are scant to the point where everything that is not illegal or unethical is optional. As illustration, Fools are free to PYOD, pick your own device. The technology department provides everyone with a budget and allows employees to select their technology of choice, replenishing their equipment every three years. The techs readily admit that this privilege increases their workload, but it also increases the productivity of employees since they are using tools with which they are familiar.

Rules of Engagement

The management scholar Warren Bennis calls respect one of the two essential attributes of effective leadership; trust is the other.[11] Employees agree. Employees value respect more than anything else in the workplace, and yet fewer than half of employees say they feel regularly respected at work.[12] This is a troubling statistic as it reflects the difference between feeling seen and appreciated versus insubstantial and expendable. Take Maritza, whom we met at the elite flavors company FONA (Flavors of North America). Maritza started working at FONA and found her true passion in facilities, where she has risen to supervisor. "I never thought I would find a place to grow and where people respected me. People made fun of my speech and writing [she is a native Spanish speaker] at my last job [with another employer]. Here, people just want to help." The same story is true for Alberto, who has been promoted five times since being selected directly out of high school. FONA believes in people and does not rely on superficial characteristics and invalid impressions of true abilities to guide its decisions.

Respect means taking people seriously, treating them as responsible agents, and giving earnest consideration to their points of views and personal interests. Showing consideration acknowledges that we are alike and share "hands, organs, dimensions, senses, affections, passions" as part of the genus human being.[13] "Respecting someone, we take care not to do various things to him or to let various things happen to him."[14] TCG, a premier IT consultancy to government agencies, would concur. When clients treat TCG's employees poorly, the company intercedes. TCG expects everyone with whom they do business to adhere to high ethical standards, not as self-righteousness but to protect the work experiences and dignity of its people. Indeed, federal law holds employers responsible for shielding their employees from the capricious actions of clients. Companies like TCG, Cisco Systems, and others put the onus on the client to change, or risk getting dropped.[15]

One of the ways to show respect is to be polite and considerate. Practicing good manners toward people is essential to truly respecting them.[16] In all companies we visited, rudeness was taboo. No screamers, fit-throwers, or bullies. Many of the companies subscribe to a formal "no jerks allowed" doctrine and are quick to dismiss the unredeemable.

Good companies have informal rules that collectively set out the base requirements for productive social living. As outlined below, these rules summarize expectations about common decency and assert the personal responsibility of all members to conduct themselves according to accepted norms.[17]

Relational rules dictate how people are to interact with one another.
- Be thoughtful and kind
- Help those in need
- Avoid harming others
- Respect others' opinions and decisions
- Keep promises
- Be honest, and do not deceive others
- Respect others' property[18]

Structuring rules pertain to ongoing activities such as showing up on time, meeting deadlines, and allowing others to speak without interruption.

Protecting rules support personal and institutional safety; for example, to encrypt files, wash hands before entering designated areas, and wear proper protective gear.

Personal rules emphasize accountability for one's own behavior, such as accepting feedback graciously, not blaming others, and doing one's best.

Etiquette rules iterate proper social behaviors around customs and traditions.

An example of the latter is found at BambooHR, the formidable human resource systems developer, where the day begins with every employee high-fiving a buddy who is randomly selected weekly from another department. (As a reminder, these companies frequently switch out their cultural formulations, and this morning ritual will soon be replaced by another). Here is a very simple ritual that boosts the energy of employees and launches their day. Think about it. The day begins with an encounter with someone who is happy to see you. What's more, a high five is an expression of teaming; the implicit message is that everyone across the company works together. Five minutes for all of that. Also, there is reason to believe that starting the day on a high note will positively affect the rest of the day. We know the opposite is true. People who experience rude, uncivil behavior early in the day notice more incivility and act more uncivilly during the rest of the day.[19,20]

Politeness and etiquette are the raw materials that make social engagements pleasurable. They are essential to preserving amicable and harmonious relations on which organizations depend. Prescribing the way people are expected to interact is a crucial way to encourage thoughtfulness and restraint when one is tempted by the mood of the moment, by reactionary impulses, and by self-interest.

The all-American pastime of standing in line (the British are very good at this too) illustrates the value of etiquette.[21,22] Suppose we are in a queue for our morning coffee. Although some people in line most likely will need their caffeine fixes more urgently than others, the operative rule is "first come, first served." This rule ensures that the person at the back of the line, who may want his coffee the most, cannot walk to the front of the line to request service first. Etiquette requires people to exercise self-control and to refrain from acting on impulse according to their personal wants and desires. These sorts of politeness rituals combined with the requisite self-control, graciousness (e.g., restraint from muttering annoyingly in line), and sense of fair play prevent chaotic grabs for whatever is in reach. Line aficionados understand that they all have similar needs that will be satisfied in time equitably.

This delicate social balance of equanimity is disturbed by the person who walks into the coffee shop and heads to the front of the line where, without justification, he is served. This event becomes a moment of disbelief for those deferential line-standers who are snubbed. After repeated affronts in which a person's position and interests are displaced, he comes to recognize his secondary status in the scheme of things. If you have ever experienced a progression of late-arriving airline passengers in business class superseding your place in the economy line at the airport, or have had to settle for a poor table seating at a restaurant so that more luminous patrons can be better served, then you get the feel of the upside and downside of privilege.

The line-cutter unmasks a truth: it is possible to get one's way by overpowering others. Weaker individuals are pushed back and in some instances completely washed out of the way. Remember the photograph of Governor Chris Christie (of New Jersey) sitting with his family on an empty New Jersey beach, a beach he had temporarily closed to the public for budgetary reasons? Summer attire aside, the scene was repulsive because the governor essentially cleared the place and used his authority to meet his own interests—first and only. The communication was clear: "I am exempt from the rules that govern you and I will use my privilege to get my needs met"; that is, "You do not count as much as me." This is a harsh message. Good companies send more sanguine and comforting news.

In the past, Bill and I rarely gave much thought to life events, rituals, and rites of passage, such as marriages, birthdays, deaths, and employment anniversaries, in organizations. This may be because companies often acknowledge these events mechanistically, if at all (e.g., the personnel system automatically flags an anniversary and an American Express check is spit out with a prepared note and electronic signature). The companies we visited make a big deal of significant dates, and now we realize why: it is the considerate thing to do. Considerate companies do considerate things. It is good practice to celebrate and sympathize; to show regard for others' feelings and needs; to uplift, soften, comfort, and aid. When stuff happens, people should relish it together, lighten each other's loads, and console alongside others. Like good families, good organizations have special-occasion meals together, celebrate holidays, and recognize important life-cycle transitions such as marriages.

Such celebrations are abundant in every company we visited, helping to create and bind communities through shared experiences. These companies well understand the invaluable messages of hope, appreciation, condolence, and joy that attend life's passages.

BambooHR treats birthdays as paid holidays. N2 Publishing, a high-quality publisher of local magazines, gives newlyweds a $400 marriage stipend and continues the gift annually. Insomniac Games, an award-winning games developer, provides new parents with a custom onesie, art books, and toys, as well as a baby briefcase to help parents' keep their newborn's details well organized. Edmunds (the authoritative, independent source for all things automotive) has a weekly ritual called Cadillac Catch-Up. Every Thursday, Edmunds recognizes work anniversaries, births, new employees, retirements, and other life events, often in pictures (especially for the more photogenic subjects: babies).

Quality Bicycle Products (QBP), a major distributor and producer of bicycles and bicycle parts, readily accommodates changes in schedules so people can attend the funeral services of colleagues and their families. One tearful employee told us she would never forget how the company turned out for her father-in-law's funeral. In contrast, we recall the gregarious marketing specialist in a major insurance company who always went out of her way for others. When her mother died, many of her colleagues did not attend the funeral service. The service was in a part of Brooklyn, New York, that was inconvenient to reach. But she needed them to get there. That generous, outgoing woman was never the same at work; she never spoke to some people again. When she had needed closeness and support, the people she counted on let her down.

The celebration of, or homage to, lofty or weighty occasions are gestures that real people make to one another. Often organizations do even more, stretching far beyond considerate to the ultragenerous. Companies make special accommodations for sick employees, give extra time off when employees need it, arrange transportation when employees have lost theirs, pay medical bills to supplement a family's insurance, provide temporary housing for employees in transition, put deceased employees' children through college, and more. Truly, much more. Health Catalyst finished a basement for an employee whose baby was born with a rare immune deficiency. N2's CEO bought homes that he rents out to employees' families for one dollar so they can save money to buy their own homes (this informal program recently was replaced by a First-Time Home Buyer's Program in which N2 earmarks $7,000 toward closing costs on employees' first home purchase). When an employee at Big Ass Fans (BAF)—the premier producer of industrial and residential fans—was in a terrible auto accident in her second month of employment, the company arranged to move her from an apartment on the third floor to one on the first floor of her building, placing her possessions just as they had been before and providing her with technology to stay connected during her recuperation. The Motley Fool introduced the "Fool in Need" program. Employees voluntarily contribute a couple of dollars each pay period to a pool of funds to help others. Only three individuals administer the program thereby ensuring the privacy of those who receive aid. Concord Hospitality created an annual six-figure reserve to confidentially help employees with urgent needs. Insomniac Games has a Leave Donation Bank that accumulates donated vacation days that anyone can use for unforeseen medical hardships.

Employees know that they are not equals to the executives of companies. They know where final authority lies. However, in the best companies employees do not feel inferior. These companies downplay status and power differences among people, which can obstruct sincere, two-way communication. Executives have open-door policies ("Come and see me anytime"); work spaces tend to be undifferentiated; status symbols such as special parking places are absent, or limited; and organizational structures are flat (people see themselves more in terms of what they do than as titles or levels in the hierarchy). When employees at N2 Publishing answered our question "What do you do here?" the answers we received were, "I'm on the graphics team" or "I'm on the editorial team," and not, "I'm a graphic artist" or "senior editor." Relatedly, executives' model the equal value of people qua people. One employee told us how she saw the founder and CEO of Instructure (a leading developer of innovative learning platforms), Josh Coates, meeting with a facilities worker one early morning over coffee to discuss work and careers. Now, clearly, Josh is more important to the business than the facilities worker; but he just as clearly showed he is not more important as a person.

Leaders who dominate relationships by cornering the market on ideas and decision authority, and who emphasize the dissimilarities in position power through status symbols and special privileges, demotivate employees and generate the hallmarks of dysfunctional groups: negative affect, cynicism, mistrust, poor communication, insecurity, and divisiveness. To foster a collaborative, egalitarian environment where people freely express their thoughts, Insomniac Games minimizes hierarchy and titles, regularly seeks employees' input, supports a close-knit family feel among employees, and emphasizes group contributions. For example, Insomniac lists everyone in the credits for a released game, and everyone at Insomniac shares in the royalties from game sales to denote a common purpose and signify that "in the giant web of work, we all did this together." A remarkable demonstration of egalitarianism occurs at BAF's annual holiday party. In 2017 one employee received a check for $25,000 and another received one for $15,000—among other prizes given out throughout the eventful evening. These giveaways were made by random selection and not by criteria such as merit. Like other companies we visited, BAF distinguishes among performers through means such as spot bonuses, quarterly bonuses, annual awards, and merit, but the company decided that an annual celebration is the time and place to emphasize community and teamwork, not differences.

Relationships with power differentials do not have to be combative and end badly. Some discord is inevitable in every relationship, but relationships do exist that are pleasurable, generative, and warm—even in the workplace. Relationships built on kindness mute power imbalances and refocus the relationship on things that matter, as opposed to squandering time and energy maneuvering for supremacy and settling scores. In fact, we find that people in healthy manager-employee relationships barely are aware of the power differences between them in their daily transactions. The relationships are marked by flexibility, mutual support, close social bonds, mutual affection, and interpersonal trust.

"Managers" get it wrong. When they are given the honorific title of manager, they erroneously follow a prepared script "to manage," which they often interpret as pushing people along to predetermined destinations. This primitive conception of management is linear and controlling. Many managers have no grander scheme about human motivation than simple cause and effect, while they neglect the appreciable wellspring of effort that arises from the inner lives of people who are given due respect.

CHAPTER 2

VERGONNEN

Encourage and celebrate the success of others

The Germans have a word we rather like that captures the feeling of satisfaction in helping others to succeed: *vergonnen*. The Germans also give us *Schadenfreude*: taking delight in another's misfortune. The differences between the two are nicely illustrated by an employee we met at Regeneron: "If you trip and fall here, people are there to help you back up. I have worked at places where as soon as you fell, there would be a foot on your back".

Achievement-oriented people have ambitions. Good companies allow aspirants to pursue their goals and excel in honorable, principled ways while asking them to voluntarily put aside their ambitions when others need their help. These companies thrive on mutual goodwill with each employee encouraging and helping others to do their best work—and without people begrudging others' successes or feeling left behind.

Companies nurture a sense of *vergonnen* among employees by endorsing certain beliefs:

Abundance: There is more than enough for everyone; what others do and receive does not deprive you, and vice versa (i.e., we are not playing a zero-sum game).

Long-term relationship: We want you for the long term, during which you will do many different, interesting things.

Regarding others: It is important to keep life in perspective and to think about the needs of others.

There Is More than Enough for Everyone

The paradigm case of scarcity occurs in the familiar commons problem when too many people vie for too few resources. The resource featured in the original social dilemma of the commons was a circumscribed plot of grassland for cattle that, jointly owned, gave everyone equal and open access to the land. The *tragedy* of the commons occurs when individuals acting in their own self-interest attempt to maximize (compete for) their use of the land, thereby depleting the resource over time.[1] Independent, individual actions thus destroy the collective pasture and reduce the total amount of rich grazing land available to all cattlemen. In this scenario, everyone loses. Unfortunately, the decision of any one person to limit herself—when others do not—would not make sense, because the overall results would be the same and the individual would be worse off in the end. It is in everyone's immediate interest to take while the taking is good. The temptation is for each person to get the most she can before the resource is spent. Obviously, if there was unlimited pasture for grazing, unfettered use of the land by individuals would be far less contentious to the collective.

Conditions of scarcity generally produce unfriendly competition.[2] When executives refer to scarcity and abundance mind-sets, they are alluding to features of the environment that elicit greater or less harmful infighting among employees or greater or less cooperation. We have seen the concepts of scarcity and abundance most readily applied to the availability of jobs in companies and the ability of employees to advance in their careers. Employees often want more challenging and lucrative work associated with higher-level jobs. However, jobs in most organizations are resources in limited supply, and vacancies in positions at relatively high organizational levels occur infrequently. Given that turnover is low in these higher-level jobs, eager, ambitious employees must await the promotion, retirement, or death of an incumbent for a chance to rise within the ranks.

When few job opportunities are available, people who want a position must intensely compete for it. These circumstances usually encourage a glut of self-promotion, superficial cooperation, wasteful ingratiating activities such as "face time" (worthless time spent in the viewing range of a supervisor), and political drama; in short, time-killing diversions typically compensated for by grabbing hours out of one's personal life. What's worse, studies show that rivalries within companies promote odious acts such as unsporting behavior, deception, and unethical negotiation tactics to win competitions. In fact, the desire to win and the associated preservation of self-worth and status supplant the tangible reward as the motive for performance.[3] The words famously spoken by football coach Vince Lombardi—"Winning isn't everything, it's the only thing"—sum up the nature of the game employees play under the presumption of scarcity: doing whatever it takes to outperform an opponent. A scarcity mind-set promotes an environment that is like a bucket full of crabs. Competitors crawl over one another to reach the top. Losers in these career contests are over two times more likely than the average employee to quit the organization in the ensuing year.[4] Whereas scarcity and competition redirect individuals' attention to differences between themselves and others, abundance and cooperation direct attention to similarities among people and toward a regard for others' needs and welfare.[5]

To make matters still worse, the rarity of a good makes it more valuable and attractive, thus more highly sought-after. You know: "Buy now while our limited supplies last." This enhancement in value may be part of an evolutionary kick-start; when fused with the aggressiveness that competitive threats elicit, it pushes us to go after the things we need and covet. It was a necessary prod to our hungry ancestors' survival, but a psycho-physiological remnant that is bad for business today.

A coarse, unadorned version of the effects of a scarcity mind-set is on display every year during Black Friday, the first major shopping day before the Christmas holidays in the United States.[6] This is a day when otherwise law-abiding people turn into combative hordes. In fact, you can monitor the death toll and injuries on this bleak day by going to http://blackfridaydeathcount .com/. Bodies squeeze and contort their way through doorways too narrow to accommodate easy passage for the masses who, once through, stampede their way through the big-box maze in search of the rare and valuable. The corporate competition for scarce jobs and other limited resources is less frenzied and more calculating and refined, but even in its purified form just as brutish and nasty as rushes on limited merchandise.

Companies can minimize infighting and maximize teamwork among employees by creating a sense of abundance. Companies create a sense of plenty in two ways. First, they adopt promote-from-within policies and reserve open spots for current employees. Whenever possible, organizations that foster an abundance mind-set work hard to prepare internal employees for future position openings. These companies tend to go outside the organization for talent only when the requisite skill set does not exist internally or when the company believes it needs a fresh perspective on its products and services, and related methodologies. For example, when Big Ass Fans wanted a new perspective on testing methods, it brought in people from the automotive industry. As sensible and cost-effective as nurturing internal talent is, however, less than a third of employers post jobs internally prior to extending searches to external candidates.[7]

Second, such organizations have expansive conceptions of career advancement, and they liberally fund employee development. As opposed to conventional, narrowly defined career progressions that move people along predictable pathways, progressive organizations see careers as lattices, like jungle gyms; more academically, they see boundaryless or portfolio careers that emphasize the dynamism of contemporary professions.[8] This multifaceted concept of career geometrically enlarges the number of available job opportunities. If an employee is bypassed for one opportunity, she realizes that other chances will come along and that the organization is aware of her interests and will help her to prepare for other opportunities. Employees at these companies need not worry how others are doing and whether others' success will intrude on their own ambitions. Trust in the system allows people to unselfishly promote the interests of others without feeling deprived themselves. A fair, wide-ranging system enables people to proactively support the development of others and to savor their triumphs as their own. As we often heard from employees across companies, "I know that the company has my back."

To aid atypical redeployments, Edmunds started an experimental internal internship program. When a position temporarily opens through a leave of absence, say, employees with the requisite baseline aptitudes and interests may apply. If satisfactory performance is seen in the new role, the "intern" usually lands a permanent job in the area. With a philosophy of promoting from within whenever possible, ESL (a credit union based in Rochester, New York) also places a great deal of effort in developing people outside of predefined career paths. ESL's internal visitation program, for example, allows employees to observe the work of other departments in action and, if applicable, to obtain the requisite abilities for a career jump, working in concert with their managers for the planned move. The company may inch employees into another area with increased exposure through special projects, committees, or task forces. Clarus Commerce (a tech company that specializes in the design, development, and implementation of fully customized premium loyalty programs for retailers) does something similar in its Clarus Classrooms Program. One to two times per month an employee presents on her area of specialization, thus familiarizing the workforce with skill sets and applications across the organization.

Even in circumstances in which movement up or across areas is unachievable, progressive organizations have "in job" promotions that recognize targeted increases in employees' skills and abilities. Promotions are based on fulfillment of personalized development plans that are grounded in achieving certain skill levels, successfully carrying out specific activities, and getting results.

We Want You for the Long Term

The most direct way organizations communicate a long-term interest in the people they hire is by telling them directly, by having a hiring and orientation process that welcomes newcomers into the fold, and by investing heavily in their development. These are the actions of organizations that construe relationships as permanent.

Good organizations also tell good stories that imply a long-term perspective about the employer-employee partnership. Affirmative stories generally involve tales of personal growth and positive transformations gleaned from new experiences, knowledge, and insights. The mythologist Joseph Campbell called these stories ancient hero tales: a person embarks on an adventure that leads to salutary virtues and reformed identities.[9] The protagonists are qualitatively better off because of their quests, despite the obstacles they must endure and overcome. Negative stories involve highfliers who through hubris and avoidable miscalculations spiral downward in failure.

Stories thus have arcs that denote growth with an upward temporal slope or deterioration with a downward temporal slope. The shape of the narrative arc gives employees a way to interpret events and explain why things happen the way they do. Consider the arcs in the following two life stories. Anthony Weiner's professional life began as a New York City councilman and aid to then–United States representative Chuck Schumer. Afterward, he began a seven-term stint in the US Congress as a representative and married the powerful long-term Hillary Clinton aide Huma Abedin, with former president Bill Clinton officiating at the ceremony. Subsequently, a sexting scandal led him to resign from Congress. As he was recovering from the first scandal and gaining ground in a New York mayoral race, a second sexting case came to light. That led to a swift decline in public support, a guilty plea to sending indiscreet material to a minor, a 21-month jail sentence and $10,000 fine, and a divorce and loss of custody of their only child, a son.

Now imagine those occurrences in reverse, the story of a life that rebounds. Anthony Weiner, after leaving prison, reconciles with the public, reestablishes a relationship with Huma Abedin who, convinced of her ex-husband's reha-bilitation, takes him back in, and renews his relationship with his estranged son. Soon afterward, he wins the Democratic nomination for congressional representative in a primary runoff, wins the election, and completes his pro-fessional life as a seven-term representative to the House.

We can conceive of the two lives, covering much the same ground but in reverse order. Each person lives a hedonically equivalent life. However, most people prefer to live the life with a happy ending, and these are the stories that good organizations tell. In these stories employees use what they have learned, change the way they do things, and create a future of their own design. Despite the bad things that inevitably befall people in organizations, the company conveys the message that periodic mistakes and setbacks are not the end of the story. There is more to come, most of it good. An employee's trajectory trends upward, as the stories go.

Companies tell three future-oriented, archetypical tales, of which there are variations.[10,11] The first is a story of *agency*, mainly involving careers. Stories of agency are stories of empowerment, mastery, and control. They are stories that say, "No matter your circumstances today, if you have an interest and work hard, you can become anything you want, tomorrow." Because the company provides myriad opportunities for advancement and provisions for develop-ment, then with determination and effort an employee can chart and follow her own career path. The upward arc and positive tone of these stories prom-ise greater satisfaction for employees. Contrast that with a narrative in which employees hold jobs they expect will be of limited duration.

Consider the time perspective of HubSpot—which author Dan Lyons describes as a combination of frat house, kindergarten, and scientology—in which there is little chance of longevity.[12] Employees do "tours of duty" and receive VoRP scores as part of their annual reviews. "VoRP" comes from the world of baseball and stands for "value over replacement value." In short, it is a computation of how many runs a batter adds to his team's total throughout the course of a season over the number that an average major-leaguer would con-tribute.[13] In what is assuredly a psychometrically unsound measurement, the index as applied in the workplace essentially asks, "Is this employee worth keep-ing?" In contrast, Insomniac Games makes it clear from its anniversary sched-ule that it values people who stay with the company. Employees receive $2,500, $5,000, $7,500, and $10,000 for their 5, 10, 15, and 20-year anniversaries—to be used, preferably, for nontangible, experiential activities such as travel.

A second narrative is the *redemption* story, which involves a loss of some kind followed by challenge, transformation, and victory. Employees' mistakes make the perfect plots to see how two different story lines might unfold. One way a company can tell the story is to punish the offender for an error. In the severest of punishments the company can fire the employee. The abrupt ending signals that any attempt to do work outside of the ordinary may have catastrophic consequences. In this story the narrator tells employees to play it safe and stick with the conventional, else risk falling from the precipice into a career abyss.

Alternatively, a positive story of redemption is one in which the heroine learns from her mistakes and, using newfound knowledge, awareness, and abilities, goes on to achieve great things. The storyteller accepts the occasional mistake as a natural hazard of employee zeal and encourages people to take risks and move on. Imbued with the ability to learn from and correct past errors, our employee rethinks the problem and triumphantly ventures forth. The two stories are altogether different in tone and trajectory, one showcasing anxiety and the other possibility. One story illustrates the precariousness of the relationship, and the other its prospects.

We met Jeff, who now is a project manager for Surly Bicycles, at QBP, where he worked in the distribution center. Years earlier, as the story goes, he had clipped a sprinkler on the ceiling with a piece of heavy equipment. As water rained down on two rows of products, Jeff scaled the racks, ripped off his shirt, and tried to subdue the outpour by covering over the sprinkler, like a medic compressing a wound. Too little, too late. However, everyone began working together to remove the damaged products, fetch new products from inventory, and restock the shelves. And they filled all the orders on time. The narrative is that mistakes can be fixed and life goes on, and Jeff moved on to experience much success. The saying at QBP is, "When we fall, we fall forward." And as in the case of Jeff, they really do.

BambooHR has a novel, nonthreatening way of handling mistakes. The company asks employees to broadcast their errors without fear of recrimination. It created an Oops Email Box as a place for all employees—founders included—to announce mistakes made, what others should be aware of because of them, and steps taken to correct them. WD-40 does something similar when asking new employees to take the "maniac pledge." These vows include taking responsibility for getting answers to questions, making decisions, and admitting to mistakes, which are called learning moments.[14]

Fortunately, there aren't many Oops at Bamboo—or, we suspect, at WD-40—but the Oops outlet lets everyone know that mistakes are an inevitable part of the human condition, they happen, and they are fixable.

A third narrative theme, *communion*, is one in which progress is only possible through the performance of a cohesive group, through fellowship, togetherness, and caring. Sound relationships and working together well are fundamental to making a positive difference for the social good. Together, for example, employees at Patagonia—the producer and retailer of high-quality clothing, equipment, and accessories for outdoor enthusiasts—form a formidable collective force whose actions promote the public welfare. This communal effort can be seen in Patagonia's recent introduction of a new beer, Long Root Ale. This is the first beer made with kernza wheat. The kernza's deep roots need half the water of standard varieties of wheat, and because it is a perennial it reduces erosion and captures more carbon from the atmosphere. Similarly, Patagonia recently introduced a new wetsuit made from the havea plant. Patagonia extracts natural rubber from the plant using certified sustainable practices that are a cleaner alternative to the fabrication of the conventional neoprene wetsuit—a product made using petrochemicals and energy-intensive manufacturing processes.

The story that unfolds is one that underscores how employees with dogged efforts, and working together, are going to change the world. Change takes time, and most effective social change leads to improvements rather than resolutions. The collaborative work of social change, therefore, is future oriented, open ended, and never ending.

Think about Others

The companies in our sample devote time and money to charitable giving and community service. These companies view themselves as embedded within a larger community to which they feel a responsibility. Social responsibility is baked into their DNA, and they engage in these activities because for them it is the right thing to do. For example, TCG sponsors monthly "Charity Sprees." An employee organizes a charitable event and TCG makes a $1,000 donation to the cause. During the month of our interviews TCG had just completed a sock drive for the homeless in the Washington, DC, metropolitan area.

ESL started an innovative program by which employees can volunteer time at local charities using VTO, Voluntary Time-Off Days. To foster community giving and volunteerism, ESL allows employees to take paid time off for volunteer activities. In one recent year, employees collectively have donated something on the order of one thousand hours to nonprofits such as Habitat for Humanity, Foodlink, Life Assistance, and the Salvation Army.

Concord Hospitality also started a program that they refer to as "Share Day." This is a day when the company engages in charitable activities across its various markets. Most recently, employees prepared boxes of food for families in alliance with Feed the Children and helped renovate the homes of low-income families with Rebuilding Together. Each quarter, employees of Clarus Commerce collectively decide on and commit to a social cause within the community in a program called Clarus Cares. In recent quarters employees have updated and repaired a YMCA and Salvation Army building, gathered pledges and strained leg muscles in a fund-raising stair climb for the American Lung Association, and packed food at a local food distribution center. There is no shortage of big-heartedness at the companies we visited.

As it happens, volunteering not only helps the recipients of aid; it positively affects the volunteers as well. Volunteering fosters greater psychological well-being and life and job satisfaction in volunteers.[15,16,17] Charitable acts also build social capital among groups. They create tighter networks and closer social ties, more intense feelings of connectedness and social well-being, and greater interpersonal trust and cooperation.[18,19,20] Furthermore, people who engage in prosocial behaviors become less focused on themselves and more focused on others. In context, givers see themselves as part of something bigger, grander, and more important and therefore are more aware of others and their own actions within a broader system.

The act of helping others belongs to a constellation of spiritually charged actions and imagery that puts life into a broader perspective.[21] Exposure to nature has this same effect. Nature's splendor prompts us to reconceive our place in a grander, higher order. People who see the majesty of nature, the elegance of a theorem, the beauty of a symphony, or the urgent needs of those who are deprived become part of something much bigger than themselves.[22] Like a raindrop that falls into the ocean, we become immersed in a problem, concern, or idea of unfathomable depth and vastness.[23] For a moment, we lose ourselves and become aware of our connection to something more substantial. Our frame of reference changes from that of a solitary actor who is large and entitled, to being a smaller, intimate part of something bigger than us and more profound.[24,25,26,27,28]

In this regard, our trip to Patagonia was particularly instructive. One of the wooden steps in the headquarters' building was marked with arrows and danger signs, alerting walkers that in the middle of the step, a butterfly, now in the chrysalis stage, would soon present itself to the world. The chrysalis was placed there by children from the onsite day care. In sharing a scene of the mysterious, the children freed those who passed by from their preoccupations with the everyday, and aroused within them a sense of wonder. The children keep the rest of us grounded. They put things in perspective. They remind us that there is life beyond the all-important "me," that we are caretakers for one another and our boundless communities.

CHAPTER 3

KINDNESS

Insist on kindness

A few weeks ago, an executive confided to us that he was having an awful day. Not that anything particularly dreadful had occurred. It was one of those days when everything grates, productivity drags, and the world looks bleak. "You guys have any suggestions?" "One," we replied. "Do something kind for someone." His brow furrowed in thought. He was expecting us to say something along the lines of, "Why don't you treat yourself to a half day off, a massage, a trip to the fitness center, or nice lunch." But he replied, "That's a good idea. There are a couple of people I have been meaning to thank for some of the work they've done recently." His mood visibly changed in expectation of doing something special for someone else.

The Primacy of Kindness

Kindness is the most important attribute when choosing a mate. It is revered equally for romantic partners, close friends, fellow employees, and supervisors and is embraced across cultures and religions. In one study researchers asked participants to rate the importance of 34 personal qualities in four different relationships: close friend, romantic partner, an employee of yours, or your boss. The results showed that there was one set of qualities that people would like in any relationship: kindness. (In the study, kindness was a composite construct made up of qualities such as sincerity and compassion).[1] Similarly, researchers performed a text analysis of philosophical and religious writings from the East and the West and found that one set of values shared across cultures is love and kindness (called "humanity" in the study).[2] The essence of kindness, to have a final concern for the welfare of others, is universal. The value of kindness in the workplace is further underscored by a 2015 NBC poll which found that most people would forego a 10 percent pay hike in exchange for a nicer, kinder boss.[3]

Employees are not likely to get one. Christine Porath has been tracking incivility (discourteous, rude, condescending behaviors) in the workplace, and the problem is getting worse. Surveys show that about half of employees were treated rudely once a month in 1998; that percentage rose to 55 in 2011 and to 62 in 2016.[4] Other surveys corroborate and extend Porath's results and expose the dismal prospects for a hospitable workplace. One large-scale survey indicates that over 40 percent of employees will be insulted, shouted at, and threatened at work within a one-year period, and 6 percent of these instances will result in physical aggression.[5] Approximately 30 percent of employees will experience two or more severe incidents, such as public humiliation, harassment, belittling, verbal abuse, intimidation, work sabotage, isolation, and power plays that reduce responsibilities and career opportunities, per week over a period of 6 to 12 months.[6] These are woeful statistics collectively conveying that the workplace may be the last place an employee wants to be.

Several studies document the adverse effects of incivility on mental and physical health, job satisfaction, and performance.[7,8] In a recent *Harvard Business Review* article, Porath and Pearson list the costs of incivility based on a survey of 800 managers in 17 industries.[9] They found that almost half reduced their effort and time at work; two-thirds said their performance declined; and a fourth admitted to taking their frustrations out on customers. Perhaps no study shows the ill effects of incivility more acutely than a recent medical simulation. Twenty-four teams from neonatal units throughout Israel took part in a simulation in which a mannequin connected to medical instrumentation was depicted as suffering from a serious but common disorder called necrotizing enterocolitis, a condition in which bowel tissue disintegrates. The teams' task was to diagnose and treat the infant. Ostensibly, an expert was observing the teams' performance and could communicate with the teams. In the control condition, the expert made no extraordinary comments. However, in the rude condition, the expert exclaimed that the quality of medicine in Israel was poor and that the team would not last a week in his department. The results: composite diagnostic and procedural performance scores were significantly lower for members of teams exposed to rudeness than the scores of members of the control teams, thereby showing how modest doses of incivility can impair medical care.[10] Uncivil oversight fractures psychological safety within teams and disrupts healthy exchanges among team members.[11] In the simulation, teams in the rude condition were less likely to share information and seek help.

Once incivility and uglier forms of misconduct escape from the box, the blight spreads.[12] Coworkers and other observers who witness the mistreatment of colleagues are affected. These third parties experience increased stress and lower morale, mental health, productivity, and commitment to the company, and they perform more poorly on problem-solving and creativity tasks.[13,14,15,16,17] Further, team performance is impaired as the effects of abusive supervision of some members of the team spread to adversely affect other members.[18,19] Incivility has expansive, destructive organizational consequences. It is fair to say that incivility is contagious, ominously spreading through organizations and into family life.[20,21]

Whatever Happened to Kindness?

Our elevation of economics and material welfare in the workplace over simple virtues such as kindness will perplex future generations. Our acceptance of incivility in our workplaces will bewilder our generational successors. They will be aghast at the coarseness of our managerial and technocratic approach to the workplace, which construes employees as performance-delivery devices— a conception that gouges the humane and the personal out of the workplace. The big virtues of kindness, love, and social justice are displaced as we wander through thickets of cost-benefits and total returns.

People from our past would be puzzled as well by the demotion of kindness. From antiquity through the Middle Ages, kindness was considered a central virtue that made satisfying communal living possible. Kindness was an encompassing term that tied several related concepts together into a bundle of civic obligations: solicitude, warmth, affection, sympathy, helpfulness, thoughtfulness, tenderness, caring, and humanitarian acts. Kindness denoted a code of conduct that surpassed expectations of courtesy and extended to the idea that social living demanded that one be at the service of others in need.

However, by the time the Industrial Revolution was well in motion, kindness had been driven out of the workplace and confined to the home.

Kindness was increasingly domesticated with the advent of industrialization and transformed into graciously receiving guests, being thoughtful about the neighbors and local community, providing a soothing and supportive space for the children to learn and play, and creating a welcoming and comfortable environment for the husband's replenishment after a hard day at work. Kindness became hospitality and care of the hearth. Outside the home, kindness lost its former grandeur and seemed increasingly out of place in the hard-knuckled world of industry.[22,23]

The Positive Effects of Kindness

The diminution of kindness in the workplace is unfortunate. It exists, of course, in happy pockets of refuge, but it is rarely promoted across the company. It is common to see "energy" and "focus" on corporate placards, but kindness not so much. Kindness should play a more central role in the life of organizations because it has organizational and even life-affirming benefits.[24,25] People who are predisposed to kindness, who are mindful of the needs of others, and who engage in acts of generosity are happier and more optimistic; they experience greater satisfaction with life and greater psychological well-being; they feel more connected to others and less socially anxious; they have a greater sense of self-worth, are more understanding and less critical of their own mistakes, and tend to be more forward-thinking and motivated. Kindness also is a mechanism that fosters greater sociability, connectedness, interpersonal trust, and cooperation among employees.[26,27,28,29,30,31]

To illustrate how kindness positively affects you, think about times when you have been unusually sad and unusually happy. There is a very good chance that in the former instances you saw the world as particularly narrow and confining. It was difficult to see past your immediate circumstances as you searched for a way out of your present predicament. On the other hand, happiness filled you with possibilities. Your focus was broad and the opportunities before you appeared immense. People who are positive do not think the same way as those who are negative. Pain, whether physical or psychological, restricts possibilities to those actions that can alleviate the suffering. Alternatively, people who experience positive affect are more open to new experiences, attentive to a wider field of stimuli, and have a broader behavioral repertoire in responding. That is, happy people have a more extensive range of observations, thoughts, and actions than those who are less happy.

Acts of kindness are not the only ways to elicit positive emotions in oneself and others, but instilling kindness is one of the surest ways. In the laboratory, kindness and the positive emotions that kindness engenders can easily be produced through simple mental exercises, for example through loving-kindness meditations (such as repeating short phrases: "I wish you peace and joy").[32] What's more, the effects of kindness last. People who were asked to perform three nice things for others on a given day reported greater psychological, social, and emotional well-being two weeks later compared to control subjects.

Both positive and negative emotions are self-perpetuating. Because acts of generosity and helping others heighten positive affect and all that that entails, people who are kind find it easier to muster the resources they need to grow and flourish. Because they are more open to new experiences and knowledge, they tend to adaptively cope with stressors. Because their social relations are sounder, they find it easy to reach out to others for support. Because they are willing to stray from well-trodden paths and experiment with new thoughts and behaviors, they tend to live more exhilarating and intellectually engaging lives. People who are happier and more optimistic also differentially attend to more positive aspects of their environments.[33] Overall, the upbeat lives of those who are kind become self-reinforcing and enduring across the domains of work and home.[34,35,36,37]

We have conducted thousands of interviews and focus groups across hundreds of companies within different industries, and a frequent refrain among employees is, "They treat us like animals." In fact, we have heard several pejorative descriptors for employees over the years: machines, numbers, monkeys, robots, nobodies. All are dehumanizing epithets because they deny attributes and emotions that distinguish people from animals or, like the term "automaton," fail to acknowledge human nature altogether.[38] In our past consulting, dehumanizing tags for employees arose commonly enough to call for a new item in a culture survey we administer to organizations. The item is simply, "I am treated like an intelligent human being." Remarkably, about half of the many thousands of people who have taken the survey have disagreed with this statement.

We were aware of these frightening survey results when we wrote *Leading with Kindness* ten years ago. At that time the prevailing sentiment required managers to have tough exteriors and to contain expressions of compassion that might depict them as pushovers and in turn adversely affect business results. A dispassionate application of force was needed to "*drive* performance" or "*move* the needle." To prompt action, managers believed they had to apply some sort of accelerant (i.e., "light a fire" under employees). Managers who held generous opinions of employees' motivations and appeared to be responsive to their needs may have delighted employees but risked the disapproval of peers for being too liberal and tenderhearted to be effective.

Not the Same as Nice

Juxtaposed against the hardness of the workplace, kindness is thought of as being nice or accommodating, even as interpersonal feebleness. Some writers have gone so far as to suggest that empathy and kindness are liabilities.[39] It is better not to possess them at all. Never mind the type of person who would inhabit this dystopian, empathy-free world: we never claim that kindness is the sole criterion for decision-making. Most complex situations necessitate making judgments among competing goals and demands. A wise, centered executive will be aware of the multiple considerations that weigh on his judgment before choosing the right thing to do; not just the kind thing, fair thing, profitable thing, but the *right* thing, all things considered. For that, we prefer to make empathy, love, and kindness critical parts of the business equation.

A recurring theme in both the leadership and family relations literatures is that a leader's (parent's) behavior can be summarized along two dimensions.[40] The leadership literature refers to these dimensions as initiation of structure and consideration.[41] The family relations literature refers to the dimensions as demandingness and responsiveness.[42,43,44] The respective interpretations are the same. Initiating structure means to have firm expectations and standards, to insist on mature, ethical conduct, and to press for progressive achievements and independence. The consideration dimension is associated with warmth, noncoerciveness, bidirectional communication, and flexibility and responsiveness to the needs and interests of others; it is the emotional part of leadership that steps in to give support, guidance, and encouragement when the situation recommends it, while preserving an affective climate that is respectful of others' intelligence and abilities. Bagnoli refers to the intersection of limit setting and support as "responsible care" in which a person's immediate preferences may be respectfully overridden.[45] To illustrate this, she uses the experience of her daughter, or so we assume; as one of us has a daughter who had a similar experience to the one Bagnoli describes, she will be used as an example.

One summer one of us sent our daughter to camp, much to her dismay. Then in her teens, she did not want to go. It was a period that the family retrospectively, and humorously, refers to as "the dark year," and we believed it was essential for her to invest in a different sort of experience that summer. We were adamant and clear about our reasons. She went. Whether from a naturally burgeoning maturity or because of summer camp, the period marked a positive change for her. Kindness—responsible regard—is not kowtowing to another's personal desires; rather, it is preparing people to be healthy and successful. The respect one shows for another is for a future person who presently has the stuff to do and become much more.[46] If you kick a soccer ball to another player in stride, your aim must account for where the player will be in the future, or else you risk badly missing the mark. The same holds true for others' interests and needs.

Care and concern without standards and limits is permissiveness. A permissive leadership style is one that is excessively lax and affirmative toward others, placing little emphasis on personal responsibilities and few demands on conduct. These leaders exercise little control and allow others to regulate their own activities, while in turn too mildly sanctioning or dismissing outright violations of rules and norms. It is a style that asks others to discover their own interests and desires and to follow their own pathway to personal fulfillment. Kindness has become associated with the consideration dimension of leadership. However, this mistaken conception omits the fact that kindness also includes a notion of development that ought not be left to others' own devices. Growth requires the imposition of standards, adherence to norms, and mature, responsible conduct. Kindness mandates what family therapists and leadership pundits have called authoritative leadership. It implies a healthy mix of emotional support and indoctrination for socially wholesome and capable human beings. Coldly and dispassionately directing others is autocratic, and nondirective coddling is acquiescence, not kindness.

Kristin van Ogtrop wrote an extremely funny article in *Time* magazine that describes the differences between authoritative and laissez faire or permissive governance.[47] She uses holocracy as her foil. Holocracy is, in theory, a transparent, self-organizing system of distributed authority in which employees flexibly adapt to the work to be done. In practice, it can look like no one really knows what he is supposed to be doing, and no one feels responsible for not doing it (although this loose anatomy of overlapping roles has its defenders).[48] Van Ogtrop imagines how the system would work in her home. She contemplates the system breaking down when no one answers the phone or feeds the dog, since presumably these tasks are believed to be outside everyone's distributed ring of authority. Every family and every organization needs a CEO for whom behavioral induction and discipline are part of the dynamics of value creation and decision-making. Nothing is inherently wrong with structure or hierarchy. In fact, they provide the clarity people need so they can spend more time doing and creating as opposed to groping in the dark.[49] Employees are most satisfied, productive, and creative under authoritative leadership—a finding that can be traced back to the seminal studies of Kurt Lewin.[50]

Yet while groups require direction and need leaders who decisively serve as the final authority on matters of importance, evidence suggests that when influence is wielded as a blunt instrument, performance and satisfaction within groups are impaired. In this regard we rather like the metaphor used by Pedro Pizzaro, the chief executive at the public utility Edison International, to describe his leadership role. He sees his place not as the center of a wheel but as the rim, which holds the spokes together. The rim leads the way, keeps the group together. If the team ever goes through mud, the rim goes first.[51]

Consideration and expectations for high performance are not then mutually exclusive. PURE Insurance, a premium property and casualty insurer, exemplifies this. PURE likens its environment to a game of basketball. Success is largely determined by the level of talent, the passion of the players, and the players' ability to execute effectively as a team. The players are free to operate as they please provided they adhere to the rules of the game, which for PURE include the organization's principles. In addition to teamwork and passion, these principles include member (policy holder) centricity, personal integrity, constant improvement, and action orientation. Ross Buchmueller, one of the company's founders and the current president and CEO, added the critical fact that basketball has a shot clock. Consequently, there is a pervasive sense of urgency at PURE that reaches intense levels when a deadline is imminent.

A ubiquitous attitude of care pervades PURE, not profit, not efficiency. Its worldview is care for one another, for the customer, and for stakeholders. Ross clarifies, "Care toward employees does not mean nice or permissive; it means helping them to excel and execute to the best of their abilities—removing distractions and giving them the room they need to grow and prove themselves." Employees agree with that: "At my previous job, I felt like a piece of furniture. At PURE, I feel more like an entrepreneur—I'm told how the business is doing and given the latitude to make important decisions." And "care" does not mean that PURE will dither about business necessities. Insurance is being transformed by technology, artificial intelligence, and big data. PURE will do what is needed to remain competitive. At the same time, its corporate benevolence means that it will not forsake people because of changes in the workplace. It will continue to invest heavily in continuing education and help guide people into newly created jobs. To rejoin the basketball analogy, PURE wants to win. And it wants to win in a way that will produce the best experiences for everyone through reputable values and the aptitudes of its people.

Another of our companies, FONA, also clarifies the difference between kind, or nice, and effective. As we were meeting with people in the FONA offices, we noticed blocks of wood on employees' desks and shelves. The blocks had the name of the employee etched into ornamental bronze plates on one side. Each block was precisely two inches by four inches. We inquired and were told that these blocks and their dimensions represent any number of the company's ambitions: double the profits in four years; double employees' knowledge and capabilities in four years; double the number of clients in four years, and so on. The wood blocks conspicuously sit as challenges to be taken on. These goals did not seem practical to us and we questioned their feasibility. We were told, "We have done it before."

FONA describes itself as a kind, or caring, meritocracy. Yet the people are, indeed, tough on themselves. For example, the company only awards quarterly bonuses when a sales record for the quarter or month has been broken. But FONA is not the sort of organization that leaves anyone behind. Whether ambitions are met or not, the blocks of wood continue to stand for possibility and they expectantly push people on while reminding everyone that increased profits will only be possible with a continuously improving workforce.

Similarly, Concord Hospitality underscores the point that a kind regard for others does not imply being "soft on performance." It does imply being "constructive" and "well intentioned." In fact, Concord meticulously tracks hotel performance and takes remedial action if statistics show that a hotel is not getting its fair share of the market. As one person told us, "We are hard on issues, soft on people. We try to catch people doing the right things: twice the praise and half the critique."

Our modest purpose in *Leading with Kindness* was to expose the twisted logic that posits kindness as a barrier to accomplishment. One of our objectives was to point out that the inner lives of employees matter to organizational performance and that leaders profoundly shape the affective tenor of the workplace. This seems self-evident now. However, it was just a short time ago when there was an express hostility toward sentiments unless packaged and presented in a highly intellectualized form as data points or as a cerebral exercise in business ethics. When the idea of emotional intelligence was popularized, for example, many executives with whom we were working shunned the concept, not on substantive grounds but because it contained a word that agitated them: "emotion." Today many leaders can say "emotion" aloud without gagging.

People who are superior at perceiving and using emotional cues are more effective, personally and interpersonally, than those without those capabilities. Many studies have revealed the advantages of emotional intelligence (EQ) in work performance, leadership effectiveness, customer satisfaction, academic achievement, problem-solving, well-being, and life satisfaction.[52] Teaching people to be more self-aware and to modulate their emotions is a prescription for more enjoyable social interactions and more effective job performance.[53] Progressive companies such as PURE Insurance now make EQ a fundamental part of their leadership development programs.

The capacity of social traits to dramatically influence results was neatly illustrated by William Muir, a biologist at Purdue who was trying to increase the egg-laying capacity of chickens. In one test, he took the most prolific egg-laying hens from each cage, which held nine chickens each, and used them to breed the next generation of hens. He continued this process for six generations. This succession resulted in a generation of "mean" chickens that maintained their ascendency in their cages by pecking each other to death. Just a few bedraggled and relatively unproductive chickens remained in the cages; the remainder were vanquished by what Muir has referred to as psychopathic chickens. Muir was not surprised by the results, as he was selecting on the individual traits of the so-called super chickens. In this case what he got was an aggressive supremacy whereby the dominant chickens outperformed their peers by killing them off.[54]

Muir repeated the experiment, but rather than select the top chicken from each cage for breeding, he selected all of the chickens from the top-producing cages of chickens. Six generations later, the progeny were healthy and 160 percent more productive. In this case he was selecting on group traits: chickens that were hospitable toward one another and collectively more productive over time. He had created super-chicken teams. There were individual differences in the chickens' performances, but importantly the selection of hereditable traits produced a milieu that enabled the chickens to perform better year after year.

We recall Itzhak Perlman, the virtuoso violinist, who once demonstrated that great notes do not make beautiful music. Beautiful music is created by what comes in between the notes—how one note is passed to the next. The same can be said for chickens, and people. Talented people become "beautiful" when they learn to exquisitely pass and receive skills, materials, and information to and from one another.[55] Who is on the team is of course important, but it is what goes on between team members that makes the ultimate difference in performance.

CHAPTER 4

UNRULY

Adopt zero tolerance for destructive people

In the spring of 2018, the United States announced the appointment of the president's personal physician and director of the White House Medical Unit (WHMU), Ronny Jackson, to head the massive Department of Veterans Affairs, which oversees healthcare for veterans. The medical unit at the White House has approximately 25 people, who are active-duty military physicians, physician assistants, registered nurses, medics, and support staff. Dr. Jackson joined the staff in 2006 and was named the director sometime around 2012–13, coincident with an internal power struggle with another physician, who subsequently left the unit.

The Secretary of Veterans Affairs is a cabinet-level position that requires confirmation by the United States Senate through the Veterans Affairs Committee. Prior to the hearings, the committee interviewed 23 current and former colleagues of Rear Admiral Jackson, most of whom were still in uniform. The final report raised many concerns about the appointment, one of which related to Dr. Jackson's temperament and ethics. In an annotated portion of the report provided by the *Washington Post*, Jackson was described as "the most unethical person I have ever worked with," "flat-out unethical," "explosive," "100 percent bad temper," "toxic," "abusive," "volatile," "incapable of not losing his temper," "the worst officer I have ever served with," "despicable," "dishonest," having "screaming tantrums" and "screaming fits," someone who would "lose his mind over small things," "vindictive," "belittling," and "the worse leader I've ever worked for." The day-to-day environment was like "walking on eggshells." As Jackson gained power he became "intolerable." One physician said, "I have no faith in government that someone like Jackson could end up at VA [Veterans Affairs]." A nurse stated, "This [working at WHMU] should have been the highlight of my military career but it was my worst assignment." Another stated that working at WHMU was the "worst experience of my life."[1]

We invite readers to draw their own conclusions. We happen to believe that the allegations, above, are true because we have seen many instances just like this one. The terrible, horrible, no-good, very bad manager terrorizes others, but keeps his job. Our goal in this chapter is to explain how this happens and the price companies pay for their egregious errors of omission.

We were overly optimistic in our prior work. We erroneously thought that the testimonies and practices of illustrious leaders who subscribe to kind leadership would win converts. Perhaps they did, but certainly not enough of them. We have good reason to believe that an ample inventory of incivility is still in the workplace. Surveys continue to portray troubling work environments. In one recent survey, 36 percent of employees said they have managers whom they would describe as "dysfunctional." Not "bad" or "incompetent," mind you, but "dysfunctional"![2] This makes sense given that 75 percent of employees say their boss is the most stressful aspect of their jobs.[3]

Appallingly, we continue to hear stories of managerial tantrums, hurled objects, public affronts, and systematic abuses. We listen to managers who are contemptuous of the aged, quick to forsake the underperforming, and who mock the ambitions of millennials. The stories of outlandishly poor managers from the people who have lived through the tumult keep on coming. You would think that three hundred years after the Enlightenment we would have devised more refined institutions. And yet the poignant experiences of employees continue to convey a great deal of personal anguish. Their accounts represent many lost opportunities for better lives and greater organizational success.

Many possible reasons exist for unfriendly workplaces. The business environment is intensely competitive; offices have an excess of angst and urgency; financial necessity overwhelms social propriety; and subtle changes in the workplace (e.g., the change from business to casual attire) have obscured traditional cues for proper behavior. However, organizational pathologies are far-reaching and cannot solely be attributed to factors largely outside managers' control.

For the past ten years, organizational improvement lay in the hope of an engaging work environment. Unfortunately, there is scant evidence to suggest that "engagement" has left an imprint of any notable size on the workplace. Although individual companies may have remade themselves into more scintillating enterprises using engagement as the springboard, these changes have come through sensibly improved human resource practices. These practices underscored employee growth and development and were complemented with a generous mix of nouveau perks such as gym memberships, spa services, and free food. However, once engagement was seen to entail little more than compilations of practices that had been used in the past, the onetime engagement mystique began to settle in as part of the ordinary. We have found its allure as a cure-all beginning to fade.

The engagement-performance connection is a seductive formula because it is well dressed in business-friendly attire. It has an explicit utilitarian message. If people feel more connected to the organization and energized, they will be more productive. But despite offering the proverbial win-win outcome, where everyone seemingly gets what they want, the entire affair appears to have been exchange oriented and instrumental; decency and personhood could be traded like commodities at the local bazaar.

While we still have a long way to go before universal decency prevails within management, kind leadership provides a new model that is consonant with these times of stiff competition and with our human need to be valued and respected. It is possible to attend to human needs without giving up organizations' money-making rationale and without having to justify the treatment of people as people on its being profitable. It is high time to flip the organization on its head and create institutions that conform to our better selves; to introduce a cultural ambience in which unbecoming behavior is counternormative and disrespect for people out of place. What if, for a change, we assumed that what people really want is to be treated, well, like people, and we really meant it this time? In advocating for a new people-centric organization, we want to revive what always has mattered to employees as real people with real lives, as someone's son or daughter, husband or wife, father or mother.

We saw firsthand the generational reach and grace of one caring organization. When we arrived to meet with Sam Mogannam, the co-owner of San Francisco icon Bi-Rite Market, he was working out front of his store, a historic Art Deco building from 1940. When Sam took over his parents' store, he thought about changing the original neon Bi-Rite sign. "The name is old-fashioned and the illuminated sign is kitsch," shared Sam. He reconsidered. Bi-Rite is an institution in the Mission District of San Francisco. The store is a fixture in the historical neighborhood. Sam is too. Today the name is the same; however, Bi-Rite has evolved along with the community in which it sits and still serves.

With Sam we entered the building next to the storefront. The first floor has lockers for employees and storage for the inventory. There isn't much inventory since the produce is locally sourced and fresh from farm to shelf. Several employees exchanged warm hellos with Sam as they passed by one another. These were not hellos between boss and employee. These were it-is-really-nice-to-see-you greetings.

Many employees have generational attachments to Bi-Rite. Some employees affectionately call Sam's parents Mom and Dad. Several children of long-time Bi-Rite employees now work there or return to 18th Street each summer as seasonal staffers. We were at Bi-Rite on a day of orientation for new employees and interns. We overheard the educational pedigree of two of the summer staffers: Harvard and Wellesley. Whoa. This is what happens when people invest in people, as Bi-Rite does. The generations prosper. Bi-Rite pays San Francisco's living wage (minimum is $15, starting in July 2018), 100 percent of employees' health insurance, matching dollars on a 401(k) plan up to 4 percent of income (with lenient vesting terms), and profit sharing that ranges in value from 2 to 6 percent of salary. Full benefits are available to those who work at least 20 hours per week. This hourly minimum for benefits is extremely generous, as many employers set the cutoff much higher.

Bad Management Finds a Way

The reaction of employees who have a first encounter with a managerial madman is, "Is this really happening?" "Is this for real?" These episodes are unlike anything anyone could dream possible in the 21st century. How can behavior in organizations be so unruly? How does the ugly and hostile penetrate the boundaries of ethics and etiquette and allow the unfathomable to occur? The flippant reply is that we allow bad behavior: once bad managers advance and begin to disassemble a culture, it is difficult to put things right. This is true, but it's an incomplete explanation for the occupation of institutions by poor management. There are several other reasons. First, senior executives do not recognize that something strange is happening. That is an uphill battle. Twenty-five percent of employers do not believe extreme behaviors such as those exemplified by bully managers occur in their organizations.[4] The stories they hear are dismissed as the exaggerations of dissatisfied and perhaps vengeful employees. They chide accusations as farfetched embellishments made without full understanding of context and circumstances. Did the manager really wipe the employee's desk clean with his arm in a fit of rage? Did the manager really denounce the employee as "stupid" and "useless" in a meeting? Did the manager really have his shoes shined in his office during a one-on-one meeting with an employee? Yes, in each of these instances, he *really* did.

A second reason that destructive managers can persist in organizations is because they offer something of value. Often this value comes in the form of revenues, profits, or innovations. The recent onslaught of sexual harassment charges against corporations' stars revealed the complicity of these organizations in safeguarding their revenue streams. Sure, organizations argue, these managers may have a few quirks and cause some distress in the ranks, but a molehill of upheaval is a small price to pay for a mountain of money. In fact, it might be theorized that mini-explosions are necessary to power the organizational engine of growth and advancement. We have heard the naïve theory and its corollaries over the years that a little wackiness, interpersonal discord, tough (unsavory) love, belittlement, and threatening will motivate people. But in fact, the widespread tensions and gloom evoked by pernicious managers have no net value to organizations. Poor management overshadows any benefits derived from the destructive workplaces they create.

Third, people tend to believe in a just world in which people are presumed to get what they deserve and deserve what they get.[5] This outlook has one problematic consequence. To preserve our faith in the inevitability of justice, we often blame victims for the troubles that befall them. In one case, authorities told a female worker who had received sexually explicit messages from her boss to not give out her personal cell number again, and to change it to prevent future occurrences. Similarly, if a manager has targeted an employee for intimidation, observers are quick to infer that the employee must be "uncooperative" or "difficult," or have done something that provoked the manager. Observers conclude that there is something wrong with the *victim* as opposed to the *perpetrator*.

A fourth reason poor management persists is that employees are reluctant to seek help from official organizational outlets. Fewer than 10 percent of employees ever do.[6] Perhaps they intuitively understand what movie-watchers know about horror and science fiction plots: the authorities are not much help. In fact, the authorities might be part of the problem or duplicitous in some way. Indeed, research evidence shows that employee visits to internal administration often make matters worse. The employee's divulgences alert managers to the treachery while leaving the employee helplessly exposed to potential retaliation. Consequently, only 15 percent of employees who bring their troubles to administrators for help say they are satisfied with the results.[7]

A fifth reason that poor managers endure is because they have enablers. These managers are unable to inflict damage alone. They need help from people who will watch over them, keep them safe, and do their bidding. Someone must put Dracula to bed. Often these are the obsequious protégés of senior managers who are shaped in their bosses' image and rewarded for their diligent enforcement of loyalty.

Bill and I resist the temptation to call kind leaders saints, but it is easy to see, through the stories employees tell, why gifted leaders have earned the allegiance and commitment of their staffs. We recently spoke at a human resources association meeting and listened to the awful stories of poor management and oppressed and beleaguered staff. The enterprising callousness on display was shocking. One man asked his boss for an afternoon off to be with his son during surgery. The boss replied, "Why? There's nothing you can do." (The employee eventually was given the day off, but the damage was already done.) At last, one participant rose and spoke about how her organization was much different. She told the crowd about special work accommodations, retraining funds to avoid layoffs, special aid to families experiencing hardship, progressive developmental and advancement opportunities, and more.

Organizations struggle to curb risks and increase quarterly profits. In a highly competitive global marketplace, we would think that sensible changes that provide an edge would make a lot of sense. Having exceptional people in managerial roles who can help people realize their full potential would be one strategy. Andrew Haldane, the chief economist at the Bank of England, has claimed that one proven way to increase GDP growth is to improve the quality of management.[8]

It is time to obliterate the idea that the way to motivate people is through kick-in-the-rear tactics and tit-for-tat exchanges. The best way to get results and mitigate risk is to respect employees as sentient adults, create a brand of management grounded in kindness, and promote cultures centered on people. At the same time, it is necessary to get rid of the managers who transform decent companies, business units, and departments into arid, soulless landscapes.

Paying for Damages

The damage done by malicious bosses is not at once noticeable. Even when managers' outbursts are public, the psychological incisions are concealed within employees. The victims are forced to sit outwardly unperturbed to preserve their livelihoods. But the cumulative damage done by deficient management is significant, to individuals and to organizations. Studies show that workplace bullying decreases job satisfaction, commitment, and performance, while it increases turnover and absenteeism.[9,10,11]

Managers can be destructive in different ways ranging from dereliction to incompetence to subversion. A corps of highly flawed managers can reduce once-able workforces to the lowest common denominator, driving out the best performers while holding on to loyalists of suspect quality. A term exists for this filtration system: the Cesspool Syndrome.[12] The Cesspool Syndrome refers to the inability of organizations to keep their best and brightest, resulting in a stagnant pool with dreck at the top and sludge at the bottom. Indeed, psychologically compromised managers target and discard those who are most likely to challenge their authority or who remind them of their own deficiencies— the better performers or "tall poppies" that must be cut down to size.[13,14,15] These managers chase high performers away by assigning frivolous work or using other hostile covert measures such as withholding information, sabotaging work, and excluding the best people from important meetings.[16,17] The idea of extinguishing worthy competitors is long-standing and may date back to Herodotus (*The Histories*, book 5, 92e–g) in which the despot, Thrasybulus, demonstrates a key rule of domination by chopping off the tops of the tallest wheat stalks in a field.

There is more. Poor leadership causes devastating psychological and physiological harms by creating chronically stressful conditions. Abusive, unkind managers instill fear. To illustrate the effects of threat on a population, recall (or imagine) the widespread anxiety and fear produced in communities in upstate New York when two convicted murderers escaped from the maximum-security prison. For three weeks, the normal routines of the now hypervigilant communities were disrupted. When the convicts were caught and the onerous psychic burden lifted, the relieved communities once again could enjoy the safe embrace of daily living.

Researchers have likened the atmosphere of high-threat workplaces to state-induced paranoia.[18] A pall of harm and persecution settles in, anxieties increase, and a steady watchfulness and monitoring of the environment ensues.

Think of how the warehouse workers Bill and I once worked with must have felt while under the constant scrutiny of management—to the point of having to punch in and out of bathroom breaks, which supervisors liked to see average less than three minutes. We would be jubilant, too, if these conditions of watchfulness and enforcement were eliminated and replaced by feelings of security, freedom, and companionship.

Threats, whether from managers in the workplace or murderers on the lam, induce stress. The more unpredictable and uncontrollable the threat, the greater the stress response.[19,20] Our bodies mobilize their defenses by changing glucose levels, cardiovascular output, blood flow, respiration, and such to prepare for fight or flight.[21] These reflexive mechanisms, however, are designed for short-term maneuvers to repel or escape harm. Yet employees must venture into the workplace every day, which for many is a continuous, gut-wrenching ordeal.

The adverse effects of long-term exposure to stressors are well documented. A prolonged state of high arousal can produce the following symptoms: decreased concentration, sleep disturbances, fatigue, weight loss, depression, headache, backache, gastrointestinal complications, musculoskeletal disorders, and cardiovascular disease. Employees stuck in a job and pinned in place by a venomous manager suffer real illness and feel real pain. In fact, the psychological onslaught of dysfunctional managers can be so severe that employees display symptoms of post-traumatic stress disorder (PTSD) long after their supervisory relationship has changed or they have left the company. One core symptom of PTSD is a reexperiencing of the traumatic event. One employee we interviewed described how she would bypass the building where she once worked to avoid pronounced feelings of helplessness and anger and to avert the agonizing ruminations that a drive past her former office building produced.[22,23,24,25]

Clearly, employees cannot perform optimally when under persistent duress. The size of the problem is tabulated by the estimated costs of stress due to bad bosses, interpersonal conflict, role ambiguity, role conflict (multiple expectations), and work overload. Stress-related costs attributed to absenteeism, turnover, declines in productivity, and increased healthcare expenses are between $200 and $300 billion annually in the United States alone.[26,27] In the United Kingdom, stress contributes approximately 43 percent of lost days at work and $60–$70 billion in costs.[28] These costs do not count retaliatory behaviors of employees, which include theft, fraud, and sabotage as well as long breaks, tardiness, legal expenses, drug and alcohol use, excessive socializing, and cyber-loafing. Nor do these costs include the reputational damage unhappy employees can do. Recall the 2009 video, which went viral, of Domino's Pizza employees abusing takeout food; or the 2012 video of a Burger King employee standing in a tub of lettuce in filthy shoes with the caption, "This is the lettuce you eat at Burger King." Or consider the IT worker who, learning that he was on a list for layoff, created a backdoor into the system from home, where he was able to manipulate and publish files and affix attachments such as pornographic images. More insidious, some experts suspect that the hack of 40,000,000 personal records from Target in 2013 was abetted by insiders. Recently, a disgruntled employee sabotaged Tesla's manufacturing systems causing substantial damage.[29] Indeed, some of the largest debacles in corporations have been due not to competitive miscues but to the perverse actions of employees out for revenge.[30]

If companies want better management, they will need to pay more attention to those whom they have entrusted to lead, and perhaps be a little less forgiving of the bullies who blaze a fine path to personal glory while leaving dead bodies in their wake. Despite the notable body counts, deeply flawed managers expertly avoid detection. Since they understand that it is impossible to squash things bigger than themselves, they have a knack for ingratiating themselves with their bosses, who are unaware of their actual practices. Consequently, if you really want to find out how well a person manages, it is imperative to collect the opinions of those they manage.

Clarus Commerce is an example of a company that takes the selection and ongoing evaluation of managers seriously. Clarus will wait for the right person rather than fill a position with someone who imperfectly fits the culture. This is true for any position, but Clarus is especially cautious when it comes to managers. Understanding that managers are the primary guardians of culture, it hires them carefully and evaluates them regularly. Clarus conducts 360-degree assessments on every manager annually (these are assessments that include direct reports, peers, and superiors). Curiously, most organizations do not ask employees what they think of their managers. We are astounded by this oversight and are unable to account for this neglect except to infer from comments we have heard that bosses view such evaluation as the sole prerogative of management. Presumably because of their unique angle and special understanding of leadership, superiors view their perspective on managerial excellence to be exclusive, even though looking down and looking up yield two very different realities.

At Edmunds, the automotive information service, managers are responsible for maintaining the conditions of the "highway." Their primary role is to keep highway surfaces smooth, allowing employees to handily move forward and grow. Each year, through a highly visible leadership program called "Pave the Road," managers are assessed on standing criteria. These criteria include managers' ability to inspire, develop, and connect employees (to resources, people, committees) while preserving their welfare (not burning them out). The ratings are cross-validated by interviews and three winners are selected and announced at the annual all-employee meeting. The company produces videos of employees describing what they have enjoyed about their managers and how these managers changed their lives. The award presentation is briefly interrupted with levity and humor to keep the proceedings from becoming too sentimental, and the award itself is highly coveted and received with warm, often tearful regard.

Many employees are resigned to face daily trials and count on their coping abilities, resilience, and mental toughness to endure their desperate circumstances. Fortified by will and armed with strategies for handling difficult people, employees engage with their managers in day-long psychological warfare on the borders of normality. All this, when there is a fix: installing and developing leaders who have the requisite attributes for managing well and who will actively promote cultures that allow people and organizations to flourish.

Culture by Default

The thing about culture is that every place has one. Of necessity, they must. Behaviors are regulated by conventions, norms, and practices. These practical constraints preserve order when the propensity for chaos is high. At intersections in the road, drivers take turns; at ticket booths, we stand in line according to the order of our arrival; when boarding planes, we enter by class. If there were no prescriptive behaviors for any of these things, people would devise new rules. Otherwise, no one would be able to get on the highway, and there would be riots at ticket booths, and passengers would experience greater delays in departure times. All cultural voids are filled. In the absence of intentional forces, cultural compositions will form that—rightly or wrongly—favor certain behaviors over others.

In a similar vein, without adequate controls the wrong people often are promoted and obtain power—or more power. In many organizations the people who tend to rise are frequently those who most crave power, control, wealth, or other forms of idolatry. This "cream" at the top, described in its biological form, is a light-weight, fatty globule with little substance. It needs to be skimmed off.

The void that allows the proliferation of bad management includes a failure to set standards and limits on conduct. These "chaotic" organizations are typified by laissez-faire leadership that has abdicated responsibility for establishing ethical ground rules and social order.[31,32,33] Planning is poor, information flows are poor, role clarity is poor, and the cleanliness and orderliness of the work environment is poor. Inadequate and hostile strains of management reproduce because corporate decision-making is scattered, poorly constrained, and loosely watched, allowing managers throughout the company to decide for themselves the best way to administer business.[34,35]

It is remarkable how easily and quickly cultures can deteriorate. Yet it is a well-known phenomenon in psychology. The spontaneous acquisition of a behavioral repertoire is perhaps most fatefully illustrated by the Stanford University Prison Experiment.[36] The experiment randomly separated student participants into prisoners and guards in a simulated prison environment. Although the prison guards had prescribed duties, experimenters did not instruct them on how those duties should be carried out. The experiment was prematurely stopped because of mounting aggressive behaviors displayed by the guards.

This demonstration of behavioral change showed that people who we would regard as ordinary on the street might act in unusual and alarming ways under certain circumstances. For many student participants there was nothing especially revealing in their character that would have predicted their treatment of the prisoners—and fellow students. Researchers have offered different explanations for the results of the prison experiment. One explanation posits a capacity to objectify others as categories, as opposed to seeing them as individuals, and to impute to a group certain characteristics that make members seem less than human—deserving of, or impervious to, harsh treatment.[37] Another explanation points to a loss of personal accountability. When in groups, people tend to adopt the prevailing norms of the group. If the norms of the guards are to be tough with the prisoners, then that is the way they will behave.[38] However, this explanation does not say why a norm of intimidation should form.

Recent work by Keltner and associates suggests that differential power may play a role. He finds that more powerful individuals are more likely to engage in rude, selfish, and unethical behavior.[39] What's more, it does not take much to elicit the differential authority of leaders over others. Imagine three people who just met, one of whom is casually selected as the designated leader by the experimenter. While the trio are working on a presumed writing task, the experimenter places a plate of four freshly baked cookies in front of the subjects for a snack. Guess who eats the extra cookie?

Keltner suggests that the indulgences and abuses of the more advantaged and powerful are significant. Evidence unequivocally supports his claim, as bullying disproportionately occurs between people at different organizational ranks and with differential power.[40,41] Part of the reason for this may be that people of rank *can* exert control over others; however, they also seem to be less sympathetic to and distressed by others' predicaments than those without similar authority: the social distance between people appears to widen their emotional distance.[42] We have seen power's hammer enough times to realize that the phenomenon is real. On several occasions we have seen friendly, charming employees transformed into fiends once they were promoted into managerial positions.

One of the primary ways to control the incursion of the obscene into the workplace is to put a premium on leadership and on those leaders who enforce respectful relations among members of the workforce. We get the people we deserve as leaders in our governments and organizations when we do not take our commitments to values and to each other seriously, and when we allow those who care about neither to fill the void. The best chance for our institutions is to mobilize our greatest weapon: a mission-driven community based on the governing premise of kindness. It is a community that thrives on the energies and abilities of people and that resists giving in to those whose motives reduce purpose to daily survival.

Not everyone who goes to work each day will find meaning and personal satisfaction in what they do. Yet everyone should find respect and safety. Showing respect is not so hard. It entails expressing interest in what employees want for themselves, listening to what they say, sincerely considering their perspectives, figuring out ways to use and grow their talents, and showing appreciation for what they do. When we swaddle our blue- and pink-capped babies, we wish simply for their future happiness; we do not expect that there will be those, similarly born, who will prevent that from happening.

The advantages of a people-centric brand of kindness should be self-evident. All else being equal, wouldn't you rather work for someone who is kind? Wouldn't you work harder and do more for someone who is kind? Wouldn't you trust in and be more committed to someone who is kind? Companies that invest in kindness will be giving themselves an advantage. Employees who choose to work at a kind company will be doing themselves a favor.

CHAPTER 5

COMMUNITY

Attend to the needs of the whole person and foster a climate of appreciation, collaboration, and security

Most people have regrets. We have ours. They aren't big but they are nagging. For several summers one of us worked in a camera shop. The store had taken in a Yashica camera on trade. Most readers probably have never heard of the brand (and although the company is gone, the name lives on with a new Kickstarter digi-film camera). The camera had a few nice features but it was not a make to be found among the most elite. The manager of the store who had acquired the camera told the employees all about its wonderful properties and that we should try to sell it. He would sweeten a sale by offering three times the normal commission. A customer, whose appearance I faintly recall to this day, came into the store looking for his first camera. He was looking for something in the midmarket range, what we would call a prosumer camera today. Well, that was his lucky day because we recently took in a camera on trade that would be perfect for him. Perhaps the customer ultimately was delighted with his Yashica, but I know for a fact he would have been more delighted with a Canon, Nikon, or Olympus. The store manager heartily congratulated me on that sale, but I wish I had that moment to do over again.

Tending to the Whole Person

According to the economist Emily Northrop, the goal of maximizing profit became ubiquitous in the business literatures when econometric models entered the scene and certain assumptions, such as maximization, had to be made to work through the equations.[1] There is nothing prohibitive about "making a profit" as a goal of business to clear space for other concerns and values to enter the decision calculus. This modest reframing helps contain a rapacious form of capitalism that the moral philosopher Adam Smith warned about. It might prevent inferior mixtures of cement and dead batteries and broken switches in backup systems on oil-drilling platforms (recall the *Deepwater Horizon* oil spill), or the dumping of waste in preference to more costly investments in clean technologies. It might even prevent salespeople from passing off inferior products to customers for personal gain.

As a society we have been making poor choices. Indeed, our vision is so tarnished by an ideology of monetary exchange that it is hard to imagine another way we might exist: a way where people are seen as much more than convenient apparatuses or fleshy machines; a way within the dog-eat-dog world of business, in the words of Robert Solomon, where we can forge relationships more like those we have with real dogs—warm and mutually rewarding;[2] and a way where economic activity buzzes within communities in which there is pride of accomplishment and reciprocal devotion to craftsmanship and one another.[3,4] As broached by Jay Coen Gilbert, founder of the B Lab (the certifying organization for B corporations), there is an urgent need to correct a defect in the source code of the corporation: shareholder primacy.[5]

"Profit is necessary, but it is not the goal," Duane Hixon, the founder and CEO of N2 Publishing, said to us. "Our purpose is to help people live better lives. There is not a higher priority in the company than the people. Profit, like air, water, shelter, and food, is a necessity, but not the raison d'être for being. We are not living to merely survive but are searching for something deeper and more enriching—purposes, not necessities." The end for N2 is to help everyone realize their potential, to live authentically, and to succeed in life as healthy, contributing members of the community.

Ben Peterson and Ryan Sanders, the cofounders of BambooHR, spent the first three months of the company's existence in a room the size of a common garden shed envisioning a business that would enable them to live rich, full lives and keep their priorities centered on those things that mattered most: family, friends, and the people around them. Their goal is to live healthy, meaningful lives and to offer the same possibilities to those with whom they work.

BambooHR's perspective of total life satisfaction influences the way it approaches business. The values of the organization are not the ones you usually see because the values that were adopted are meant to make both the organization and its people better. Some were not even born in the workplace. One value had its birth as one of the founders lay in bed one night, angry with his wife, believing she had said something hurtful. He bristled, then reflected. "Would my wife ever say anything to purposely hurt my feelings? Why should I think she has done that here?" Thus, the value "Assume the Best" in others was born, as well as its cousin, "Be Open," direct, and truthful in communications—maxims of value for any time, any place. Indeed, the crossover effects of consistently held values in the home and workplace yield comments such as one we heard: "I have become a better father since I started working at Bamboo."

BambooHR has seven core values, but two have been prominent since the company's beginning: "Grow from Good to Great" and "Enjoy a Quality Life." The aims are for people to be happy and to become socially, physically, emotionally, intellectually, and spiritually better people. Consequently, the concept of work-life balance is foreign at BambooHR since the idea of balance invites the awkward division of people into two, who act out different versions of themselves in different places—one of which cannot be authentic. Indeed, neither may be. These woeful changelings act out one ethic and personality on the job, and adopt other sentiments, demeanors, and traits at home. Never living full, true lives anywhere, they fit into the roles dictated by their surroundings. They are splintered personalities that do not become qualitatively better or feel more alive. In contrast, the goal at BambooHR is for people to enjoy one well-lived life of passion, purpose, and value.

The employer who wants the entirety of a person says: "We want you to be who you are and to become a better person in all ways and in all of life's domains. We want you to be a healthy, successful person here at work as well as at home. The person you are outside of work is the one we want here, and vice versa—physically, mentally, financially, spiritually." The narrative of the whole person is an evolving adventure of self-discovery, attainment of wisdom, and feeling comfortable in one's skin. To enable personal growth across life domains, the organizations we visited offer an array of nontraditional programs. BambooHR fashions a part of its training around general life skills, such as a nine-week course in financial acumen called Financial Peace University, which includes budgeting, building up emergency funds, and dealing with debt. One employee confided, "That course saved my marriage." FONA sponsors programs in estate and financial planning, mental health (First Aid USA), and personal guidance through a spiritual lens (Corporate Chaplains of America). N2 Publishing conducts regular lunch-and-learns structured around three themes—financial security, relational and physical health, and professional development—and offers a care team known as Life-Work-Care made up of volunteers who are always available to lend fellow employees a listening ear. SAS, the premier statistical software, analytics, and data visualization company, provides employees' children with college preparation and guidance and offers employees counseling in grief, eldercare, depression, finances, divorce, and so on through a Work-Life Center on the SAS campus staffed with social workers. And Patagonia teaches environmentally sensitive and socially conscious employees how to engage in peaceful activism. To support employees' commitments to responsible causes, Patagonia also will pay the bail and legal fees for employees who are arrested for civil disobedience.

Building Community

Employees at Edmunds refer to their community as a "culture of swarm," an apt allusion to the single-mindedness of a bee colony—one team, one family, one Edmunds. Employee requests from outside departments are not placed into a pile where they sit indefinitely as burdens to be tended to whenever time allows. Rather, people within Edmunds are equally responsive to requests regardless of where they originate, as if no boundaries exist at all; it is one giant "Department of Edmunds." Regeneron similarly has a metaphor, also biological, for community. As explained to us, the organization is like a cultural amoeba that absorbs people. People are part of a single organism and are inextricably attached to one another and to the whole.

The companies in our sample nurture strong employee bonds and convey a strong sense of family through the attitudes they project and the actions they take. As the CEO of FONA, Joseph Slawek, told us, "When we hire, I think of us as hiring a family, not an individual." Highly functioning organizations, like highly functioning families, have certain telltale characteristics. They are enduring, cohesive, caring, and mutually appreciative; they communicate often and effectively, spend time together, and share values and points of view; they adapt and deal constructively with crises, working openly together to solve problems and overcome hardships; they are sensitive to one another's needs, supportive and encouraging about one another's growth, and enthusiastic about one another's accomplishments. And high-functioning families and organizations emit a firm sense of emotional and physical safety and security in which, no matter what, everything will be all right.[6,7]

Family certainly was on the minds of Insomniac Games when they created the Better Halves Program.[8] Although the gaming industry has been the target of searing critiques on the issue of work-life balance in the past (an onslaught of negative commentary about the industry was unleashed by Erin Hoffman in 2004 in what became known as "The EA spouse web post," which recounted the brutal hours gamers worked), Insomniac Games is attentive to the issue while it has more than held its own in an extremely demanding industry. The employees we spoke with confirmed that the scheduling flexibility afforded at Insomniac Games allows people to meet their most important needs at work and at home. Employees also mentioned that game developers have real schedules and deadlines. There are crunch times. Insomniac Games tries to cushion the stresses of these periods by making life more predictable for families. Accordingly, Insomniac started the Better Halves Program. This program is a calendar of important dates, such as production cycles, that spouses and partners can access so that they know when work activity is likely to increase and when social events inclusive of family members will occur. Plus, Insomniac Games closes during the second half of December, providing a nice mind-clearing respite for employees and worry-free time with family members.

The companies we visited are, unapologetically, businesses. They are in business to fulfill aims about which they are passionate by supplying products and services to consumers who need them. Yet the solidarity of family invariably pokes through. Corporate memorabilia are proudly displayed in waiting areas, and cherished "family" photos are neatly hung on walls. The first thing you see when entering the offices of QBP is a series of serpentine bicycle chains mounted on the walls with 750 2×3 portraits attached. The faces and names of every employee are neatly displayed in chronological order from their date of hire. We have been to companies where simply asking for a printout of current employees' names was a chore, and trying a visual depiction like that found at QBP would have been like solving a Rubik's Cube involving the impossible assembly and disassembly of faces. Here at QBP, with orderly spacing and artful consistency and precision, was every employee.

At The Motley Fool, one hallway includes a photo of all employees that is prominently visible from where the board of directors meet. Our chaperone informs us: "Oh, that's to remind the board during their meetings that their decisions have real consequences and will impact the lives of hundreds of Fools. We got the idea from Dogfish Head Brewery."

And then there are countless opportunities for families to mingle and to get to know one another. FONA has a Bring Your Children to Work Day extravaganza. FONA loves the day when the kids come. The day is well choreographed to direct the energies of the children. The event gives children the chance to color and flavor frostings for cupcakes, create gummy candies, and concoct fitness drinks. Insomniac Games has Food Truck Fridays when the company provides lunches to entire families. QBP has a family cycle-cross every October on the company's premises. The lawns and parking lots fill with foods, music, games, and an obstacle course for the littlest bike enthusiasts. TCG not only includes families at many social events, but it thoughtfully remembers spouses and children on special occasions. Children receive freshly minted $10 bills on their birthdays, and when employees are hired the company sends spouses notes of gratitude which convey that they too are valued members of TCG.

More than anything, though, families help families. When tornadoes knocked out the electricity, phones, and internet in the entire county where *INTUITIVE* (an engineering and technical solutions consulting firm) resides—during a payroll period—the people in human resources rallied. They packed up their computers and drove south of Huntsville to a home with power and internet to make payroll on time. Human resources wanted to ensure sufficient funds in employees' accounts in case employees had automatic withdrawals. During that devastating tornado disaster, human resources initiated the company's planned crisis management response and the company found every employee in impacted areas within hours (including checking on people via four-wheelers where roads were impassable) to make sure they were safe. Following another tornado, when the company discovered that an employee's home had been severely damaged, *INTUITIVE* employees joined in to help. Some showed up with tools, some with pizzas, and all were there to help an employee who had only just started at *INTUITIVE* two weeks prior to this cataclysmic event.

The Extended Family

Companies are embedded within communities, and studies show that the ability of the community to support employees' needs and in turn accommodate their sense of responsibility toward the local community affects employees' psychological well-being, their commitment to the company, and satisfaction with their work. That is, employees' attachment to the community positively relates to their experiences at work. The ability to give to and take from the community is part of the employee experience.[9,10] The community becomes an extended family, so to speak.

Our tour of Bi-Rite Market and of the immediate area around Bi-Rite started in its main building, in the commissary, for lunch. An assortment of hot and cold foods was laid out cafeteria-style. Daily lunch is free. A long picnic bench serves as the table. We sat with Sam among five employees, discussing the foods that some of the people sitting at the table had made. Foods and people kept coming throughout the hour we were there. In that span of time, we met a dozen employees. The room is small; the picnic table fills half of it. People who enter are immediately absorbed into the conversation. Sam just wanted to make sure we were fed, but this stop served as lesson number one on how to create community through food, the mission of Bi-Rite Markets. The following lessons came when we began our walk through the neighborhood. Outside the store, five women huddled in a circle. The ends of freshly baked breads were peeking from the tops of their bags. Other smaller groups clustered nearby. "Community center," we thought.

We crossed the street and followed 18th toward Dolores Park. Here were more clusters of people, this time holding ice cream cones made at Bi-Rite Creamery, a San Francisco landmark appropriately placed on the tourist route. We stopped to talk to a man and woman, grandparents who were out with their grandchildren. They had usurped a piece of the sidewalk and nearby steps as their platform for conversation in between licks. People walked by. "Hi Sam." "Hi Sam." "Hi Sam." Our next stop was a few buildings down. It is a space for the nonprofit organization Sam cofounded in 2008 called "18 Reasons" (don't even try to figure out the name). The organization uses the space to provide classes on food preparation such as how to cook a dinner using fresh ingredients for ten dollars, or how to debone a chicken and make stock.

As ESL's CEO, Faheem Masood, told us: "It is not always possible to anticipate and measure the real contributions a decision can make to a community. We believed that as a community institution, building our headquarters in downtown Rochester was the right decision for us." In hindsight it proved an enlightened decision, but it was a daring investment at the time since downtown Rochester was faltering from the shrinkage of its big three employers, Eastman Kodak, Xerox, and Bausch + Lomb. ESL's commitment to build in Rochester was the first major development in the city in ten years. Faheem added: "Communities are symbiotic; we count on employees, employees count on us. We count on Rochester, and Rochester counts on us." We think of it as triggerfish that meander among coral reefs for their sustenance while helping to replenish the coral: when all organisms are healthy and engaged as one, they all flourish. Today ESL's 175,000 square-foot LEED-certified structure with its gorgeous two-story atrium has notable business companions along the strip of downtown that now is known as Rochester's Wall Street. M&T Bank, KeyBank, and Five Star Bank all have elegant presences in the area.

Communication

A strong sense of unity is predicated on a set of foundational elements in high-functioning organizations. Specifically, these involve wide-ranging methods of communication and the induction of gratitude, cooperation, and security among members of the workforce.

The companies in our sample openly share information with employees, including sensitive financial details. All the organizations we visited are transparent regarding the financials, providing regular updates—for some companies, daily updates through intranet posts. The openness can be surprising to newcomers. One employee joined Health Catalyst on the day Dan Burton, the CEO, was giving his monthly update on the status of the company. The company is operationally transparent and Dan was providing information about the finances of the organization. Feeling uncomfortable, the employee whispered to the person seated next to him, "Am I in the right meeting? Should I be here?"

Insomniac Games supplements financial disclosures with other programs, such as "Ask Me Anything." In this program, employees submit questions directly to the CEO on any matter whatsoever, and he will answer them—or ask someone who is more familiar with an issue to respond. Employees may submit questions anonymously and the questions and answers are posted on the company's intranet for all to read. The accessibility of vital information quells hearsay, welcomes employees into a restricted sanctum as insiders and copartners in the enterprise, and provides a foundation of truth for employees to reflect on and use in their daily affairs.

Within our sample of companies, employees are regularly included in decision-making processes, as appropriate, and are asked for their opinions on matters of importance. The thoughts and ideas of employees matter, and are acted upon. The companies in our sample understand that listening to employees is important, but that taking in information without ever acting on it would amount to nothing more than a test of auditory abilities. Good ideas must lead somewhere for employees to care enough to offer them. Several companies have action-oriented committees that take in employee ideas and find appropriate internal sponsors to research an idea further and to foster development and implementation if it is approved for production. QBP established an internal, rotating committee (GRIP, Great Results Improvement Processing) staffed by employees to ensure that suggestions are vetted and directed to the right parties for further examination and, if practical, execution. The benefits of allowing the free expression of ideas, suggestions, and opinions are well documented. A large-scale study showed that open, two-way communication in organizations is a boon to team decision-making, creativity, and agility.[11]

At BAF, there are no trappings of status and no titles to speak of to squelch dialog. When one person needs to talk with another, the communication does not have to weave a circuitous route through political correctness. Clarus always is probing for feedback and listening through daily exchanges, employee and customer surveys, employee lunches with the CEO, formal reviews, and the digital suggestion box that routinely gathers ideas for improvements. The ideas employees present for consideration are well informed since internal classes ensure that they understand the industry. Similarly, QBP conducts monthly briefings on issues ranging from logistics to product development, and holds three major town hall meetings each year to discuss the state of the organization. At Health Catalyst, team members are polled every six months on a given set of questions designed to measure employee interests and motivations. Senior management frequently conducts other, informal polls on a variety of topics throughout the year whenever it uncovers a need to understand the "voice of the team member."

And just so employees never miss out on information, Edmunds produces a weekly "Rest Stop Reader" that conveniently is posted at eye level in men's and women's *rest stops*. Concord Hospitality creates monthly posters of announcements and events that they distribute to their sites. If anything, the companies in our sample might say they overcommunicate and overcollect information. The openness and frequency with which information is shared, however, is an important means to keep conversations from going underground and to prevent suspicions about company motives and actions from arising and spreading.

Gratitude

A couple of the executives with whom we met at Concord Hospitality had experienced life-altering events that made them appreciate everyday pleasures and the people in their lives more deeply. Kevin, the SVP of marketing and sales, prematurely lost a wife to cancer, leaving three small children behind. "When the two-year-old comes into your room and asks for pancakes, you put one foot down on the floor, and then the other, and make pancakes." (Kevin wrote a memoir about love, loss, and keeping a family together called *Daddy-Can-You-Make-Pancakes.*) Kevin well understands the obligations close relationships impose and the necessity to care for those in need.

Matt, the EVP of operations and development, turned the tragic loss of an eight-month-old daughter into a celebration of life, spreading a message of gratitude for each day and a boundless, loving devotion to each person. "I'm never surprised by great results." That is because employees give back all they can, knowing that Matt is there to help them overcome barriers and succeed both at work and at home—and realize that Concord will never give up on people or discard them if they make a mistake. Concord Hospitality exudes unshakeable kindness, gratitude, and love.

Feelings of thankfulness, whether toward specific individuals, a group, or life more generally, increase happiness, life satisfaction, optimism, connectedness with others, and altruism.[12,13,14] Literally counting one's blessings by recording daily the things for which one is thankful heightens well-being.[15] One study that tracked adolescents over four years also found that as feelings of thankfulness emerge, so does children's prosocial behavior. The more gratitude they felt, the more likely they were to, for example, stick up for other kids who were in trouble.[16]

The cycle of kindness and gratitude creates a glow of goodwill among people and begins a train of prosociality that builds trusting relationships.[17] The nonspecific, unscored give-and-take is part of the binding power of friendships.[18,19] To demonstrate this, Grant and Gino had students ask professionals to review cover letters for jobs.[20] Twice as many professionals agreed to help when the request included an expression of gratefulness. Interestingly, when the researchers had another student ask the same professionals for help, twice as many who originally had been thanked agreed to help. The professionals felt appreciated and so were willing to help others. A naturalistic study showed the same generalizability of goodwill. Select employees were asked to perform random acts of kindness toward a designated group of employees.

The recipients of the kindnesses not only were happier than control subjects (employees who were not targeted for benefit) but acted kindlier toward others. Their incidence of kind acts increased by almost three times beyond the giving behavior of controls.[21]

Arkadium, a builder of interactive content experiences for all kinds of media partners, from advertisers and news publishers to brands and tech giants, is a very appreciative place. People openly and naturally express gratitude and warmly receive it. Evidence of a culture of gratitude is shown everywhere by the "Thank You" stickies that tile people's desks and frame their computer screens. These small, preprinted notes are used by employees to thank one another for their work and generosity. The notes unexpectedly appear on desks as refreshing tributes.

Arkadium never misses a chance to celebrate holidays, but Valentine's Day and Thanksgiving are special for a tradition of giving thanks. During Valentine's Day week, each person has a large heart on a wall with the words "What I love about [name]" written on it. The hearts fill. On Thanksgiving, the department heads thank the people on their teams, saying what they are thankful for.

FONA gave us a printed copy of a 70-page annual called "FONA Accomplishments and Gratitude." This book of gratitude is part of a day of appreciation, which starts on the Wednesday of Thanksgiving week at 10:30 a.m. It is a white linen tablecloth day that is fully catered and staffed by a third party. It is a day when members of the organization express the things they are thankful for. These thanks, which can be for anything and to anyone, are recorded (by department and unit) and published in the annual. It would be impossible to convey the impact of this book by selecting a few entries from the thousands included; it is a very moving text on gratitude and the things, large and small, to be thankful for. Employees told us that this is the most important day of the year for them. However, it is not the only day of gratitude. The company summarizes financials every month, and in greater detail every quarter, in all-employee meetings. The quarterly meetings offer a public venue for employees to thank one another for their services and accomplishments, in or out of the workplace. The day we were there, one employee thanked a teammate for rescuing him from the interstate roadside when his car broke down. Another employee thanked a teammate for taking over a project when she had to go out on leave.

Sometimes fondly referred to as business spouses for their like-mindedness, the cofounders of *INTUITIVE*, Hal and Rey, are humble enough to recognize that the successes they have achieved were not solely of their own doing.

Accordingly, one of the conference rooms at *INTUITIVE* is named after a former mentor of theirs. That is gratitude!

Cooperation

Regeneron gives itself the best chance of success by, as one person put it, "taking as many shots on goal as possible"; by generating many scientific ideas and then pursuing the most promising. Regeneron's culture encourages its players to take their best shots within a field of play that may be likened to a giant jazz ensemble in which people are identified by their specialties and expertise, not their ranks. Like jazz musicians, the people at Regeneron skillfully execute and improvise, with each member "playing" in a way that helps others to showcase their skills and perform at their best. It is a mutual aid society. Helping one another is an organizational given in Regeneron, an ideal that is aptly reinforced by recognizing effective collaborations.

People assume that in a tough, competitive world, the kind and cooperative most assuredly will not inherit the earth. They will get their clocks cleaned. That is not what the research shows. Game theory (in which multiplayer games reveal how the decisions players make affect their behaviors) shows that while self-interested players in repeated games will accumulate more rewards in the early rounds of play, cooperation wins out. To demonstrate these relationships, the paradigm game "Prisoner's Dilemma" envisions two prisoners, who if they both remain silent (cooperate) will get off with a lesser sentence for a lesser crime. If they both talk, they each get modest leniency but for their most serious crime. Therefore, they each receive a longer sentence than if neither talked (mutually assured destruction of sorts). However, if one prisoner talks while the other stays silent, the betrayer is released and the other is sentenced to the harshest penalty possible. The best result for an individual, then, is to defect (talk) in the hope that the other player cooperates (remains silent). Many games begin in this way. But over repeated trials this pattern does not persist; instead, these games degenerate into unanimous self-interested actions—If you get me, I'll get you.[22,23,24,25,26] The game devolves into a pattern of destructive competitive play with the result that each of the players receives the lowest possible outcomes over successive trials. When experimental conditions give players an opportunity to switch organizations into a new game environment, the players invariably do. The multiplayer games they leave behind collapse from the exodus.

In the real world, too, self-maximizing behavior is only rewarding over time when not everyone is playing by the same self-interested rule, but again that changes quickly with experience. People will get even and, if made to look foolish by a betrayal of their trust, more than even.[27] What's more, people will not help those who they believe will not help others, or who are seen as "unhelpful." In one study set in a grocery store, experimenters wanted to see when customers with various loads of groceries would allow a confederate with one item (a bottle of water or a bottle of beer) to move ahead of them in line.[28] The more groceries in their baskets, the more likely they were to allow the confederate to move ahead. In this case, the perceived need and value of assistance was greater. However, this was less likely to occur for the confederate with the *beer* versus the water. Why? The shoppers attributed certain characteristics to a purchaser of a single bottle of beer as a person less likely to "pay it forward." People selectively channel aid to others whom they perceive as being helpful themselves. These findings have been replicated under more controlled experimental conditions and have shown that generosity spreads with at least three degrees of separation—from person to person to person.[29] People are more inclined to help those who they believe will help others.[30]

Insomniac Games developed a creative way for employees to celebrate one another's successes in a novel pay-it-forward scheme, thereby underscoring a norm of doing unto others. As one focus group participant summarized, "At Insomniac, one person's failure is not another person's success, and vice versa." Insomniac brilliantly started a peer-to-peer recognition program in which the current recipient of the award, which is a trophy of an oversized wrench—an iconic nod to Ratchet (of game fame)—names his successor on the basis of a meritorious action. The successor recipient keeps the award for a week, then once again passes it along. We asked employees in a focus group if they knew who had the trophy. "Nigel has it." They knew.

Security

We are social actors who are primed to help others.[31] We naturally respond to the distress of our children, for example. We certainly have the innate ability to go beyond simple niceties to comfort and support others in need. Other people's distress, however, only becomes noticeable when we can recognize their need for help. We are much less likely to see or respond to others when we are too busy in our blip culture to notice, or have big problems of our own to which we are inclined to attend to first. We only have so much in our psychological reserves that we can give, so when we are mustering resources for our own benefit we do not have the time or desire to devote to the troubles of others. A precondition then for going to the aid of others is feeling relatively safe and secure. Security provides a solid psychological foundation that allows an outward focus without being overwhelmed or incapacitated by the extent of others' suffering. Research in fact shows that people who feel supported and secure are more compassionate and likely to help others.[32] Indeed, an internal study conducted by Google found that the largest determinant of team performance was feelings of psychological safety and security among team members.[33] These feelings gave members a sense of ease with open, uncensored dialog within the group, resulting in up to a 50 percent increase in revenues versus less secure groups.

"Security," however, is not a word we associate with the transitory, angst-ridden workplace of today.[34] Yet the people at INTUITIVE know they are safe. While they worry about satisfying clients, helping others to succeed, and improving the company's operations and themselves, they know INTUITIVE is there for them. For example, INTUITIVE does not lay off consultants. The company depends on reliable long-term subcontractors for routine or one-time niche work and hires people for the high-value slots as long-term employees. It does not hire a cohort of people for new projects then let them go when the funding dries up. When the government shut down for a week a few years ago, most contractors sent their people home without pay. In contrast, INTUITIVE kept everyone on full pay and used the week for employee training.

In 2008, when the economy began its sharp decline and employers were throwing their most valuable assets overboard, Jim Goodnight, the CEO of SAS, made an announcement. SAS would not lay anyone off. "People are not disposable" is deeply engrained in the SAS psyche. Goodnight continued, "In fact, we will grow." And they did grow. Goodnight asked for thrift but assured employees that SAS would not hold back and would keep moving forward.

Unfortunately, when the moment is viewed purely as a business decision, companies give laid-off workers what is necessary by policy, and seldom more upon separation. The supposed greatest assets have become chattel. The parting words of employers reinforce that very point: "It's nothing personal." This is a great rationalization. It would be harder on the executioners if the layoffs were conceived as personal. For it is "personal" for people who cannot afford healthcare for their children or are forced to sell their home.

Philippa Foot's moral dilemma of the trolley nicely illustrates the difference between personal and impersonal.[35] A trolley is heading down a track toward five people. If you pull a lever you can divert the trolley to another track. Unfortunately, there is a person on that track who would be killed. Would you pull the lever? Most people say they would. On the other hand, suppose you are standing on an overpass and see a trolley heading toward five people. The trolley could be stopped if a heavy object impeded its path. As it happens, a very big man is standing beside you directly over the track. He is leaning over the bridge to watch the event unfold. You could push him off the bridge onto the track to save the five people. Would you? Most people say they would not. Calculations change when the nature of the relationship changes. It all depends on how closely you stand.[36]

CHAPTER 6

BASIC NEEDS

*Ensure an adequate standard of living
and generational prosperity for families*

If you had a chance to start a business but realized that the only way you could earn the kind of money that would make the enterprise worthwhile to you would be to pay employees the least amount allowable by law and provide negligible benefits, would you start it? The answer was clear in the companies we visited. In the words of Ben Peterson, cofounder of BambooHR, "That would not be a win for us."

Many people's aspirations for better, more satisfying lives are thwarted by the pursuit of necessity. Even modest disturbances in financial security or job stability can impair a person's ability to work creatively and productively. A survey of a large energy company found that the more secure and safe employees felt, the more they could appreciate the satisfying components of their work, finding their jobs more pleasurable, interesting, and intrinsically satisfying.[1]

Minimum Wage

Whereas companies like BambooHR rhetorically ask, "What would be the point of starting a company where we profited at the expense of others," other companies are not as introspective and will compensate employees at levels they are ostensibly willing to accept. That compensation can be as low as the federal minimum wage ($7.25). To put the minimum wage in perspective, a primary wage earner in a two-person household would be working at a rate below the poverty line (less than $16,460 per year in 2018). Employees in these positions typically are excluded from formal training programs and have limited advancement opportunities. They often work in physically or emotionally demanding jobs that deplete their physical and psychic strength and reduce their ability to perform over time. According to the Department of Labor, half of low-wage employees do not have paid time off and about a third of those employees do not have employer-provided health or retirement plans. Even when employers sponsor health and retirement plans, the out-of-pocket costs can be prohibitive to low-income wage earners.

Congress established the minimum wage as part of the Fair Labor Standards Act (FLSA) in 1938 to counter employee deprivation and raise people's quality of life. That standard was $0.25 at inception with scheduled increases to $0.40 by 1945.[2,3] The phase-in was part of a political compromise, but the prevailing logic was that current wages were not enough to sustain families and that the increased purchasing power of more people—including those who might opt into the labor market at the higher wage rate—would provide the needed impetus for the economy, which was climbing its way out of a recession. Unfortunately, legislators did not build in automatic adjustments for inflation, so the minimum wage has been a politically contentious issue since 1945. Nevertheless, from its beginning to 1980, the minimum wage was adjusted regularly and on average was equivalent to 48–55 percent of the median wage. From 1980 to today there have been lengthy periods during which no adjustments to the minimum wage were made, and today the minimum wage stands at 38 percent of the median wage. Of the 35 participating countries in the Organisation for Economic Co-operation and Development (OECD), only Estonia and the Czech Republic have lower ratios.[4]

Economists have recognized the need for a minimum wage (185 out of 193 UN countries have them); otherwise, the markets could drive wages so low that the only work people would be able to get would be too meager to adequately support themselves. The US Congress recognized the perils of the markets and the need to set up a minimum wage rate, as had already been done in Australia, New Zealand, and the United Kingdom. When the FLSA legislation was passed, Congress had determined that one third of the US population was "ill-nourished, ill clad, and ill-housed."

Governments considered the minimum wage to be a mechanism for bringing wages back to levels that provided an adequate quality of life for employees and their families. However, the stasis of real wage growth among the lower 50 percent of earners in the United States, coupled with an anemic minimum wage, has placed more and more people at risk of homelessness, food insecurity, and so on. In fact, the real wages of the lowest 20 percent of workers have declined over the past 40 years even while worker productivity has increased. In theory, productivity gains should be returned to employees in the form of wages; in recent history, that has not occurred. Indeed, since 2001 national income in the United States has fallen from a historical steady state of 64 percent of GDP to 58 percent, or about $7,500 per worker. Economist Alan Blinder speculates that divergence from historical trends may be attributable to downward pressures exerted by global competition.[5] Even with consistent declines in unemployment since the Great Recession of 2008—and in the United States in 2017 the lowest rate of unemployment since 2000— hourly wages have barely budged, rising more slowly than the growth of the economy for 90 percent of all workers.[6,7,8]

The seemingly simple solution of raising the minimum wage has proven difficult to enact, mainly over concerns that raising wages will increase unemployment. This is an arguable issue among economists and it is easy to find support for and against the harmful effects of compensation on employment levels. The Phillips Curve says higher wages should reduce employment; however, lately the curve has not been obeying historical principles. (One reason given for the curve's break from norms is a historically low labor participation rate: working-age people who have dropped out of the workforce are at a 30-year high.)[9] Studies have shown little to no adverse effects of increased minimum wages on employment or significant decreases in hours worked.[10,11,12,13] These results are consistent across developed countries.

Some researchers believe that higher compensation expenses can be offset by savings and revenue enhancements attributable to lower turnover, absenteeism, and recruitment and training costs, plus higher morale and productivity. In some cases, companies may be able to absorb higher labor costs. They could, for example, accept lower profit margins, transfer internal expenses, or charge consumers more for their products and services. The effects on prices may be lower than imagined. For example, one recent study showed that the effect of raising the minimum wage from $7.25 to $10.10 (33%) in the fast-food industry would result in a 3 percent increase in the price of a burger, or 10 cents.[14] A more recent analysis of fast-food businesses came to a similar conclusion.[15] A staged increase in the minimum wage over a four-year period to $15 per hour was fully absorbed by the businesses without job cuts, through reductions in turnover, trend increases in sales, and modest incremental price increases. Similarly, a study of restaurants before and after a 25 percent increase in the minimum wage in San Jose, California, found that the increased costs were entirely passed on to consumers (a 1.45 percent increase in prices, on average) with no significant employment effects or shift in economic activity from San Jose to nearby areas.[16]

Although the issues of income are complex and worthy of debate, we warn of the social tsunami that awaits if we treat people as expendable and do not make the right investments in human capital. We find it difficult to envision how a democratic society can persist that leaves so many people behind. A livable hourly wage can go a long way toward meeting the basic needs of employees and giving people choices in life that exigencies now deny.

Money, Happiness, and Life Satisfaction

Social scientists have devoted substantial attention to the relationship between money and subjective well-being.[17,18,19,20] As it happens, there is a strong and persistent relationship. Researchers have found that the direction of causality primarily is from the money to subjective well-being, versus the other way around. The nature of the relationship between money and subjective well-being differs depending on which aspect of social well-being is under investigation. Subjective well-being has two parts. One part consists of a person's affective experiences in life or, more generally, degree of happiness. The other part pertains to how a person evaluates her life: how well she is doing in life given her goals and aspirations.

With respect to happiness, the relationship with money is curvilinear. At lower levels of income and wealth, there is a direct relationship: more money means greater happiness. However, once a person has a certain amount of money, more money has declining effects on happiness. Economists refer to this type of association as diminishing marginal utility, in which each additional dollar contributes less and less to happiness. Thus, happiness goes up with increases in income and wealth then begins to level out once a person makes a certain income or has accumulated a certain level of wealth. People at higher income levels are more or less happy, but not because of money. Other factors, such as the quality of one's relationships, become more important. The upshot of these results for lower-income individuals is that every little bit of extra money helps. Money can buy resources that can make life easier, provide more leisure activities, and allow greater time with friends and family. At lower income levels, money makes a difference in people's lives by unshackling them from the perpetual quest for security for themselves and those they love. Unfortunately, happiness is an elevator ride for people in the lowest quintile on income. It is not uncommon for the wages of low-income earners to change by as much as 50 percent from quarter to quarter because of, for example, changes in the number of work hours scheduled or unexpected increases in childcare or transportation expenses.[21]

The relationship between money and life satisfaction is more straightforward. In the early 1960s, psychologist Hadley Cantril interviewed over 20,000 people in 13 countries, culminating in a book, *The Pattern of Human Concerns*. The pattern revealed that people saw money and possessions as instrumental to an improved quality of life. As part of his study, Cantril developed one of the most interesting and widely used measures of life satisfaction, Cantril's Ladder. Visually, it is a ladder that extends from ground level ("0") up ten rungs to the top. The top of the ladder stands for the best possible life a person can imagine, and the bottom stands for the worst possible life imaginable. The task of respondents is to situate themselves on the ladder according to the way they now view their lives. Research has shown that the greater a person's access to money, the higher they place themselves on the ladder. People with more money say they are living better lives than those with less money.[22,23] It is easy to imagine how money can help. Money affords greater freedom from the mundane; more choices and options; resources that can be deployed to reduce stress or enhance convenience; a sense of security, autonomy, and control; and acquisition of goods that can be applied to meeting one's personal needs and goals.[24,25,26] Given the advantages of income and wealth, it is not surprising that money positively relates to better mental and physical health, and negatively relates to mortality.

If organizations administered Cantril's Ladder as a matter of course (which we think they should—and QBP conducts annual surveys on happiness), they could see for themselves how near or far employees are from living the kind of life they envision, and how little sense it makes to exhort employees to try harder while they are resource constrained and preoccupied with an abundance of worries.

Each year the United Way of Central Maryland runs a poverty simulator that provides middle-class Americans the chance to complete a set of tasks amid a set of constraints that are confronted by the working poor: using transit to get to and from work, doctors' appointments for children, or stores; relying on family for childcare; managing afterschool activities for children; researching eligibility for government programs and submitting the necessary paperwork; balancing a budget that partly depends on a teenage wage earner's money, and so on. Participants in the simulation often discover what poor workers know for a fact. It cannot be done. The choices and barriers are too weighty and insurmountable: to miss work, to go hungry, to leave a child alone at home, to be evicted from an apartment and go homeless, to have utilities and phone service disconnected, to have unmet medical needs for family members, to have home upkeep and repairs left unattended, and so on. For example, low-income wage earners are more frequent visitors at food banks because they have traded assets for other needs that have left them low on food.[27] Just imagine having a sick child, no health insurance, and no car and being told that you do not seem to be giving your all at work. Circumstances should not force people to choose between work and home or between food and shelter in a modern, compassionate society. We are asking low-income wage earners to do the impossible at great cost to themselves and their children.

Companies such as Bi-Rite Markets try to do their part by creating a community of employers who share a concern about the quality of life of their employees. We tasted strawberries at Bi-Rite Market in San Francisco. They are strawberries from Swanton Berry Farm. Every employee at Bi-Rite knows that. Employees visit the farms, ranches, and docks where the food in Bi-Rite comes from. They see firsthand that the foods come from places where employees are treated fairly, animals are handled humanely, and the land and waters are properly cared for through sound environmental practices.

Supermarket berries are bred for size, color, shelf life, and disease resistance. Strawberries are one of the fruits most heavily treated with pesticides. We are told that pickers vomit when the ground is stirred. The cheery-looking strawberry is a low-lying fruit, so pickers hunch when working. It is backbreaking work for about $10.00 per hour, or less. Agricultural work is exempt from the Fair Labor Standards Act, so minimum wage requirements do not apply to the 2.6 million direct farmworkers.

Why does Bi-Rite buy from Swanton Berry Farm? The farm produces great strawberries and treats its employees well. A guiding precept of the farm is the dignity of farm labor. Swanton Berry Farm was the first organic farm in the United States to contract with the United Farmworkers of America AFL-CIO. It provides farmworkers the best pay scale in the industry with an hourly wage (versus piece rate), a medical plan, a retirement plan, vacation pay, and holiday pay. It switches workers among crops to keep the work more interesting and to prevent overuse of specific body parts to reduce strain and injury. And employees receive unlimited time off to take care of their children's and their personal needs. The farm also offers low-cost housing, which most employees take advantage of. All of this increases the cost of strawberries but, as studies by agricultural economists conclude, not by much. Consumers can put their own activist dollars to work by purchasing from producers who shun the monolithic, mega-agrifarms to do what is right.

Living Wage

Because the federal minimum wage has remained low—neither keeping pace with inflation or returning full productivity gains to workers as compensation—states and municipalities began to set their own minimums. Starting in the 1980s, states and municipalities decided to break from federal guidelines and set their own wage standards, called living wages. The terminology of a living wage is a little confusing because originally it was an argument for a higher minimum wage, so they were once seen to be one and the same. The ideas of a living wage and a minimum wage were more closely bound together from the turn of the 20th century to midcentury. Today the living wage often is more objectively connected to requirements for an adequate standard of living.[28]

A living wage generally refers to an income level that allows a wage earner and her family to be self-sufficient, to have a predictable quality of life free of persistent anxieties and insecurities, and to engage in the life of the community. The wage is intended to mitigate the poverties of opportunity and enable people to fashion the life they wish to lead.

Starting in Baltimore, the contemporary living wage movement spread to approximately 140 municipalities and communities.[29,30,31] Communities often peg the wage to the poverty level for a family of three or some multiple of the poverty level, such as 30 percent above it. In 2018 these would translate into hourly wages of $9.99 and $12.99, respectively. Living wages often increase at fixed annual amounts or by the inflation rate. The number of people covered in these ordinances originally was small, sometimes covering only recipients of public funds such as contractors, and on occasion extending to all low-wage municipal workers. Many states and urban areas now have living wages (or higher minimums than mandated by federal law) that cover more employees. For example, the city of SeaTac, Washington, which lies between Seattle and

Tacoma, sets the minimum wage at $15.64 for hospitality and transportation employees. That wage has not deterred development, as nine new hotels are under construction. Owners say that the economic outlook of the area and availability of a stable, skilled workforce are more critical determinants for expansion than the minimum wage.[32]

On the basis of our reading, the literature on the effects of living wages on local communities is inconclusive. We have seen limited definitive evidence one way or another on employment/disemployment, purchasing power, and local sales, or on internal organizational benefits such as boosts in morale. However, living wages do not appear to have had much of an impact on poverty rates, likely due to the low proportion of urban workers covered by living wages.[33] Additionally, poverty rates are determined by family composition; however, living wages are assigned only to workers at the company. The employee may be part of a big or small family whose other members may or may not be employed. Therefore, the degree to which a specific wage helps to move people out of poverty depends on family circumstances and household earnings.[34]

Poverty and Basic Needs

As we see it, a bigger problem with the living wage is pegging it to a specious poverty rate. In many instances, the living wage is insufficient, particularly in areas with high costs of living. When public opinion and consumer expenditure surveys ask people how much it would cost to live a minimally acceptable lifestyle, estimates routinely exceed the current poverty threshold by more than two times.[35] The trouble with living wages as typically defined is that they are still not high enough. Many beneficiaries of higher minimum wages remain in the chasm between officially impoverished and self-sufficient: the working poor.

The working poor are those who have full-time jobs and whose households technically are over the poverty line, but who rely on social aid to get by. Their pay lifts them over the poverty line but does not provide enough to liberate them from everyday trials. One of the purported goals of instituting a living wage is to make life livable for people without the need for public assistance. However, neither the minimum wage nor the living wage as employed are adequate to cover individuals' basic needs.

Most definitions of basic needs include the costs associated with housing, food, transportation, and healthcare. Some calculations include childcare expenses. Other necessities, such as clothing, insurance, educational supplies, personal care, entertainment, and household items, are estimated as a percentage of core basic needs or from existing data furnished, for example, by the US Bureau of Labor Statistics. These calculations do not include rainy-day funds, set-asides for retirement, enrichment activities, college savings, or unexpected expenses such as car repairs. If a family wants to fund these latter activities, it must live frugally to do so. For the most part, basic needs are those things we once thought a job could buy.

Pinning wages to basic needs is the ideal way to establish minimums, although as applied they too are indifferent to family configurations and employment statuses. Commonly, a company like Patagonia that pays a living wage will pay at a level for the single wage earner using one of several calculators for living wages. Patagonia uses one developed at MIT, appropriately called the MIT Living Wage Calculator. Other indices include the Self-Sufficiency Standard, developed at the Wider Opportunities for Women; the Basic Needs Budget Calculator, developed at the National Center for Children in Poverty; and the Basic Family Budget Calculator, developed at the Economic Policy Institute. Variations exist among the calculators; however, the intent behind each is the same: to assess how much money an individual or family needs to live a self-sufficient life.

We have characterized needs in the context of employer-employee relationships; however, we do not think that a social problem of the magnitude of poverty is the private sector's alone to solve. Although we are not able to say how social responsibilities should be balanced, we can say that a helpful way to start would be to establish basic needs as a new national guideline to replace a concept of poverty that has outlasted its usefulness.

Mollie Orshansky, an economist working within the Social Security Administration, created the poverty line (which varies depending on familial configurations and ages).[36] President Johnson adopted it as the official measure of poverty in 1969 as part of his War on Poverty, and it is the same index used today, updated annually by increases in the Consumer Price Index. The measure is based on the most economical nutritional diet for a family of three, based on figures supplied by the Department of Agriculture in a 1955 report. The dietary plan Orshansky used was intended for short-term emergency use and not for long-term sustenance. As food constituted one third of a family's budget in the 1960s, by multiplying the "basket of foods" by three she could estimate the total income required for short-term subsistence living for a family of three—and then modify poverty levels for other types of family units by using similar assumptions and multipliers. Orshansky understood that the measure was imperfect, warning that it is easier to determine what is too little as opposed to what is enough. In 1963, when she made her original calculations, the poverty line was 50 percent of median income for a family of four. Today, the ratio is 25 percent.

The poverty line provides a convenient standard from which to make year-over-year comparisons; however, it is not a good index of poverty. It is based on a bare-bones diet and is uniformly applied throughout the continental United States regardless of differences in the cost of living. It does not accurately reflect today's expenses, in which families spend proportionately less on food and more on housing, transportation, childcare, and healthcare. For example, housing now consumes 41 percent of the budget within low-income households.[37]

Based on the U.S. Census Bureau's 2016 "Official Poverty Report," the official poverty rate is 12.7 percent. That rate has been relatively constant since 1970; most of the gains from the War on Poverty were made in the first few years of the national assault on poverty. According to the National Center for Children in Poverty, about 15 million children in the United States, or 21 percent of all children, live in families with incomes below the federal poverty threshold. This is one in five children. But if the current poverty level underestimates the true requirements to live a satisfying life by 25–50 percent, as some believe, the number of children who live in impoverished environments would be higher.[38] How much higher is hard to say because poverty statistics do not include noncash benefits from programs such as EITC (Earned Income Tax Credit), WIC (Women, Infants, and Children), SNAP (Supplemental Nutritional Assistance Program), and Medicaid. The statistics do include income from direct cash transfer programs such as TANF (Temporary Assistance for Needy Families). Among the cacophony of programs and labyrinth of eligibility guidelines, however, studies find that one third of the people who are eligible for benefits never apply for them.[39] We are back to our original suggestion. Let's produce a clearer picture about what people need and then figure out the best way to meet those needs. As the Cato Institute concluded in a recent report, we have been throwing life preservers to low-income individuals, but we haven't been pulling them into the boat.[40]

Benefits Employees Want

Companies try to lift the load of employees by offering benefit plans in addition to compensation. Although companies' nouveau perquisites are nice-to-haves, surveys of employees show that the traditional benefits matter most to them. Healthcare comes first, followed by flexible work arrangements and paid time off in its various incarnations; for example, sick days and vacation days.[41]

Healthcare

Healthcare is not only the benefit most sought by employees; it is the most expensive. According to the Kaiser Foundation, the average family premium in 2016 was $18,142.[42] Of this, employees contributed $5,277 on average, with the employer covering the balance. The average deductibles are approximately $1,500 but surpass $2,000 at smaller organizations. Expensive.

Companies valiantly try to figure out ways to hold down costs and keep coverage affordable and practical for employees. Nevertheless, given the historically large increases in the cost of healthcare, employers have been gradually shifting more and more of the premium expense to employees, increasing out-of-pocket expenses such as copayments and deductibles, reducing provider networks, and pulling back on prescription coverage. Overall the increased healthcare costs for employees have gobbled up a sizeable portion of their earnings. In a recent survey, employees described the effects of rising healthcare costs: 28 percent reduced their retirement contributions; 25 percent reported difficulties paying for basic needs such as heat, food, and housing; 27 percent said they had used up all of their savings; and 30 percent said they planned to postpone retirement.[43]

Although the costs of healthcare are painful to many wage earners, they can be extremely problematic for the working poor, particularly if they do not qualify for Medicaid. The Affordable Care Act sought to expand Medicaid coverage and create a national standard for eligibility at 138 percent of the federal poverty level. However, states have the right to opt out, and 18 states still maintain their own eligibility criteria. In the United States, attempts to make healthcare more affordable have faltered as policy fixes became stuck in a political quagmire. In addition, people who work less than 30 hours per week often do not qualify for healthcare or paid time off (about two-thirds of part-timers are excluded from benefits programs). This is especially true in low-hour industries such as accommodations, food services, personal services, home healthcare, arts and entertainment, and retail trade.[44]

When it comes to healthcare, the companies in our sample are generous, with most paying for the preponderance, or all, of the costs. Instructure pays 100 percent of employees' healthcare premiums and supplements this coverage with nutritional foods and a robust wellness program called PandaFit (the panda is the company's mascot), which includes an annual high-profile weight-loss contest. In addition to a stellar healthcare plan that is also 100 percent company-paid, INTUITIVE sponsors a "Care Day" each quarter in which various healthcare providers are brought to the company. Caregivers have included nutritionists, optometrists, nurses, pharmacists, physical therapists, reflexologists, and more. Employees make appointments in advance and receive full check-ups or assessments at no cost. INTUITIVE also has an on-site gym with showers, bike groups, running groups, weight-loss competitions, and so on. Plus, there are weekly fitness classes. While we were there, we saw advertisements for bar exercises, piloxing (Pilates + boxing), and yoga. PURE Insurance pays 70 percent of employees' health premiums and, in exchange for a few simple tasks such as contacting a tele-doc, will reimburse employees 100 percent for their deductible expenses. BAF offers an on-site full-time nurse with prescription-writing privileges and an excellent employee assistance program that includes a host of educational programs such as smoking cessation. The company has comfortable lactation rooms (not overhauled closets, but real rooms), ball chairs and heating pads for people with back problems, and special parking for pregnant women. SAS, one of the first employers to be employee-centric before these types of companies were being praised as fashionable exceptions, offers 85 percent health coverage for families and has a free on-site healthcare facility, pharmacy, pool, and fitness center.

Flexibility

According to a National Study for the Changing Workforce survey, 87 percent of employees said flexibility is critical to their job choices.[45] This makes sense given the socioeconomic changes that have occurred over the past 75 years. In 1960, one out of three women were in the workforce. Two-thirds are today. In 1960, 73 percent of children were in households with first-time-married parents. That number is 46 percent today, with 34 percent of children now in single-parent households as opposed to 9 percent in 1960. Today women are the primary breadwinners in 40 percent of households with children. The level was 10 percent in 1960.[46] Dual wage-earner families also are working a combined ten hours longer per week than in the 1970s. The stay-at-home mom is long gone. In fact, households need her more than ever in the workplace. But she, and he, need help—as surveys reveal. A survey by the National Partnership for Women and Families found that 40 percent of respondents regularly experience conflicts between home and work.

Flexibility broadly involves the ability to decide when and where a person will work, and the length of time a person wants to devote to work tasks. This incorporates flex-place, mainly telecommunicating, and flextime. Flextime refers to any program that deviates from the standard fixed schedule, and includes job sharing, compressed work weeks, and working variable hours. The use of flexible work arrangements consistently is associated with greater job satisfaction, employee commitment, performance, psychological well-being, and physical health. Patagonia recently introduced a win-win-win scenario in its hours of operation at headquarters that gave employees and their families more time to engage in their passions on weekends. Employees recently voted on a change to a variant of a compressed work week called 9/80: 9 hours of work a day with every other Friday off (or 80 hours, rounded).[47] This modest but highly intuitive modification has increased morale, supported current productivity levels, lowered operating costs, and reduced the company's carbon footprint.

Flex-place, or telecommuting, can solve quite a few cost problems, and studies show that managers' greatest fears (shirking from home versus working from home) are unfounded. Companies save on rents, and employees who work from home are more productive, take fewer breaks and shorter lunches, and start punctually each day. Research also suggests that telecommuting works best when days are taken as needed or restricted to certain days of the week rather than taken habitually; chronic use over time seems to erode home-work boundaries and interfere with the completion of work goals. However, many low-paying jobs are customer-facing or involve tasks performed on the premises.[48,49]

A discussion of time in the workplace could itself be the subject of a book. Our goal is to make a few points on a couple of salient issues. First on the list is parental leave. If you ask, "What parental leave?" you would have a point. Of 15 developed economies studied, the United States is the only country that does not require paid maternity leave, and one of two without paid paternity leave. Some leaves in the developed world are six months or longer, and paid at a rate of 70–100 percent of current salary for an average range of 14–20 weeks.[50]

The Family and Medical Leave Act (FMLA) in the United States requires that employers provide 12 weeks of unpaid parental leave and reserve the individual's position until the parent returns to work, but the act only applies to businesses with more than 50 employees, and employees must have worked

1,250 hours during the prior year (about 25 hours per week). Consequently, only about 50 percent of workers qualify; and getting those meager provisions through the U.S. Congress took many years of partisan tussles.[51] Apart from the law, a recent exposé in the *New York Times* discusses the surreal obstacles pregnant women face in the workplace and their treatment as "lepers" versus people giving life.[52]

A prolonged period without pay creates a hardship for many employees. New mothers will use their sick time and vacation days, if available, to absorb some of the costs of being away from work. As a result, American mothers and fathers without the necessary financial support return to work earlier than parents in other countries. The sooner mothers return to work, the less time they spend bonding and nurturing their newborns; the less likely they are to breastfeed (as research shows, breastfeeding is associated with a lower incidence of infections, respiratory problems, and allergies, and enhanced neurological development); and the higher the child mortality.[53] Their commitment to the organization also declines.

Once again, the companies we visited come to the rescue. Edmunds has introduced programs that underscore the importance of family. Most notably, it has implemented a progressive maternity (and paternity) leave policy that gives six months of paid time off for primary caregivers and two months of paid time off for nonprimary caregivers. Finally, a policy that rivals those offered elsewhere in the Western world! There are also flexible ramp-down and ramp-up periods for two months before and after leaves to smooth transitions out of and back into the workplace. These ramps are likely to help with adjustment and lighten return-to-work regrets. Abrupt and early returns to work are taxing on new mothers and magnify other stresses the employee experiences at work and home.[54]

Childcare

When lower-income mothers return to work, they likely discover that many childcare arrangements made prior to their return to work are impermanent and the alternatives of accessible care of high quality are expensive. The "New America Care Report" estimates the average annual cost of daycare to be $16,554.[55] That amount consumes $7.94 in hourly earnings, and in some instances a person's wage does not offset the expense for childcare (the *childcare squeeze*). If a family is eligible, subsidies and credits for childcare exist, but they often are insufficient to ensure a level of care that would positively affect the child on cognitive abilities, social development, and academic achievement. Quality is essential, but so is accessibility, as one third of the lowest quintile of wage earners do not own cars. Companies are aware of these difficulties, and 20 percent of employers with one hundred or more employees now have on-site or near-site childcare facilities, though many are not subsidized and are unaffordable. Difficulty in securing childcare is one of the chief reasons for turnover among lower-income employees (families in the lowest 20 percent in household earnings).

The benefits of quality early childhood care are indisputable. James Heckman, the Nobel Laureate, led a team of researchers who tracked children from low-income families who were provided free, quality childcare over a 30-year period. Compared to controls, the grown children from the program earned more, had fewer misdemeanor arrests, and were less likely to be drug users or to have high blood pressure.[56]

Universal childcare is expensive. However, the United States devotes the smallest percentage of GDP to childcare of any industrialized nation. Overall the United States expends 1.6 percent of GDP on family benefits, which places it well below the mean of all OECD countries. For all of the rhetoric about the importance of family that oozes out of Washington, the fact of the matter is that the United States is not politically kind to children and families.[57] We could afford more. An increase in family income (or equivalent) of a mere $3,000 for the first five years of a child's life is associated with a 20 percent increase in that child's earnings later in life.[58] A $1,000 increase for a period of 2–5 years increases children's achievement scores by 5–6 percent of a standard deviation. Besides, the roof is leaking. If we wait and do too little now, little leaks are certain to become big, expensive ones later.

A window in Patagonia's cafeteria is oddly placed. It's worth a look. On the other side, little children are sitting on little chairs at little tables. Their over-sized parents seated at the miniature furniture look on, or color, or build with their children. Patagonia has been running its own on-site childcare facility since the company's start. Patagonia has found that many of the barriers that have dissuaded other companies from venturing into childcare facilities of their own are not true. The program is not inordinately expensive; insurance has never been a problem; and becoming an accredited program was straight-forward. The company never questioned the wisdom of its choice. Patagonia does not want work to separate families, and this is reflected in the childcare center and in the company's generous paternity leaves (12 weeks' full pay) and maternity leaves (16 weeks' full pay). The childcare program is a noticeable part of Patagonia. The outdoor play area extends outward from the headquarters. It is a well-stocked playground that in the hands of experienced workers can easily engage creative minds. In fact, professional childcare workers staff the program and are employees of Patagonia entitled to the full array of Patagonia benefits. Those benefits include retirement savings and employer-paid medical premiums for all employees, with no hour restrictions. The childcare workers enjoy their work, are compensated fairly, and stay.

To make the program accessible to all parents of children ages eight weeks to eight years, Patagonia partially subsidizes program costs on a sliding scale by income level. Later, we discovered that the childcare center is a feeder for future employees. Patagonia now employs 15 workers who were once graduates of the childcare program and who presently have their own children enrolled. Patagonia thinks of it as long-term succession planning. The childcare center also fulfills one other function: it brings the parents of the children together and is the stimulus for lifelong adult friendships. Children are the epicenter of parental affiliations, providing the foundation and rationale for social engagement outside of work.

Time Off

BambooHR was settling into its new building when we arrived. The building still had that new-home feel with room numbers taped to doors, posters and prints leaning against walls, stuffed pandas (again, a mascot) lounging in hallways and on chairs, and voices echoing off barren surfaces. The open architecture with exposed pipes and vents reflected the simplicity and functionality of the company's software and the humility and unpretentiousness of the people. If an archaeologist was asked to decipher the sparsely furnished building, she would readily note the democracy of the open floor plan, consistency of materials and supplies, and undefined seating arrangements. An especially astute archaeologist also would notice that the standard accoutrements of technology companies are missing, namely game tables, large funky commons areas with overstuffed chairs and thinking spots, and a storehouse of foods to outlast a year of deprivation. The primary reason for the countercultural décor is that BambooHR wants people to go home. It wants people to use their time well during work hours and leave by 5:30 p.m. BambooHR does not want people to assemble in commons areas to conduct talkathons without purpose or agenda. It doesn't want people playing Ping-Pong or shooting hoops with the expectation that they will make up for lost time at the end of the day. And there is no need for an oversupply of goodies: go home for dinner, go out for dinner, but just go. Bamboo does not like to mandate much, preferring to make most meetings and events voluntary; however, it told a new hire who reliably worked late that his behavior was inconsistent with the values of the company, and that he had to leave work sooner. Other companies in our sample of organizations have similar outlooks. At *INTUITIVE*, working long hours is a sign of a problem. Long hours suggest that activities may not be appropriately distributed to the right people, that the project is not staffed correctly, that work is being performed which wasn't specified in the contract, and so on. A problem exists somewhere in the system that needs fixing. One of the things we noticed across the companies we visited is that there is plenty of time in a day to get one's work done if all of the extraneous nonsense is purged from the workplace, people remain focused on a few essential goals, and time is managed efficiently.[59]

People have their preferences regarding how much they want to work. The points we wish to make are that not working all the time is a good thing and that you do not have to at the companies in our sample.

All companies allot employees short, discretionary paid time off in the form of sick days, personal days, and vacation. Most developed nations grant four to five weeks of vacation a year. Companies in the United States tend to phase in vacation schedules. Years of service determine the number of vacation days available. Clarus Commerce is an exception, giving vacations of three weeks for all new employees, which incrementally increase at anniversary milestones. This sort of arrangement makes sense to us, as newer, younger employees often have the most urgent need for time off. Often, though, employees start with ten days of vacation during their first five years of employment. Even when vacation days are available, Americans are reluctant to take them all, for the same reason they tend not to use other flexible arrangements: they are afraid it will negatively affect them. And it does. (America isn't called the "No Vacation Nation" for nothing.) People who use more of their flexible time receive lower performance reviews, smaller increases, and fewer promotions. Only 19 percent of Americans take all their days, leaving an average of 3.2 days on the table, or 429 million vacation days in total.[60,61]

Good companies want people to take breaks and do not hold it against them when they do. Penalizing people for taking advantage of the programs that the company itself created is counterproductive. Employees will engage in activities that are bad for their health and decrease performance in the longer run. To avoid the semblance of being undedicated, employees will work while on vacation, shorten their maternity leaves, come to work sick, strand children at daycare, and so on. The unspoken prohibition against attending to personal needs over work worsens employees' stress. Consequently, the companies we met with want people to use benefits to the fullest and not to worry that their use will negatively affect their standing in the organization. Organizations that offer family-supportive benefits must therefore encourage their use. For example, FONA does not deduct points from people who are unable to be present at work because of personal injury or commitments to family members. The corporate reflex is not to bemoan lost productivity when people are not able to perform at their best, but to ask, "How can we help you?" The solution can be as simple as giving people the time they need: "Please, don't worry about anything here; just go and take care of your father." One employee told us about his chronically bad back and multiple surgeries that had sidelined him from work, off and on, for many months. The company approached him about a new job in inventory—working on computers—that he could perform with his disability. "I never worked on computers before. When they [FONA] say, don't worry, they mean don't worry. They will find a way to help." Today that employee is thriving in his new role.

The Motley Fool once considered whether it should make employees take a minimum number of vacation days but thought that solution was too invasive and decided to just let people know that it is okay to take vacations. To underscore this commitment to time off, The Motley Fool sends a select employee on a "Fool's Errand" each month. A person is randomly chosen (the number of entries a person has in the raffle is equal to his or her years of service), given $1,000, and told to take two consecutive, completely unplugged weeks off within the month. This proves that the company can make do with temporary absences and that the employee has permission to relax.

BambooHR wants people to free their minds and enrich themselves in ways they are not able to at work; thus, their novel "Paid Paid Vacation" program. The repeated word "paid" is not an error: BambooHR pays people $2,000 to go on paid vacations. This benefit provides employees with memorable, life-enhancing experiences for themselves and their families and gives their bodies and minds much-needed breaks from daily routine. The time off reinvigorates and frees previously occupied mental space for creative thoughts and ideas. Not only do employees take their full vacations, but they document their travels with photos using the social media site Yammer, which employees use internally for personal correspondences.

The HR team at Edmunds are masters at behavior change. Their interventions begin by asking a few straightforward questions: "What do we want people to do? Do we want our employees to take vacation?" Simple. Offer a $500 use-it-or-lose-it "Trip Cash" reimbursement for employees' vacation expenses. "Do we want employees to take better advantage of the range of benefits available to them?" Okay, hold a beer garden benefits fair prior to open enrollment for benefits. Create a beer sampling station for each benefit—with advisors present at each—and have people circulate through to obtain the information they need. It works.

Providing family-supportive benefits that ease employees' conflicts between work and family responsibilities is one way companies make a whole life possible. For most, these benefits and programs have the effects intended: they reduce the discord between work and family obligations and enable employees to be more committed at work, more satisfied with their jobs and their lives, and less likely to leave the organization.[62,63,64]

PART 2

HUMAN NEEDS

CHAPTER 7

BELONGING

Be inclusive

National surveys conducted over the past 30 years indicate that happiness in the United States is gradually declining. Indeed, a recent United Nations report on national happiness (http://worldhappiness.report/ed/2018/) reveals that the United States fell four places in the rankings from the prior year, to 18th happiest in the world. Although income per capita has more than doubled since 1972, happiness has declined. Like individuals, once societies reach a certain economic level, further increases in wealth have little to no effect on happiness (this relationship is referred to as the Easterlin Paradox). Chasing after more and more wealth with the thought that it will buy greater happiness is a red herring.[1]

Decreased feelings of social connectedness causally relate to declines in happiness.[2] People belong to fewer groups and associations, marry at lower rates, and have fewer social contacts. As a country we slowly are losing the social nourishment we require for our happiness and well-being.[3,4]

Feelings of inclusion, companionship, and social acceptance are significant to employees and employers. People who feel a sense of belonging are more committed, giving, and satisfied and report greater well-being (they are happier, less anxious, and less depressed) and optimism than people who feel excluded.[5,6] And people who feel socially connected experience lower stress levels and exhibit better coping in response to traumatic events. For example, for members of emergency response teams and firefighters, the tighter the teams' bonds the less distress they experience and the quicker their emotional recovery following acute events.[7]

The human drive for connectivity is potent since we have an evolutionary hunger for contact.[8] Closely connected groups offered a mechanism for survival. Our bonds afforded communal protection, mutual support, temporary refuge and relief, information exchange, and divisions of labor that made securing food, providing shelter, and making clothing more efficient. Humans organized around identifiable social groups whose members could be depended on to contribute complementary skills to ensure collective comfort, safety, and sustenance. Being in a group was literally life-sustaining, and therefore belonging is recognized as a fundamental human need.[9,10]

What It Means to Belong

Belonging to a group entails much more than simple membership. A membership card will gain a person entry but will not ensure the depth and quality of relations one feels in belonging. To feel a pivotal part of a group, a person has to feel wanted and valued; to believe he is able to make substantive contributions to the whole; to be of concern to other members; actively engaged in the affairs of the group; and confident that his needs will be satisfied through participation within the group.[11]

Healthy organizations realize that their effectiveness relies upon the goodwill and solidarity of groups, so they put quite a bit of effort into social outings and rituals that recurrently bring people together. These are not the forced activities conjured up in annual meetings or the dreaded teambuilding exercises poured from prepared packets as instant trust and friendship. They are not, as one employee at Health Catalyst described, "funishments"—rare and artificial teambuilding exercises that people are forced to take part in and required to enjoy. Such attempts to manufacture happiness are misguided. In a study that had people listen to classical music, for example, those who were told to try to be as happy as possible ended up in worse moods than people who were told to just listen.[12] The good social stuff that builds the joints and connective tissues of teams, which in turn enables members to move nimbly and effectively in unison, occurs regularly and spontaneously in the organizations we visited, without continuous prompts for togetherness. The social outings and extravaganzas conducted by companies in our sample are freewheeling and not overly engineered. A fabricated environment would disrupt the spontaneity on which growing relationships depend and would interfere with what people can learn about themselves and others through play. An employee at Clarus Commerce told us of one adventure the company took to a foreboding zip line involving a wobbly 30-foot ascent, a 1,500-foot line, and a 40-mile-per-hour rail ride. Had a chant of his name not arisen from the ground below, he might never have taken flight. If not a momentous event, it is one that the employee remembers as an episode of accomplishment: of doing what he thought to be undoable through the urging and support of his colleagues.

Social extracurriculars may appear contrary to real work and as senseless wastes of time. Certainly the no-nonsense Type A people see it as time that could be better spent putting fingers to keyboards, or nuts on bolts. But forming meaningful relationships is real work that the best companies do because they realize that personal affinities and deep social bonds are failsafe measures against team breakdowns and are essential for top team performance. Engaging in activities with others also is important for mental health. A couple of years ago, experts compiled a report for the UK government that describes how to improve general well-being. Simply stated, the "Five-a-Day Program" outlines five things you should do each day to improve your psychological health. The first two items instruct you to connect with others and to actively do things with others. The next three items are to be mindful and aware of the sensations around you, to learn something new and experience joy, and to commit to one act of kindness each day.[13]

The hosting of social events is thus important and thoughtfully enacted in our sample organizations. People get to know, like, and trust one another through repeated, gratifying social encounters. BAF sponsors monthly outings to baseball games, comedy clubs, and off-Broadway shows; encourages employees' involvement in clubs such as kickball, sand volleyball, and bowling; and holds colossal family events such as a summer amusement jamboree and a Halloween pumpkin patch festival. Regeneron has spring flings, summer barbecues, a cheesy-Hawaiian-shirt day, holiday parties, and a multitude of company-wide assemblies that celebrate advances in science. Clarus Commerce schedules quarterly events such as bowling excursions, happy hours, dodgeball tournaments, and whirlyball (a team sport played a little like lacrosse—except using a whiffle ball—while driving bumper cars). *INTUITIVE* hosts food-sponsored events such as a spring fling where executives become grill masters for the troops, and a chili and cornbread cook-off where the company honors the best cook and runners-up for their culinary prowess. It also sponsors a farm day, where kids invade a pumpkin patch; "*INTUITIVE* at the Movies," where once a year the company rents out a movie theater and shows a movie of choice; and an end-of-year formal holiday party.

Feelings of belongingness are particularly challenging in organizations where telecommuting is prevalent. TCG is such a company. In addition to supporting employees' personal preferences to work remotely because of the time savings and flexibility it affords, Dan Turner (the company's founder and CEO) decided he would rather spend money on staff than on a central office where everyone could work. So TCG has had to be creative in establishing a collaborative, cohesive environment. In this regard, the company conceived of a new department for the task of building employee rapport: the Department of Employee Happiness. We rather like the name of the department because of its obvious connection to a large body of social science research in positive psychology and subjective well-being. The department is broadly concerned with employees' general welfare and should not be seen as an institutional agent for merriment. The department's real mandate is to forge strong inter-personal bonds among community members, generate a heightened sense of belonging within the workforce, ensure that employees progress devel-opmentally and thrive, and further employees' identification within a fuzzy corporate presence. And, too, it wants people to have fun. Accordingly, TCG introduced several meaningful touch points among employees that include daily standing meetings with teleconferencing, quarterly business briefings and socials, monthly charitable and social activities, and tickets to most major entertainment and sports venues, which are available to employees.

The Pain of Exclusion

It is easy to underscore the importance of belonging by recalling the times when you were not invited to the party, not asked for your opinion, not included in a meeting, or not asked to be on a team. The sting of exclusion and rejection is appreciable and includes harmful physiological reactions in autonomic func-tioning.[14,15] To borrow an analogy from Arthur Schopenhauer, we are like por-cupines huddled together for warmth. Our craving for society brings us together but our proximity also introduces dangers—the occasional quill in the side.[16] The quills that push members away can be problematic in organizations. The prick of rejection can instigate retaliation, especially if there is no hope of reentry into a group either because the ostracized member does not wish to return or because the member's presence is too disruptive to the group to allow reconciliation.[17]

One reaction to exclusion is to aggress against the group or engage in anti-social behaviors to repair the personal injury activated by rejection. Researchers use different methods for producing feelings of exclusion in laboratory settings. One is cyberball. With this technique, subjects play a game of virtual catch with fictitious others who limit the number of times they pass the ball to the participant. Another is the "get acquainted" technique in which study confederates ostensibly state their desire to work with the subject following a brief period of interaction; for example, "I hate to tell you this, but no one chose you as someone they'd like to work with." The results of these manipulations are consistent under different experimental ruses: subjects who feel excluded give more hot sauce to study confederates (who said they did not like spicy foods); deliver louder and longer noxious sounds to confederates; and stick more pins into a voodoo-doll representation of a confederate. This research also illustrates that revenge is indeed sweet. Getting even attenuates hostile feelings and restores people's moods to equilibrium.[18,19]

Research also shows that feelings of exclusion heighten unethical behavior. People who felt excluded through the cyberball paradigm were more likely to lie about solving (unsolvable) puzzles in a later task. A field study by the same investigators revealed a similar pattern of results between feelings of exclusion and unethical behaviors. Employees who felt more ostracized in the workplace were rated by supervisors as more likely to be involved in questionable ethical practices, such as falsifying time reports.[20]

Although removal from a group is personally hurtful, aggression, anti-social behaviors, and social withdrawal are not the most common ways that people respond to excommunication. The usual reaction is to atone for whatever one did wrong to get back into the group. If there is hope for reintegration into the group, excluded members try to become more attractive by being more compliant with the group's attitudes, more complimentary of the group, and more accommodating and helpful to the group. Affiliative motives are strong and people generally want to renew broken relationships, particularly if no appealing alternative group is within reach.[21,22]

Belonging or Bondage?

As much as we embrace belonging, there is a dark side. A desire to belong produces conformity. Leaders who, for example, may want complete acquiescence to their authority can use people's urge to belong as a powerful instrument of control. Inclusion becomes contingent on towing the line; those who do not are cast adrift.

As coming-of-age movies convincingly show, people will go to great lengths to be included in groups that are important to them, and groups will exert tremendous pressure to ensure that their members adhere to group norms. Solomon Asch in the 1950s illustrated the power of group influence in a series of classic experiments.[23] In the most acclaimed experiment, the experimenter asked groups of six to eight people to compare the lengths of three lines to a target line of a given length. The task of the group was to say which of the three lines was closest in length to the target. In most instances there was no question about the correct answer. All of the people in the group were confederates of the experimenter except for one lone subject, who after hearing the answers of the confederates had to publicly state which answer he thought was correct. Each session involved 18 matching trials with confederates giving the correct answers in only 6 trials. In the control condition, when answering alone, subjects said the incorrect answer less than 1 percent of the time—a small deviation from perfection that might be attributable to a mistaken report-out or other human error. However, when responding as part of a group, subjects gave an incorrect answer an average of 37 percent of the time.

This experiment shows that there is a fine line between belonging and compliance. We often yield to the opinions of the group. We yield because we want to be liked, to be accepted, to fit in, to not be left out. The results of conformity experiments apply not only to physical stimuli such as line lengths, but to moral questions as well. People will modify their opinions to follow group consensus on issues such as free speech, the use of torture, and other moral dilemmas.[24]

Conformity is most likely to occur when decisions are public, the group is desirable, the group consists of more than three people, and the group is unanimous in its opinion. However, there are ways to guard against blind conformity. One way to protect against counterfeit consensus is to implement formal procedures designed to question decisions. In the 1500s the papacy had decided that the canonization process was getting out of hand when Guinefort achieved sainthood. St. Guinefort was a dog who had saved a baby. In 1587 Sixtus V set up the office of Promoter of the Faith. The role of the office was to raise logical and analytical objections to proposed saints so that only the truly worthy would be granted sainthood. Because the duty of the office's occupant was to oppose sainthood, he was said to be taking the side of the devil, or was the Devil's Advocate. How effective was the position? Very. Pope John Paul II eliminated the office in 1983 and more people were canonized during his tenure than in the previous five centuries combined. The formal adversarial system was instrumental in sustaining the strict definition of sainthood.[25,26,27] In a similar vein, one of the executives we spoke with at SAS reserves a portion of each meeting to dissenting points of view or, as placed on the agenda, "diverse opinion time" as a formal means to critically counter-argue points of view.

A second way to combat conformity is to build an irreverent, transparent culture. The Motley Fool is named after Shakespeare's professional jester, Touchstone, in *As You Like It*. Motley was a form of dress, typically a woolen fabric of mixed colors. That mode of dress lay outside the sumptuary laws of Elizabethan England, which restricted the wearing of certain luxury goods and essentially mandated that a person look the role he was assigned to in society. The licensed fool, however, was an individual of great wit who lived outside of society and who, because of that, could speak truthfully about society, even to royalty. We have thought that every CEO should have such a licensed pro by his side, although we have seen spouses ably step into the role. Practically speaking, the founding brothers of The Motley Fool, Tom and David Gardner, dispensed with the fool and instead infused their corporate creation with Foolishness. The Motley Fool, which has no dress code other than "to not wear anything that would embarrass your parents," has internalized the honesty of its investment insights in its workforce by enshrining honesty as one of its core values: always tell the truth—especially to "royalty," which is an expectation for every Fool.

Third, simple, straightforward dialog, which is diligently promoted at Instructure, can forthrightly deal with the real issues and keep debate open and honest. Call them essentialists, but the people at Instructure distill the overly complex and stick to the clean and uncluttered in discussions. Lengthy correspondences that risk obfuscation of messages are marked "TLDR" (too long, didn't read). "TLDR" works as a verb in Instructure, meaning "get to the point" and "do not add extraneous facts that unduly complicate or mislead."

A fourth way of preserving an environment of clear, open debate is to hire smart, spritely dissidents who value truth. PURE Insurance has placed many of its chips on the quality of its people. PURE is prudent about who it hires, concentrating on people who are passionately curious, critical thinkers; these are people who have active and engaged intellects and relish probing for truth. Since like begets like, a large proportion (about 40 percent) of new employees come from a highly successful employee referral program. Similarly, being academics at heart, the people of SAS and Regeneron are practitioners of the precepts of science, embracing knowledge sharing, earnest deliberations, independent thinking, meticulousness, and truth.

The companies in our sample rarely get hiring wrong and preserve a healthy cultural milieu through astute recruitment and selection practices. Since people make mistakes in choosing organizations, and organizations make mistakes in hiring employees, separations will occur. The organizations we met with recognize the inevitability of errors on either side of the employee-employer relationship and exercise "no fault separations." PURE Insurance admittedly is a hard club to get into, but it wants to make it easy for people to leave as well. Trapping people who do not want to be at the company makes no sense. Departing employees, of which there are few, receive a percentage of their base salaries based on tenure (which totals more than typical severance policies) in addition to a host of career transition options: PURE will extend benefits coverage, assist with résumé preparation, facilitate networking, provide coaching and advisory services, and cover relocation costs. Similarly, if for reasons of performance or cultural incompatibilities a team member is asked to leave Health Catalyst, the company has set the minimum severance to generally be three months of pay so that life may go on for the employee without putting the employee in financial peril. These practices support honest communication between employees and their employers, ease tensions that may arise during separations, and promote a happy league of alumni.

The Person-Organization Fit

Given that a sense of belonging is critical to the health and welfare of employees and promotes employee citizenship, job satisfaction, and performance, organizations will want to ensure that people fit in and feel a vital part of the organization. Concord Hospitality has perfected its hiring processes over the years to ensure that it lets the right ones in, particularly people who have a "hospitality heart." In addition to an employee referral program, Concord conducts "hiring sprints," a standardized method of quickly reducing the number of potential employees from a dozen or so to just a few, with the latter invited to a succession of on-site interviews. The sprints consist of web links that take candidates to sites that, using standard questions (per position), give them the opportunity to tell the company more about themselves. In turn, candidates have a chance to learn more about the job and the culture of the institution—and to self-select out of contention if the corporate value system and performance expectations do not jive with their own.

Edmunds preserves its highly collaborative culture by effectively screening and culling the noncollegial types—egocentric, insensitive jerks for whom Edmunds has extremely low tolerance—from its ranks. These bad actors are kept to a minimum by taking a job candidate's cultural fit into account from the moment he or she expresses interest in Edmunds as a place to work and then continuously reinforcing corporate values and behavioral expectations once inside.

At N2 Publishing "fit" minimally means that a candidate is approachable and friendly and possesses certain attributes such as collegiality, humility, self-discipline, and integrity. A candidate also must be a "radiator" as opposed to a "drain." The symbolism is stark. Drains are biting, gloomy actors who pull others down. N2 defends against the people who deenergize relationships and upend performance through difficult, frustrating, irritating, or rude behaviors.[28] On the other hand, radiators . . . radiate. They are people who heat the place up with their buoyant and lifting spirits. The company looks for people who will augment the capabilities of the organization and make those around them better.

In selecting people, Health Catalyst works hard to ensure that future team members will be well suited for the corporate culture. People selected into the organization have the necessary technical skills as well as sound moral sensibilities, natural curiosities, a solid work ethic, and humility that let people nurture and take delight in others' successes, assume the good intentions of others, and remain open-minded when discussing ideas and proposals. Health Catalyst has purified the workplace of interpersonal toxins by selecting well. One employee emphatically stated, "There is a notable absence of hidden agendas, Game-of-Thrones politics, and malignant personalities at Health Catalyst," an observation readily seconded by others in the focus groups we conducted. Several employees we met reflected on their past employers and reported how much time they had spent simply working through the noxious cultures and dysfunctional people. An employee at N2 told us, "I was afraid if I stayed [at my last company] I would become one of them."

Recruitment at Instructure is a rigorous staged process in which only a tiny percentage of applicants are selected. Not only must candidates prove technical excellence and that they will be able to add a new voice to the collective conversation; they also must be a consensus fit with the corporate values, code-named COOTIES (customer experience, openness, ownership, trust, integrity, excellence, simplicity). Given the stringent technical requirements for engineers, that tiny percentage shrinks further for these positions. Instructure is very picky. However, once an employee is in and acclimated, it is a good bet that he would no longer survive for long in a traditional company. The inside joke is that once employees experience the liberating feel of ultratransparency, flexibility, and autonomy afforded at Instructure, they are irrevocably broken, incapable of returning to the staid, rigid, and impolite nonsense of a typical workplace. Indeed, employees across companies told us about "being broken" or "going native" with reference to the fact that they would never be able to return to an ordinary company after feeling the freedom and inclusiveness afforded in each of the companies in our sample.

You get the point. The companies we visited take culture seriously because they are aware of the large damage that ill-suited tyrants, genius jerks, or talented terrors can do. As Hal, one of the founders of *INTUITIVE*, said to us, "The best way to minimize employee problems is to not hire them."

Socialization

Socialization is a process of acquainting newcomers to a culture and introducing them to the norms, practices, and expectations of the organization. Socialization is the process where outsiders become insiders and learn what to do, how to do it, and why it is done a particular way.[29] During this initial period, organizations present their first factual rendering of what they are really like. Until this time, employees have received only glimpses and hearsay to form their impressions. Done well, socialization will increase work productivity, social integration, and organizational commitment.[30]

If social engagement and feelings of connectedness are not your thing, it is doubtful that you would find happiness at The Motley Fool. The socialization process there starts before a person's first day at work through the Foolienation (orientation) process. The company sends new hires a survey to complete in advance of their first day, which quizzes them on myriad interests, hobbies, investment experiences, and so on. The hiring manager also calls to answer any last-minute questions and to reiterate instructions for the first day. When employees arrive on their first day, their desks are adorned with objects they might fancy, these being based on the survey results. Favorite foods, favorite sports teams, and favorite pastimes all find representation on a very crowded desk.

Employees always start on a Friday so the orientation fare tends to be light, though it includes a tour of the facilities, lunch with Fools from other departments, a team party, and $100 to take friends or family out to dinner to celebrate the new job. New employees also receive stock in the company and $1,000 to invest (plus a six-week training program on how to analyze stocks and make investments). On the following Monday, the organization assigns the new employee a buddy, who is a seasoned Fool, to help navigate the company, culture, processes, and systems. Buddy and employee jointly participate in a scavenger hunt that involves answering questions, solving riddles, and following clues—nudging employees to explore different parts of the company and to meet different people. And, of course, discussions about expected performance and further integration into the local team continue.

New employees soon discover that the social fare continues with regularity. Here is a sample of what we unearthed during our visit:

- Monthly all-Fool activities (camping, theater, skiing, etc.)
- Birthday Celebration Day (first Friday of every month)
- Pizza Day (last Friday of every month)
- Mani-Pedi Day (once a month)
- Haircuts (once a month)
- Fooliversaries (a celebration of a Fool's anniversary)

TCG has several ways of bringing people together and keeping them meaningfully linked to the company, beginning with a thoughtful onboarding process and ensuing celebratory observances for newcomers—movie tickets after 30 days, a book of choice after 90 days, and a basket of fruit after 180 days—continuing monthly for a year. A gift that keeps on giving is a nice reminder of organizational membership and a way to repeatedly confirm that the employee is wanted. At the end of the first year, and every year thereafter, the employee receives a nicely crafted anniversary card from the company that enumerates the employee's many accomplishments over the year, including kudos from clients.

The primary facet of the socialization process is building relationships.[31] What employees learn about their work, the context of the work, and how the work is to be done is affected by the quality of relationships new hires form through their early encounters. The triumph of selection and the ensuing socialization process is that newcomers feel welcome, wanted, and included and will quickly become contributing members of the group.

Socialization unfolds in three identifiable phases with the intent to reduce uncertainty and increase confidence, accelerate learning, and support adjustment, satisfaction, and performance.[32] We refer to the first phase of socialization as the anticipatory phase, in which the goal is to alleviate the newcomers' anxieties and reassure them that their decisions to join the organization were good ones. We liken this first phase to an invitation into someone's home. To make a guest feel comfortable, you would want him to know what to wear, what to bring, when to come, who will be there, and so on. Similarly, the organization provides digestible pieces of information to newcomers, proactively provides support and answers questions, and sets expectations for the first week or two.

The best companies—those in our sample—carry out these initial tasks with pizzazz. All new hires at Insomniac Games receive a welcome kit of Insomniac-infused swag, such as shirts and mugs, and a thumb drive that has teammates' photos and biographies, a description of whom the new hire will be working with and what he or she will be working on, and a message from CEO Ted Price about the studio's vision to create games that have a positive and lasting influence on peoples' lives.

The second phase, the orientation phase, is the period to acquaint the new hire with the workplace and communicate the importance of having the employee as part of the team. The circle widens in this phase: the core team becomes central to the socialization process with extended organizational members becoming involved, as needed.

Several companies we visited assign mentors to newcomers to assist with psychosocial adjustment (role modeling, acceptance, counsel, friendship) and career-related guidance (sponsorship, exposure, coaching, challenging, skill development).[33] These mentors usually are from outside the newcomer's area, are known for their abilities to coach, inform, and direct employees, and have been through a comprehensive internal training program. Overall, mentors are safe and trusted advisors who through various relationship functions, such as friend, advisor, and instructor, help to transform a neophyte into a fully functioning member of the organization.

The use of mentors early in an employee's tenure is helpful. When bundled with a well-designed socialization process, mentoring eases adjustment, lowers turnover, and increases organizational commitment, job satisfaction, and performance.[34] Anyone duly trained and dedicated may serve as a mentor; however, seasoned employees who may have reached their career pinnacle can play important roles as mentors. Becoming a mentor is not a consolation prize or one step from being put out to pasture, but central to the development of the next generation of talent. Mentoring also is something that worldly experts want to do. Mentorship offers a new challenge in response to a genuine need and gives the mentor the satisfaction of prepping the next generation for success. In fact, the act of compassionately guiding others and seeing their transformative growth may have tangible, restorative, physiological healing powers for the mentor.[35]

The final phase, the integration phase, is a time to further expand and build relationships, strengthen a sense of identity with the organization, and enhance productivity. Belonging to a prosperous, culturally lush, and multi-talented organization enriches employees' identities through the company they keep. The characteristics of a group rub off on an individual to the point where the attributes of others become one's own. There are several theories about why and how group attributes become incorporated into individuals' personal identities; essentially all concern the fact that the boundaries between the group and the individual are permeable.[36] The attributes of important groups seep into our psyches and help to define who we are, raising our self-concept while we belong and lowering it when our membership is lost.[37] The degree to which we have assimilated others into our personas is evidenced by how eager we are to talk about where we work, whom we are married to, and so on. If we work for a notably smart, innovative, and successful company, we will look for ways to slip the name of our employer into conversations.

The stories that employees hear early in their tenures are central to the formation of their organizational identities, as these stories say quite a lot about whom the organization hires and the way employees are expected to behave. Twenty-five years ago, Insomniac Games almost never happened. Ted Price, now CEO, and a colleague had developed a game demo that they then shopped around to publishers. After a succession of no's and increasingly bleak prospects, their tenacity paid off just before the fledgling business exhaled its final breath. Insomniac's first game, "Disruptor," was born. This near miss is now the stuff of legend—a story that everyone knows and tells. The legend reinforces an image of boldness and persistence. It defines Insomniac's employees as people who will persevere until they get everything just right—"ten times better than anyone imagined," as one employee put it. They are nearly 300 strong ("Spartans," as another person described the workforce) and will fight to the death alongside, and for, Ted and Insomniac.

At Instructure, employees aren't just going to do things the way everyone else does them. A man in a panda suit is walking around with a military-grade flamethrower. His vision is impaired by the fire retardant he has doused on himself and that has coated the panda's eyes with a thin film. Every time he depresses the trigger mechanism, three feet of flames pulsate from the barrel. Companions standing on each side of the panda orient him, like aligning a table or straightening the edge of a rug: "To me, to me. Now a little back. Turn it slightly to your right." When the panda's position is settled, he releases a stream of fire that incinerates the midsection of ribbon stretching in front of him. Instructure's new building is open for business.

The panda emerged as the company's mascot early in Instructure's history through a preoccupation of an employee with the endangered species, thus accounting for the panda's puzzling presence on each of Instructure's floors and its periodic appearance in full body suit. Underneath the menacing panda on this inauguration day is CEO Josh Coates, who with typical flare dedicates a building the Instructure way. The singed cement still marks the building's threshold. The scar that people pass over daily reminds them of the uniqueness of the company and of the talented, independent thinkers who labor within it. The people are committed disrupters whose charge is nothing less than to change the way people learn through the company's online platforms. The message of the story is clear: the people of Instructure are going to do things their way.

Companies stay closely in touch with newcomers to ensure all is going well and as planned. Insomniac Games stays abreast of employees' satisfaction and career goals by meeting with every employee in one-on-ones, on a rolling schedule, in "IF" (Insomniac Future) sessions. Human resources meets with everyone in the studio on a continuously rotating cycle, once employees have been with the studio for a minimum of six months, so that it can keep abreast of their work, career goals, and their suggestions to improve the studio, work environment, and culture. These meetings provide a chance to learn from employees what the studio could do better or differently and for human resources to learn what employees want for themselves. This is then imparted to team leads.

Similarly, the "Employee Happiness" staff at TCG meet with team members to celebrate birthdays and unbirthdays (six months after an employee's birthday). This ensures that top management (the head of Employee Happiness is a vice president in the company) checks in with each employee at least every six months. These are informal one-on-one get-togethers that allow the company to respond to any concerns an employee may have, and to ensure that employees' developmental needs are being tended to.

The value of hiring and socializing correctly is quantifiable. The cost of bringing in a new hire who washes out is between 50 and 300 percent of base salary depending on the availability of prospects and the position level. Even when a company picks the right person, there are monetary differences between companies that integrate new employees well and those that do not. A successful socialization process produces people who understand their roles, are confident in their abilities, and feel accepted. These employees are more productive, and sooner.

Given the right precautions, everyone wins through organizational efforts to be inclusive. Inclusiveness increases the social capital of the organization and enhances employees' well-being, which together make strong communities possible. Social integration and fulfillment of interpersonal needs promote a positive sense of togetherness for employees, one that is rewarding, pleasurable, and sustainable over time. At the end of a lengthy career, many employees will look back most fondly on the people with whom they worked and the bonds that were created. Having others in our lives who genuinely care about our welfare is a wonderful elixir. Little did employees know at the time that these relationships were helping everyone to live healthier, longer lives.[38]

CHAPTER 8

MEANING

*Help people to find and do work
that excites and matters*

The gods condemned Sisyphus to eternal toil for leaking secrets to mankind. The punishment for his crimes was to roll a boulder up a hill and then retrieve it when it rolled back down—before he reached the top—and then begin rolling it uphill again, endlessly. If Sisyphus had been asked to fill out a survey that questioned him about the meaningfulness of his work and life, we are pretty sure he would have given low marks.[1]

The Greeks were masters at sending us messages. In this instance, one message could very well be that what Sisyphus was experiencing in death, we may be experiencing in life. We can surmise that the Greeks were speaking to us and not the dead, and that the haunting act of stupefying repetition is a horrifying way to live out our days. The insightful moral philosopher and father of modern economics, Adam Smith, recognized the problem of mind-numbing labor when discussing the 18 discrete steps—each performed by a specialist—to make a pin.[2] He worried, as did Marx after him, that the separation between the conception of work and its execution would cause people's initiative and intellect to atrophy. A now-classic study by Arthur Kornhauser of Detroit autoworkers showed precisely that. Repetitive work had deadening effects on workers' lives.[3,4] The author describes how the rigid daily regimen extinguished workers' ambitions and eliminated their pursuit of meaningful life goals.

Meaning is a tricky topic since it is intensely personal. What thrills one individual and fills her with purpose may have lesser effects on others. Still, meaning is not altogether a subjective experience and therefore cannot exist wherever a person may wish it to. For one thing, when people search for meaning they are not just looking to change their minds about what they are doing; they want to change what they are doing. For another, we can generally agree that activities like pushing boulders, collecting tire air caps, or copying the dictionary in longhand lack significant purpose, even though each may provide uncommon people with pleasure.[5]

We can imagine a version of Sisyphus who gleefully pushes a boulder up a hill and spiritedly romps back down to the hill's base to start the cycle anew, ad infinitum. Rock rolling just happens to be one of the things that fills him with joy. Given the idiosyncrasies of humankind, the gods most likely were not concerned about sentencing Sisyphus to eternal happiness. It seems they were more interested in condemning Sisyphus to a preposterous, meaningless life, which is different. In fact, although studies show that happiness and a sense of meaning are related, they are not the same. Meaningful events may be those that are the most satisfying and uplifting, but often some of the most penetrating and declarative episodes in life can be terrifying, calamitous, and sad; not happy occasions at all but gut-wrenching affairs that give us a new-found awareness and reroute our energies in more value-laden and meaning-ful directions. Indeed, one of the hallmarks of meaning is poignancy.

We recently attended the retirement of an 80-year-old nursing professor at a prestigious university. She had volunteered for the war in Vietnam and spent years tending the troops. When she returned to the United States to resume her career, she chose oncology as her field. Having watched people die, she thought she could do the most good by helping people comfortably pass through their final phase of life—meaningful and gratifying work, but not light.

Having a Purpose

Surveys show that employees value meaningful work more highly than income, job security, promotions, working conditions, and hours.[6] And for good reason. Meaning heightens life satisfaction, job satisfaction, and performance and increases personal well-being by reducing stress, anger, and depression. Longitudinal studies also reveal that people who live purposeful lives have lower risks of heart disease, stroke, and death (within the timeframe of the study), correcting for education, lifestyle variables, and such.[7] What is it that people want in work that is meaningful? Employees say they want work that provides a sense of purpose and directs activities toward ends that (1) are perceived as important (including building relationships and helping others); (2) have a social impact or make contributions that matter to someone; (3) are consistent with one's values and identity; (4) stimulate and draw on individuals' intellectual and creative powers; and (5) allow people to develop to their full potential.[8,9,10,11,12] Once again, we have bad news to report. Forty percent of employees say they work in jobs that make no difference.[13,14]

Meaningful work is similar to a calling, in which a person feels she is doing the work for which she was intended and that suits her abilities.[15,16] The individual engages in a significant cause she believes she is destined to pursue in light of her special gifts. The work is a summons (more like a discovery) to a life in which she finds fulfillment to the point of sacrificing time, money, and comfort.[17] Meaning does not have to be big with a capital *M*; it can be the small *m* of the craftsperson who makes or performs with elegance and skill. We admire and appreciate the aptitude and composure of the accomplished waiter, the mechanic, the dancer, the carpenter, the machinist, the paperhanger, and the stonemason who are in full control of their arts. People want to be able to give something of themselves that takes a material form and that matters to others—to leave a trail they can proudly point to and claim, "I did that."

Victor Frankl made it his life's endeavor to understand the origins of meaning in life, arguing that one of the primary ways we find meaning is through what we give to the world (e.g., deeds, accomplishments) that reflects a life of worth.[18,19] Most people simply want to make a difference using their unique gifts and be remembered for what they achieved of value. Regeneron is a perfect example, where making a difference is in fact its mission. We had never heard of cryopyrin-associated periodic syndromes (CAPS) or fibrodysplasia ossificans progressiva (FOP) until our visit to Regeneron. The former is an uncomfortable, disabling allergic reaction to cold (jumping into a pool in summer, entering an air-conditioned building, and holding a cup of ice coffee in your hand count as cold). The latter is a condition in which muscle and connective tissue (e.g., ligaments) become ossified—turn to bone. Neither is common in the population; nevertheless, when scientists at Regeneron believed they had found large-molecule (proteins) solutions to each disease, the leaders of the company gave the green light to carry out tests. Regeneron may never make large sums of money from these treatments for rare diseases. However, the company's goal is to relieve the suffering of others without further qualification such as "when it is convenient to do so" or "if we are reasonably assured of an acceptable ROI." The purity of its position makes a big difference. The people at Regeneron have a genuine sense of purpose, in which they feel passionate. That purpose—that they are working to improve the lives of millions—energizes the workforce. A single note from a grateful beneficiary of Regeneron's science, such as, "Thank you for helping my grandfather to see again," is fuel for a lifetime. Helping others to heal is much more motivational than making a buck. As often articulated in our interviews with employees, "It is not about the money for us." In fact, the company publicizes much of its science in peer-reviewed journals, inviting any scientist who can find a cure using its results to find it. If Regeneron cannot find a way to use the power of science to improve patient health, perhaps someone else can.

Regeneron lets people do what they like doing best: science. "Science is first, last, and always." Science is the nucleus of the enterprise. Rather than exclusively focusing on particular disorders, the scientists at Regeneron are instructed to "follow the science." That is, the company is "disease agnostic." Sometimes the hunt will lead to treatments for rare conditions in which the return will be psychological as opposed to financial. However, with intelligent, independent thinkers at work, the company gets its fair share of big FDA-approved hits as well. Regeneron has had six FDA-approved drugs in its relatively short 30-year history. Over a dozen more drugs currently are in clinical testing. Given that it takes about 10–20 years and billions of dollars for a drug to go from discovery to patient, Regeneron's successes seem especially good. Further, since the probability of a compound making it out of the lab to human testing is roughly one in a thousand, it takes an abundance of passion to have the will and staying power to attempt the improbable.

Allowing scientists to work in conceptual proximity to their training has the advantage of deploying people in ways that make the best use of their abilities, rather than trying to shoehorn people into preconceived compartments according to expected monetary yields, which they may be well suited to execute but for which they have no affection. Many told us that they found their dream jobs at Regeneron: "Being here is like being back at MIT, where I have room to satisfy my curiosities. I have been here 15 years and I still learn something new just about every day. I love it."

Many other employees in our sample of companies felt a keen sense of purpose. "People outside the company [SAS] who think of us as workplace pioneers forget that we make things. Our products touch so many lives in positive ways." In fact, the global software and data analytics company routinely saves lives and money. For example, SAS worked with Duke Hospital to simulate decision-making in the hospital's neo-intensive care unit. The data models showed that doctors could improve medical outcomes at lower costs by extending care by three days.

Ten Ways to Destroy Meaning

Sadly, organizations can also present serious barriers to meaningful work.[20,21] To prevent undercutting employees' sense of meaning, here are ten precautionary don'ts for companies:

1. *Don't promote mediocrity.* Countless ways exist to produce or deliver goods in an inferior manner. The most prominent is to abdicate all semblance of professionalism and place profiteering atop the values hierarchy. This is achieved, say, when parts are switched out for cheaper replacements of lower quality, or when a hospital sends a patient home prematurely to free up bed space. In general, meaning is impaired when companies urge actions against employees' better professional judgments, thereby reflecting a willingness to cut corners and degrade quality and service in a bid to elevate the bottom line.

2. *Don't succumb to SDD.* The acronym SDD stands for "strategic deficit disorder." This disorder refers to an organization's propensity to abandon courses of action, reverse courses of action, or forget about courses of action by not following up on progress. Initiatives are either contradicted later or stopped altogether, leaving employees with a sense of "What's the use?" Work has no chance of having much meaning if the actions of the organization are chaotic and make little sense. Research has demonstrated that people readily convert conceptions of orderliness and predictability into assessments of meaning—or meaninglessness.

3. *Don't act like the Keystone Kops.* In Max Sennett's slapstick silent films, the Keystone Kops were well-meaning, rambunctious, bungling buffoons who raced around with intensity but without direction. They clumsily went nowhere fast. This is what happens when there is no script or plan of action to follow. Actions fizzle out from haphazard implementation or are thwarted by unforeseen barriers and conflicts. The consequence is a lot of activity with no results.

4. *Don't set unachievably high goals.* Some organizations aspire to achievements that far exceed credulity. They tout aspirations that are unfeasibly

higher than realistic, challenging goals. We once worked with a midsized consultancy that had printed signage promoting a 60 percent organic increase in revenues over the next three years. The problem was that revenues had not changed over the prior five years and there were no new plans in the offing to suggest why they would change over the next three. The signs became Instagram classics among the workforce, who passed messages among one another ridiculing the fantastical aims of the company.

5. *Don't assign pointless work.* This is work that no longer serves the original purpose for which it was intended, or is unusable in its current form, or is only performed because the company is inefficient and hasn't taken steps to eliminate it. Examples: employees receive information in paper form and have to transfer some of the information onto new pieces of paper; because records management is poor, employees spend hours looking for missing documents; because of inaccurate forecasting, a retailer spends an inordinate amount of time processing returns. Pointless work would not have to be done if something else was done properly or better.

6. *Don't marginalize contributions.* This is a simple one and easy to fix. Employees wonder if what they are doing is of value since no one ever says it is, or isn't. Employees toil in obscurity hoping that in some way they might be providing something of value. People like to hear that they are needed and that the company would not be the same without the contributions they make. Meaning comes from someone acknowledging that what a person is doing matters.

7. *Don't override employees' judgments.* We once sat in a meeting led by a manager who blustered about being a participatory bloke. We were treated firsthand to how this worked as we observed a two-hour discussion about new marketing pieces for a product. When the options had been reduced to two sets of materials, the manager called for a vote on which choice to pursue. The ten people in attendance voted one way; the manager voted the other. The manager's preference won the day with approximately 10 percent of the vote. Not only was this a soul-crushing affront to the team, but the team was now responsible for executing a marketing approach to which all members were opposed. Work is not very meaningful to employees when there is no connection between their ideas and the outcomes.

8. *Don't assign illegitimate tasks.* These tasks involve asking people to perform duties that are well outside their work role norms, which would be difficult to conceive as including the doing of one-time favors.[22] They are

managerial requests that are conspicuously and unreasonably out of context for the job. Examples might include requesting an administrative assistant to drop off clothing at the dry cleaners, or asking a postdoctoral fellow to wash the lab floor. Such requests minimize a person's professional status and devalue his or her role in the organization to that of a nonessential flunky.

9. *Don't cheapen excellence.* The social philosopher Joel Feinberg once commented that valor in battle is recognized with medals, not increased pay.[23] Certain forms of recognition are not only inappropriate for the occasion, but they are offensive as well. Some things we clearly do not do for the money and do not expect to be incentivized for our performance in hard currency. The use of money as a ubiquitous form of recognition can be vulgar and a surefire way to kill employees' appetite to do anything unless for the money.

We were speaking with Sunny, an analyst at Arkadium, when our conversation was interrupted by an awards ceremony. Arkadium was naming honorees based on a two-day "jamkadium" session (like a hackathon) that had taken place a few days prior. The votes were in. Team awards are based on the difficulty of the problems addressed (Tough Award), the expected qualitative and quantitative effects of solutions (Impact Award), and the ingenuity with which business problems are approached (Creativity Award). In addition, one award is given to the individual who best exemplifies the corporate values. Sunny won the individual award for values and accepted one of the group awards on behalf of her team. Clearly everyone at Arkadium is playing for bragging rights since the awards are small rubber duckies that people accept to much acclaim and display on their desks with personal pride. Rubber duckies!

Similarly, Concord Hospitality devotes a week to thanking nonprofessional employees for their contributions (Associate Appreciation Week). During the week, everyone receives a gift. All hourly employees also are eligible for the prestigious annual President's Award that goes to eight to ten people whom the company selects through a comprehensive nomination and review process. Award recipients and guests are invited to the National Leadership Conference to receive their honors (and bonus) and a pin for their achievements, which they wear throughout the year, and thereafter. The recognition is nice. The pin, even though it is just a pin, is a permanent marker of excellence and of the value these select individuals bring to the company. (Higher-end department stores used to do something similar, bestowing daily roses to salespeople to affix to their lapels as regard for their proven expertise.)

One showcase of individual achievement is the Lunch Pail Awards ceremony held at N2's annual holiday party. This whimsical, yet significant, award goes to the outstanding performers and pure exemplars of institutional values. The award is a metal lunch pail from the 1930s with the person's name etched into the side with car keys.

All of these awards have one thing in common: they have much greater perceived value to the recipients than their true economic value. The properties built into pins and duckies and lunch buckets that money alone does not capture are time, effort, thoughtfulness, and the nature and quality of the exchange relationship.[24]

10. *Don't fail to enrich work.* The dimensions that give work meaning comprise an area of applied psychology that is mostly settled. Still, it takes considerable thought and creativity to enrich jobs with the requisite meaning-making elements. The ensuing paragraphs describe aspects of the job that influence employees' satisfaction and their sense of meaning.[25]

Ways to Enrich Work

Task identity. Task identity is the ability to take pride in the complete assembly or completion of work from start to finish, or to work closely within a group to complete a job in its entirety. Henry Ford pioneered the division of labor and the assembly line. By breaking down work into unitary tasks, workers could quickly learn how to install auto parts without regard for the order of the predetermined assembly. Workers quickly and efficiently performed their designated function as cars rolled past on an assembly line. Honda Motors has brilliantly changed all of that in its newly built plant in Thailand.[26] Workers now move with the car in a cell (Honda calls these "assembly revolution cells"), doing the work that was once done by five workers separately. These processes are less expensive to install, cheaper to run, and more flexible to switch in and out of the manufacturing processes, while providing small teams of workers with more complete responsibility for a significant part of production.

Consider how a young Leonardo da Vinci must have felt when as part of a workshop of artists he was asked to paint half a canvas while leaving the other half to another painter. These paintings, recently on display at the Yale Museum of Art, illustrate the extraordinary talents of the young da Vinci when juxtaposed against the lesser skills of another up-and-coming artist of the period. Da Vinci could not have been pleased by the end results. Even if the other artists had been as good, it would have been difficult for da Vinci to have taken much pleasure in these paintings, which were, after all, only half his.

Task significance. Task significance is the degree to which the job has impact, positively affecting the beneficiaries of the work. Frequently, jobs have impact but the effects are not salient: they are too remote or ephemeral for employees to notice. Companies must work at making the importance of these employees' work real to them. For example, a study by Grant showed that the call time and revenues of fundraisers increased by 142 percent and 171 percent, respectively, as a result of spending five minutes conversing with a beneficiary, a scholarship recipient.[27,28] Similarly, radiologists wrote longer, more diagnostically comprehensive reports after they were shown a photo of their patients.[29] Organizations can increase the meaning of jobs and people's performance by making the results of employees' work tangible; for example, by showing employees a homeowner walking into her new home, a child receiving its first bike, or a medication that has relieved a person's discomfort.

Simply associating work with positive consequences such as helping others increases the perceived meaning of one's job. In one study, people rated their task as being more meaningful when they could give the proceeds from their participation to a noteworthy charity, compared to control subjects who performed the same task but who kept their earnings.[30] Associating work with the public good thus adds purpose and meaning to work. This is exemplified at Patagonia. Patagonia was the first B-corporation in the United States: a for-profit corporation that meets the stringent standards of social and environmental performance, accountability, and transparency. Our unscientific survey of the parking lot suggests that the Prius is the car of choice. That seems right given Patagonia's sensitivity to the environment, as shown by contraptions on the premises such as water coolers that pull water from the atmosphere rather than reservoirs. Social responsibility for and care of the environment have been the impetus for Patagonia's workforce since its inauspicious beginnings making reusable pitons in the blacksmith shop that still stands on Patagonia's grounds.

Several years ago, Clean the World, a nonprofit startup, approached Concord Hospitality about all those unused, or half-used, products in hotels. Did you ever wonder what happens to all of them? Entrepreneur Shawn Seipler wondered as well. The products used to get thrown away. Today they are collected by Concord (and now most other hotels), sent to Clean the World, remade into hygienic products such as soaps, and then shipped to developing countries. Each year Concord sends employees to a developing country to see how their efforts are helping families thousands of miles away. During our visit to Concord, we were shown photos of employees helping Clean the World in Guatemala. Social responsibility and community are central to Concord's identity and are key aspects of what gives employees' work meaning.

Skill variety. Skill variety refers to the ability of an individual to use the full complement of her knowledge and skills versus repetitiously using narrow competencies from her repertoire. This aspect of the job, when designed properly, requires employees to exercise an array of what they are able to do and accomplish. Defining a job too narrowly has two major negative repercussions. First, as might be expected, rote work is viewed as meaningless work. Second, it also is boring work. People who are bored report lower psychological and social well-being and higher rates of anxiety, depression, loneliness, and helplessness.[31] Indeed, boredom may be the opposite of flourishing.

Work autonomy. Autonomy relates to what, how, and when work is to be performed. Work autonomy means having a say in what needs to be done and the best ways to proceed. An employee will be unable to do everything she is capable of if her thoughts and actions are regulated by others or by a rigid set of rules that leaves no room for judgment. Autonomy, then, partly concerns giving people the opportunity to decide what is best for themselves. When Health Catalyst's lease was about to expire on its offices, the company contemplated a move to another location. But executives refused to dictate an answer when the result would have such a profound effect on their employee population. Health Catalyst plotted distances from peoples' homes to each of three potential sites, surveyed and interviewed employees, assessed costs, and so on. As it happens, the company renewed its lease and stayed where it is; yet Health Catalyst realized that nothing is more demoralizing than forcing others to accept a decision in which they have had no say and which has been made without regard to their interests and needs. The company's instincts are well founded in research results that show the uplifting, or distressing, consequences of having, or not having, a voice in one's own affairs. People without a voice who are exposed to harsh conditions may feel like the crew on Henry Hudson's ship, *Discovery*, must have felt. Despite the crew's entreaties to return home as scheduled, Hudson prolonged his search for a western passage to Asia. Due to the delay, the ship was grounded in ice during a harsh winter in what is now called Hudson Bay. As the ice thawed, Hudson again hesitated to return home. The dying, sick, and starving men mutinied (it was later discovered that Hudson was hoarding food for himself and a few select others), setting Hudson, his son, and a few crew members adrift in a small lifeboat with minimal provisions before returning to England (where they were found not guilty of mutiny). Hudson and associates were never seen again.

Similarly, Insomniac Games recently began the process of clarifying and sharpening its vision. Rather than closet themselves off, executives invited employees' comments on the vision. Employees submitted more than a thousand suggestions through facilitated small-group off-sites. This led to a new internal website expressly devoted to sharing the information gathered, to elicit further discussion, and to ensure that the final vision was shaped transparently and collaboratively.

Many companies have digital suggestion boxes (e.g., Clarus Commerce) or employee wish lists (QBP). Sometimes the suggestions can be frivolous, like requests for hot tubs. More often suggestions yield helpful improvements; for example, a new, more supportive, longer-lasting, and safer shoe that was recommended for employees in the warehouses at QBP.

Challenge and responsibility: Job challenge and responsibility concern work that progressively tests a person's skills and abilities to perform, typically by adding duties that are broader in scope and deeper in complexity than currently performed. Each additional job element relies on greater knowledge, more skillful problem solving and creativity, and bigger responsibility for quantitative and qualitative results. Jobs with these characteristics are referred to as "expansive" since they involve completion of novel and challenging tasks that require the acquisition of new knowledge, abilities, perspectives, and the use of new tools and resources—all of which contribute to the feeling that one is growing and moving in a positive direction. Compare two jobs. One job is for a person to carry a Ping-Pong ball across a room by hand. The other job calls for the incumbent to cross the room using different methods and techniques each day, and on occasion directs her to solve difficult problems. One day she must cross the room with the ball using an ordinary paddle, one day with chopsticks, and one day with her foot. One day she is challenged to retrieve a Ping-Pong ball that has fallen deep into a thin pipe before she can move it across the room. The end of the pipe is buried deep in concrete, so the pipe cannot be turned over. The only tools she has are a tennis racket, shoe laces, and a plastic water bottle that is unable to fit into the pipe. Something like this experiment was carried out, and guess which job was more satisfying?[32]

A person who occupies a well-designed job will find the work to be more satisfying and intrinsically motivating, and life to be more meaningful.

Intrinsic and Extrinsic Motivation

Motivation is one of the most used yet least understood concepts in business. Any account of motivation would have to explain what propels action. Our concern is with two broad classes of motivation. One class spurs action through the performance of the job itself (enjoyment of the work is its own reward as it is experienced as more pleasurable, engaging, and meaningful), and the other spurs action through incentives external to the job, such as the promise of money. Respectively, these are intrinsic and extrinsic motivation.

Intrinsic rewards are produced through the self-reinforcing elements of the activity itself. These may include challenge, thrill, pleasure, and many other elements that fulfill individuals' internal needs for such things as learning and personal growth. Often these intrinsic satisfiers are those that concern the acquisition of new and interesting knowledge or skills, movement toward personally important goals and expectations, and new and exhilarating sensations and experiences, including aesthetic ones. These factors relate to the features of the activity and the process of doing work. For example, skateboarders describe their motivation for their sport by citing intrinsic factors such as feeling relaxed, confident, satisfied, and alive.[33]

Since people feel most satisfied and fulfilled when they are growing, engaged in what they enjoy most, and making generous use of their capabilities, the best companies always are calibrating the interests and abilities of their people to the work. Employees who are absorbed and energized by their work are more committed to the organization, perform better, and stay longer than those whose jobs are misaligned with their true interests and abilities.[34] The process of fit is like finding comfortable shoes for growing feet. Companies should resize and refit employees recurrently to preserve employee motivation and peak performance. People, jobs, and working conditions change, and to prevent the work from becoming stale, organizations need to periodically take measurements that match employees' capabilities (knowledge, skills, abilities), personal interests, and needs to the demands of the job.

The companies we visited help people to channel their energies to where they will be most effective and derive the greatest enjoyment. Employees get to do what they like and organizations get the performances they want. One interesting way we have seen companies help employees uncover their aptitudes, interests, and potential is to have employees introspectively consider times when they felt fully immersed in activities; to reflect on activities that gave them special pleasure and feelings of accomplishment.

A person often experiences intrinsic motivation as flow.[35] A flow experience occurs when a person is intensely focused, completely absorbed and lost in an activity, and unselfconsciously oblivious to time and the surrounds. Interestingly, the immersive experience of flow is most likely to happen in games, creative activities (e.g., art), and science, which we liken to solving puzzles. Flow is not something we typically associate with the workplace; however, that may be because we do not play enough in the workplace.[36]

Play, and games, have many overlapping dimensions with work. Play has rules, goals, and outcomes. Play, too, can be excruciatingly arduous and time-consuming, and involves a host of attributes such as intelligence, originality, planning, imagination, and fitness.[37] And play, like work, has consequences that can be exhilarating or humbling. The big difference occurs in how we approach work and play, which partly explains why weekends tend to be more fun than weekdays. At work, people mostly are doing things for instrumental reasons: because someone needs this or that; and companies commend and economically reward employees who produce the this's and that's. In a larger context, employees often perform work with express ends in mind: to buy food or a new car. Work therefore has an ends orientation in which behaviors are centered on getting work done efficiently and meeting goals.

Play, on the other hand, has a means or process focus. Behaviors concern thinking, maneuvering, discovering, communicating, coordinating, and rolling with the emotional ups and downs of the moment. To win at a game or sport, you must deploy your skills as best you can. The game is all about execution through a robust display of everything you have got. Given the loose and flexible association between means and ends in games, people have room to exhibit their prowess through play within an imaginative space that allows for social and intellectual development. If you lose but want to win the next time, you had better improve between now and then. To get better ends, you will need better means. It is also possible to remove the fun from a game and turn it into work. Take grudge matches. People do not enjoy playing in these contests because the wrong emotions simmer and the attention of the players turns away from the state of play to winning at all costs. Similarly, work can be transformed into play by freeing employees to engage their physical and mental resources to solve problems and enliven the work. Indeed, mixing play with work can produce a much more immersive work experience than all work and no play.[38]

One of the best companies at play is Big Ass Fans, which is already evident as we pull into the parking area. "Valet parking! Sweet." Then we read the fine print: "Want valet parking? Us, too! Show us how well you park a car, and maybe we'll hire you to do it full time." We veer into the visitor parking lot. The visitor signs have donkeys on them. Fanny, the mascot. A nifty double entendre for Big Ass Fans (BAF). We quickly discover a business where fun and function are rolled into one.

A pervasive sense of play permeates the serious at BAF. Among the dozens of patent plaques hanging on the wall in the lobby (a sample of the hundreds of patents BAF has received), we notice a phony placard that credits the company with inventing fire. We have time to talk with the receptionist for a while. Like everyone we meet, she is considerate and instantly likeable. Later we learn that the receptionist position is a short-term entry-level job and that the person we met soon would be working elsewhere in the company. That is standard operating procedure at BAF: to move people around until they find their calling, their passion. The moves happen often. In many organizations, the receptionist position would be considered a dead-end job, or no job, because it would be considered noncore to the business and populated by a staffing firm.

Just beyond the lobby entrance, the building opens. There we see nicely framed children's art—imaginative, whimsical, liberating. A residential fan with children's handprints sprinkled on the blades slowly turns overhead. It is a noncommercial variant of the successful Artisan Collection line of fans engagingly adorned by local artists. An amazing wooden sculpture of a donkey stands nearby, a gift from the groundskeeper to the founder, Carey Smith. Handmade from natural materials, the sculpture is a combination of earthiness, beauty, and craftsmanship, which is how we would summarize the entire organization.

As machines go, fans look deceptively primitive. However, producing fans of modest sizes to swirling behemoths takes a cast of computer scientists, engineers, machinists, and physicists to discover and build the most thermodynamically efficient means of cooling unique and volatile environments. Development demands a significant amount of experimentation and testing. Some tests are small-scale and conducted atop desks. Other experiments are substantial, involving invisible forces and flows. Scientists and engineers at

BAF perform these large experiments in an expansive research and development facility, a part of which BAF calls "The Kitchen"—a playful allusion to the puzzle solving and trial and error of R&D, since cooking things up in a kitchen is a rewarding, communal activity that inevitably must appeal to consumer tastes. Indeed, everything done at BAF is performed in the service of the customer. Customer problems invariably set the functional boundaries to what BAF will investigate.

Given the bounty of observable experimentation at BAF, the catchphrase for the company easily could be "Welcome to Engineering Toyland." The animated atmosphere periodically is amplified by the raw energy and intelligence of the region's premier science high schoolers vying for scholarships and internships through Rube Goldberg competitions held at BAF's facilities. BAF enhances the play-like atmosphere in other ways as well. First, all the meeting rooms are named after spaces on a Monopoly game board. If you know Monopoly, you would have an idea about the locations of the rooms since they approximate the relative positions of the board layout.

Second, work routinely is gamified. The company uses elements of games to motivate work on tasks that otherwise might not be performed or to add interest to routine events.[39] As we are sitting in the human resources area, we hear the rhythmic "ping, ping, ping" of a xylophone. The vice president of People and Culture, Samantha, looks over at us. "Someone just accepted our offer of employment." If a triangle sounded, a new position had been posted. We hear other sounds on the day of our visit. We hear a bell ringing in sales, like the one rung at the New York Stock Exchange. This sharp, prideful sound is highly significant. The bell signifies customer orders, and if total sales surpass a lofty threshold, the company opens the very well stocked beer refrigerators (we peeked) and celebrates. Everyone in the company celebrates! People listen for the bell. Importantly, these games are not meant as fun diversions from the real work; rather, they are novel practices with purpose. For example, the bell ringing in sales is a constant reminder of the centrality of the customer: it prompts employees who are not directly serving customers to serve those who are.

Extrinsic motivators, on the other hand, are equivalent to the proverbial carrots and sticks by which the frequencies of behaviors are either increased or decreased through rewards and punishments. In general, these contingencies are external to the activities performed and are distributed on the basis of the behavior's performance (although rewards need not be doled out in every instance to sustain behavior). Money, honors, praise, and awards are common extrinsic rewards. Rebukes or withholding good things like pay raises or promotions are forms of extrinsic punishments. We understand very well how these principles of learning work since they are all around us. If you go through a red light, there is a chance you will be punished to decrease the probability that you will repeat the behavior in the future. If you go to the store with your coupon, you will be rewarded with the discount. No doubt that managing contingencies is effective in regulating behaviors. However, too often managers think that this is all there is to behavior modification and rely on the so-called law of effect exclusively.

There are two noteworthy drawbacks to extrinsic rewards. First, research has found that using extrinsic rewards to change behavior decreases intrinsic motivation, which as we noted is the motivational element that makes a job satisfying and gives work meaning. In a seminal study by Lepper and Greene, children who were told that they would be monitored and would receive a reward following an activity showed less interest in the activity two weeks later.[40] For people who initially have a high interest in a task, conspicuously rewarding the activity decreases intrinsic motivation on subsequent tasks. Rewarding activities that people already enjoy doing decreases their later enjoyment of that activity (this is called the "undermining effect"). That said, extrinsic rewards can be used to increase the intrinsically satisfying elements of work such as creativity. People who are told that their work will be judged and rewarded on creativity, for example, produce more creative results.[41,42]

Second, extrinsic rewards—especially extravagant ones—are attention grabbers. A singular concentration on profit, for example, does not mean you will get more of it. In fact, there is good reason to believe that a narrow focus on monetary outcomes may be, ironically, counterproductive. Selective attention on certain aspects of our environment has been likened to the game of whack-a-mole.[43] This is a game in which moles can fleetingly appear from several holes on the game panel and the player must hit the head of the mole with a rubber mallet to earn points, which are exchangeable for gifts. A mole pops up and our sensory system quickly reorients to the objects that will deliver the greatest rewards. This, loosely, is how our attentional system works. It is extremely adaptive to have a primordial responsiveness to cues within our environment that are associated with desirable outcomes.

The game, however, depicts two hazards of our attentional system. For one, while focused on one mole, we are missing others and tuning out our wider surrounds in order to concentrate our bodily energies on a small slice of our experience. In attending to some things, we miss other things. We could make this limitation more severe by lighting a particular mole hole more brightly than others and scheduling the mole's more frequent appearance from its lighted exit. Our enhanced fixation would cause other moles to routinely slip past us. We could showcase profit in a similar way by shining a light on it through ongoing discourse, reward mechanisms, and the like.

For another, stimuli associated with rewards become attentional and behavioral priorities. We will keep whacking the lighted hole even though, say, through a game snafu it no longer is delivering rewards. Behavior will persist until we receive feedback that what we are doing is no longer effective. Attentional capture through rewards may thus lock us into performing useless activities.[44]

A person who has a more balanced perspective on the field of play will likely score higher (perform better) than one whose gaze is targeted on a specific area. The point is this: concentrating all of your thought and energy on those things associated with profit does not mean you will get the highest return through this deluxe attention over time. Thus, multidimensional (balanced) scorecards like the ones used at Arkadium (measuring people, product, revenues, and improvements) provide a clearer look at the entire game board and offer better insights into which actions are most appropriate and effective. The broader perspective duly recognizes that organizations are much more than financial institutions and that embedded within every revenue dollar is a supplier, customer, and employee—and within these, a value orientation.

Work as a Means versus Ends

Then again, innumerable people are in fact working for the money—purely for the instrumental value of hard cash, kudos from important people, and invitations to elite parties, though with scarce feelings of personal enjoyment in their work. This raises another story left us by the Greeks as a warning. The story is about Tantalus, a son of Zeus.[45] As a relative of the gods, Tantalus had access to Olympus that he unfortunately did not use very wisely. He stole ambrosia and nectar in the hope of bringing immortality and divine secrets to mankind and secretly served pieces of his son to the gods as a sacrifice. Neither act went over well in Olympus. Tantalus's punishment was to stand forever in a pool of water beneath a fruit tree. Whenever he stooped for a drink, the water receded.

Whenever he reached for fruit, the branches rose. Everything Tantalus wanted was always just out of his reach.

Tantalus is like Wiggins's hog farmer who buys more land to plant more corn to feed more hogs, for which he will need more land to plant more corn to feed more hogs, and so on.[46,47] Tantalus's everlasting punishment was to continuously work at getting something external to himself that would always be unobtainable. Here is why. People seek out happiness but can never hold on to those things they believe will satisfy them. Once a person acquires a good, the pleasure of having it slips away until she feels precisely the same way she felt before obtaining it. This pattern of ups and downs is common enough that it has a name: the "hedonic treadmill." As we reach and try to grab hold of something that we think will add a little substance and meaning to our lives—make us feel better—the pleasant feelings quickly recede once it is in our possession. The psychological lift of the new Mercedes or the pay raise is momentary. All goods promise more than they eventually deliver.

In a study of lottery winners, their initial elevated levels of pleasure and joy rapidly declined until they were emotionally right back where they started. Recent circumstances in Kenya allowed researchers to investigate hedonic adaptation in a controlled field setting.[48] A sample of 503 households across 120 villages were randomly selected to receive up to $1,525. The average disbursement was $357. That amount may not sound like much, but it is equivalent to almost twice the wealth of the average villager. The researchers took various psychological and physiological measures before and after the money transfers, which they made over a six-month period. At first, recipients reported feeling more satisfied and less depressed as a result of their good fortune. Results also showed that their cortisol levels had dropped, which suggests a reduction in stress. Follow-up a year later found that all psychological and physiological indicators had returned to their former levels, before the cash transfers. This follow-up of a year is lengthy; most studies find that pre-acquisition states are restored within six months, although rates vary with the events.

As it happens, people who believe that money and possessions are important aims and the true path to success tend to be miserable. Well-being plummets even further when people believe that money is an essential contributor to status and happiness.[49] They are less happy and satisfied and more anxious and depressed. The more material-minded people are, the lower their well-being.

N2 Publishing certainly sees the false promise of freewheeling consumption. That became clear as we toured its facilities. Becky, employee number one, sat at the first desk N2 had owned, a roadside reclamation. The conference room where we were situated for part of the day had as its centerpiece a table composed of two reclaimed doors set on supports bought at Costco. We were assured that a missing strip of carpeting that exposed the floor beneath would never be repaired. The only nice piece of furniture we saw was a desk that belonged to Katherine, the head of human resources. A woodworking hobbyist at N2, whose side occupation was crafting gorgeous wood surfboards, had constructed the lovely desk.

The lack of fashion sense at N2 is intentional. The company is rapidly growing and has plenty of cash to afford finer things. N2 purchased its sprawling office building and production center in Wilmington, North Carolina, with cash. Nevertheless, its philosophy is "function over flash." It refuses to spend on anything that is not a direct benefit to the people it serves. Employees have turned opulence on its head and transformed shabby into chic. Of all the furnishings at N2, Becky's desk is the piece that is most admired, because of its history. And employees created the Crappy Car Club, which honors the worst car in the company. Until recently, that distinction belonged to Duane, one of the company's founders.

Duane owns a small farm. He tends to the company with the same thrift as he runs his life, avoiding unnecessary luxuries as ostentatious proof of success. He encourages others to follow the same frugal lifestyle and to concentrate on things that bring happiness: friends, family, community, and having enough. N2 knows what produces lasting meaning, and it keeps what is most important in front of people—who can take it or leave it.

In one episode of the comedy *30 Rock,* Jack, the ambitious head of the mythical television station (who is played by Alec Baldwin), thinks he is dying. "I should have worked more." His line is funny because it is the opposite of the one we usually hear. But why, in retrospect, can't wanting to work more be a legitimate wish?

One of the main reasons to spend less time at work is because it resembles the horrific chase game of Tantalus. Work only for the sake of something else: a bigger home, private school for the kids, a nice watch. In *The Death of Ivan Ilyich,* Leo Tolstoy indicts the judge, Ivan, for his preoccupation with high society and for coveting the material goods that an aristocrat should have and enjoy. It is only upon death that Ivan reflects on his life to conclude, not that he should have worked less but that he should have worked better, more humanely, and for the right reasons. He could have chosen to focus on meaning, purpose, and personal fulfillment versus the trappings of the aristocracy to which he aspired. His entire life has been a false compromise, like a person who says he is working at an awful job to support his family, but because of the work is never home with his family or appreciative of being with them when they are together. Had Ivan reflected more completely on what is most important, he might have been a better person, a better judge, a better husband, and a more satisfied individual. Life could have been more meaningful.[50]

CHAPTER 9

AUTONOMY

*Give people the freedom to think,
create, and be themselves*

People give us a deadline, and we work. We plant flowers in the yard, and people look. The town lays down a sidewalk, and we walk on it. The idea of autonomy, or free will, so ardently debated in college dorm rooms is not a choice between determined and undermined behavior, but a matter of whether our behaviors are self-determined or other-determined. All behavior is determined in some way. It isn't random. Autonomy means that the locus for one's actions is internally motivated by one's values, interests, preferences, and needs.[1,2] Autonomy means choosing the life one wishes to lead for one's own reasons, deciding which desires to pursue, which abilities to cultivate, which interests to fulfill, and which to leave untouched.[3]

Authenticity

By all accounts, Han van Meegeren was a fine visual artist. Today he is known for being a fine forger. Before and during World War II, he found he could make a handsome living by creating paintings in the style of Vermeer and other Dutch masters such as Frans Hals and Pieter de Hoogh. Vermeer's paintings are highly prized since only 35 works have been attributed to the artist, who otherwise had his hands full with 11 children and two jobs (as art dealer and innkeeper). Van Meegeren's deception might have continued unnoticed had he not sold one forgery to Hermann Göring in exchange for 137 paintings from the Nazi's burgeoning art collection. Authorities unearthed the sale after the war, and given that the Netherlands considered the sale of Dutch works to the Nazis to be an act of treason, van Meegeren faced a death sentence. He confessed to being a forger instead.

Consider another exceptional forger, Zeus. During one of several conjugal visits to earth, the bored and promiscuous Zeus takes on the appearance of Alcmene's husband, and seduces her. Later, after her real husband returns from a trip, she realizes she has been had by a serial fornicator in disguise. Given that Zeus and Alcmene's husband were indistinguishable, why was Alcmene upset by the feint? Or, if a painting looks like a Vermeer, why don't we value it like a Vermeer?

One important reason we eschew fakes in favor of the real thing is that we value honesty and sincerity, which is precisely what forgers lack. We presume that a close relationship is motivated by love and that a work of art is motivated by imaginative effort. These were not the aims of Zeus or van Meegeren. We do not like frauds because their actions are not true reflections of what they think and feel, but are manipulative attempts to obtain what they want for themselves without concern for the interests of others (since it is hard to sympathize with Göring, please note that he was not the only sucker). Forgers are empty personages who execute under the impulse of ulterior motives as opposed to genuine sentiments, values, and convictions. And we do not like it when people misrepresent themselves with the idea that they will take advantage of us.

Now let's switch roles. Assume that rather than casting disdain toward fakers, our employer has asked us to be one of them. We find ourselves doing things for which we have no affection simply because they must be done—for the money or to curry favor. It may be that as calculating agents we do no harm to others other than to conceal, fabricate, or suppress what we truly think and feel.

But what if you did not have to hide who you are, what you want, how you feel, or what you think? Instead, your employer tells you, "We hired *you*, so be you." Suddenly, everything is different. As one employee said to us after moving to Insomniac Games, "I felt like I had just been rescued from the pound." Free at last.

Abraham Maslow once said, "Authenticity is the reduction of phoniness toward the zero point."[4] The more real people feel, the greater their contentment and comfort with themselves and others, and the greater their sense of individuality, happiness, life satisfaction, and emotional health (they are less anxious, stressed, and depressed).[5,6,7] When employees repeatedly told us that their organizations allowed them to be themselves, they were saying quite a lot about their peace of mind. Being authentic or true to oneself is related to greater job satisfaction, work engagement, and performance.[8]

Every summer, Edmunds hosts a developmental enterprise called Edmunds Academy. Unlike other developmental events that tend to be heavily focused on work and life skills, Edmunds Academy affords more extensive offerings. Many classes are provided by outside speakers, several of whom are luminaries in their fields. Employees themselves also offer many of the classes on a range of specialty subjects that may or may not be related to work—sailing, cheese tasting, smoothie making, hip hop, and so on. Employees told us how much they appreciate the chance to share aspects of themselves through this instruction. "I am allowed to be me at Edmunds. It's a place where you can be yourself."

N2 is also rife with extraoccupational talent, which it finds ways to showcase. The head of the mailroom is a superb rapper who composed and performed the theme song for N2. Camryn, from the talent acquisitions group, is an evening DJ. The Full Bleeds is a cover band made up of employees from the graphic design department. Marty, the wise, unassuming COO, is an avid boxer. Suzanne in human resources is a trained meteorologist and former television personality. Amanda, the head of the editorial department, is a wonderful visual artist. We saw Amanda's artistry passionately exhibited at the company's all-employee meeting held monthly. A part of this meeting is reserved for recognizing exemplary contributions to the company, and this month's award went to the entire editorial department. Amanda drew likenesses of each of her staff members wearing Marvel-esque superhero outfits and described each of their superhuman powers in a wonderful and moving tribute to her team.

Surfboarders at Patagonia periodically retrieve their surfboards from the "board room" and trek down to the nearby beach. Patagonia is equally hospitable to employees who fancy nature and the outdoors. Take Kim, who is obsessed with birds of prey. She used to keep injured raptors under her desk and nurse them back to health. Then the company's leadership offered her more space in an unused shelter on the property. The program continued to expand as fellow employees and acquaintances brought their birds to Kim for aid. Today Kim—still an employee—heads the raptor center in Ojai, California.

The fact that employees are free to be who they are brings comfort and relief. Employees, of course, realize that they will forever bump up against conventions, others' preferences, and miscellaneous confinements that restrict what they can and cannot do, but these do not necessarily prevent them from acting on their passions and beliefs. In a word, employees within our sample of companies have found a place where they can be "authentic," where they can find an original way of being human.[9]

Acting on work goals that are consistent with an individual's personal interests and values is diagnostic of greater motivation, task persistence, and goal attainment.[10] Conversely, employees' performances are depressed when the work is detached from their motives, interests, and values. In addition, a person who unstably metamorphoses with circumstances lacks sticky ethics. People who are characterologically inauthentic are morally disengaged and more deferent to the demands of circumstances. In one study, people who scored high or low on a trait authenticity scale were given in-basket tests to work on in a simulated fast-food environment. As part of the simulation, people were periodically faced with decisions. Some of the dilemmas were ethical in nature, such as the following:

- After being informed that the milk received from one supplier has likely been contaminated, the manager has to decide whether to take the milk from the market in advance of conclusive information, or wait until more information is available and only then take the milk off the market if necessary.
- A manager has to decide whether to give or withhold unfavorable facts in a report to the executive board of the company in the process of an acquisition.

Although at face value the moral resolution is straightforward, people who scored lower on authenticity were more likely to choose options that were in the immediate interests of the organization, typically choosing actions that favored profitability over principles.[11]

Ownership

Many years ago we met with the CFO of a major insurer who asked us if we could help fix his "lazy" accounting and finance staff. We asked if he thought he worked harder than they did, and he assured us that he did. We next asked if he enjoyed his work and, if he did, what he especially liked about it. He liked the challenge, the variety of work and issues he faced, the accountability and impact he had on the organization, and the discretion he had to be creative and to execute his duties as he thought best. We were young and brashly suggested that perhaps his people were not lazy at all. They just had not been given work that was very electrifying, nor the latitude to make consequential judgments given the bureaucratic labyrinth through which employees had to walk whenever they made the slightest move toward independence.

The importance of autonomy is nicely illustrated through a study that used a comprehensive national database from the United Kingdom. The database consists of attitudinal profiles of 22,500 employees gathered in 2004 from 2,300 workplaces. The data analysis showed a correlation between wage level and job satisfaction, a relationship we can look at suspiciously given results of studies on happiness and money that we discussed previously in the book. The authors of this study were skeptical too. In fact, when they added job autonomy and employee voice to their prediction model, the association between wage and job satisfaction disappeared.[12] This shows that what we undiplomatically conveyed to the CFO many years ago is true. It isn't the wages that matter; it is what frequently comes with higher wages that matters: the discretion to decide for oneself what is most important on the job and to express opinions and provide input without fear of reproach.

"Freedom to . . . " contributes a big part of the satisfaction we derive from work. Freedom to use our brains to decide the way work should be carried out is an elementary facet of job satisfaction. So too is having some control over the context of the work, such as the timing of the work and the order in which tasks need to be accomplished. Minimally, people want to have some control over the work they produce and be "free from . . . "; that is, free from coercion and related autocratic tactics such as threats (loss of promotion, loss of time off). Without suitable room for decision-making and independent action, employees will never consider the work theirs. In fact, without a sense of control over the outcomes desired, employees will never develop a sense of ownership.[13]

Executives repeatedly tell us that they want their employees to think and act like owners. The ability of employees to control aspects of their work is central to feelings of ownership. Having the leeway to rearrange, modify, improve upon, and so forth: these are attributes of possession.[14] With possession, the work is defined more in terms of what can be done as opposed to what cannot be done, comparable to the property rights afforded to owners versus renters. An owner can do just about anything he pleases with his property. However, rental agreements have stipulations that limit behaviors to preserve the property for someone else. These tenant agreements shout out, "Do not abuse your right to live [work] here." Similarly, executives who want "owners" want not only good custodians of resources, but people who can use those resources to transform the organization for the better; that is, to increase the value of the enterprise. They want people who can change the way things are versus preserve them as is, as a renter does.

An example of an ownership mind-set is beautifully on display at SAS. Today SAS resembles a college campus in look and feel. The campus sits within 900 heavily wooded acres in Cary, North Carolina—not far from the state capital, Raleigh, and the founders' former teaching institution, North Carolina State University. The land contains three hundred acres of buildings and a network of running paths, bicycle paths, streams, and side streets (with names like matrix and analytics). Ghostly landscapers keep the grounds trim while discreetly staying out of view. Landscapers have their own parcels of land to tend in any way they think best given the terrain, building architecture, and so on. It is up to them to plan and develop their plots. This is the way things work throughout SAS. The company gives employees visible assignments and then frees them to pursue their objectives as they see fit, turning to peers and management for advice and support when necessary.

The accountability that comes with managing one's own "parcel" exposes a side of SAS that outsiders do not hear much about. Caring relationships demand responsible actions: people who care for one another have certain responsibilities toward one another. The performance expectations at SAS are very high; so high, in fact, that we truly felt nervous on behalf of the employees. In just the short time we were there it became clear that SAS wants results. Pets, children, and adults quickly learn the difference between someone who says something and means it, and someone who says something without conviction. When SAS sets schedules and goals, it is obvious it really means it. And according to one employee we interviewed, "If someone says they will do something, they do it. No one ever wants to disappoint, so we all give our best."

Just about everything is voluntary at The Motley Fool. The company prefers to inspire as opposed to tell. That is a good premise for behavior. People who view their behaviors as freely chosen are more likely to alter their attitudes—to internalize their reasons for choosing to behave in a particular way.

The classic demonstration of this behavioral principle dates to the "forbidden toy" studies.[15] Children who were mildly (versus severely) warned to refrain from playing with an appealing but prohibited toy were subsequently more likely to lower their opinion about the desirability of the toy. Having ostensibly attributed restraint to free choice, the children in the mild threat condition changed their opinions about the desirability of the toy. On the other hand, children in the severe threat condition understood that the only reason they did not play with the toy was because of the punishment that awaited offenders. But they still liked the toy. In short, autonomous choice versus making people do things is more likely to lead to changes in attitude and behavior.

The Motley Fool's philosophical foundation to give employees a wide range of choices is psychologically sound. People in the company choose when and where to work and, to a large extent, what they want to work on. For example, the technology department periodically will summarize the different projects that have highest priorities and ask employees to rate their preferences for each. Given the diversity of interests and specializations among the employees, most people are able to get on projects of their first choice. And once people have become proficient in their current roles, The Motley Fool encourages employees to pursue a passion project of their own election that focuses on a problem faced by the company. Starting small, the employee gradually enlarges the initiative as the project gains wider interest, backing, and resources.

INTUITIVE also challenges its people to come up with innovative solutions to problems—any problem—through its Creative Incentive Program. The program is a way to keep employees mentally limber and to flex their independence and cerebral muscles. If the company likes an idea submitted by an employee, it will help in the commercial development. One patented prototype we tried out was a walker that easily adjusts to the size of doorways. Brilliant. As an infinitely fair company, profits from inventions are split 50-50 between *INTUITIVE* and the creators, with *INTUITIVE* supplying the start-up funding.

SAS uses various means to stimulate unconventional thinking and innovation. Oliver Schabenberger, the company's COO and CTO, trains people on giving presentations in the vein of TED Talks about their best ideas. These ideas can turn into significant projects. One recent talk led to advancements in software for the visually impaired.

In addition to the more traditional internal and external developmental opportunities available to employees, PURE Insurance introduced Passion Courses. The company gives employees $1,500 per year to explore whatever passion they choose to follow. PURE's Friday yoga classes? The instructor is a PURE employee who became a registered instructor through the program. The list goes on: one employee became a black belt in jiu-jitsu; another honed her photographic skills; another practiced Formula One racing. The program is part of a wider company effort to instill the habit of learning so that questioning, seeking, and creating are as natural as eating and sleeping: essential sustenance for a satisfying life.

PURE assigns a premium to passion and curiosity in the selection process because it wants inquisitive, interesting, and creative people who can think on their feet and adeptly interact with high-net-worth policyholders. So it requires claims adjusters and "member advocates" to be problem solvers for policyholders who perhaps have temporarily lost use of their homes or cars, or have damaged or lost personal property to which they are emotionally attached. These PURE employees search for solutions to member dilemmas by finding, for example, replacement transportation, temporary housing, or identical replacements of broken goods such as china. All interactions are unscripted. People are expected to listen to the needs and concerns of policyholders and to find ways to help them as best they can. Anything can happen. A member advocate who learned about the hospitalization of a policyholder's young son sent the boy a Lego set. She had developed a relationship with the policyholder and wanted to do something for a family that was going through a tough time. Another member advocate sent stuffed animals to two young children who were shaken (but unharmed) in an auto accident.

The same open-endedness applies throughout PURE. The staff of member services, who provide policyholders with service support, do not follow a canned sequence of questions or formulaic answers. They have their knowledge of the products and their skills to rely on. It is up to them to converse empathically and earnestly with policyholders, as one human to another.

It seems evident that superior service only is achievable when people are free to respond to people *as* people versus confining conversations to allowable utterances. PURE has found that the customer experience is better and decisions more exact when smart, well-trained people are given the independence to do what they believe is right. The research supports PURE's approach. Customers are more satisfied when service providers are more openly caring and empathic with their circumstances; they judge the providers to be more sincere in their assistance. In contrast, customers view service providers as less authentic when they suppress expressions of genuine caring, benevolence, and identity; such suppression transforms a relationship of need fulfillment into a businesslike transaction where customers feel like commodities.[16]

The ability to control one's work product by having the right applications and tools is critical to a sense of ownership as well. In Concord Hospitality's words: "All employees throughout the organization are assured that they have the tools and resources they need to be successful, and that the environments in which they work have been appropriately renovated and modernized. Nothing is more disheartening and ego-deflating than having broken down equipment in a dingy, rundown hotel. Pride of ownership loses its luster under those conditions." *INTUITIVE* has the same outlook. The executives say they carefully control the expenses that need to be controlled, and do not control those that do not have to be controlled. The latter include the tools, equipment, and resources that consultants need to approach their work in the best way. Concord and *INTUITIVE* want nothing to get in the way of people's ability to execute, whether overly rigid rules, inflexible and outdated technologies, equipment in disrepair, or problematic management. Obstructions that can encumber employees' freedom to act are removed.

The rewards companies reap by fostering a sense of ownership are sizable. Psychological ownership heightens employees' care for organizational assets and increases cooperation and helping among staff. And a climate of ownership and self-determination gets results. A large retail chain found that participative management and inclusion of employees' voices in regulating local units' actions generated positive attitudes among group members (215 work groups with approximately 13 people per group) and greater financial performance defined as percentage of net sales to plan, net sales, and sales per square foot.[17]

Autonomous Teams

Autonomy not only is essential to job satisfaction and personal productivity, but also is a key component in the superior functioning of teams. For example, the ability of a group to largely control the way it applies its skills to the realization of a goal is predictive of the quality of work life within the group and improved job satisfaction and motivation among the group's members.

Autonomous teams are different from leaderless groups. That is, they are not free from internal direction. But they are relatively free from the standards of the larger institution that would otherwise impose unnecessary restrictions on a team's activities. "Autonomous" then refers to the ability of a group to work outside of the usual procedures of the organization, defining for itself how it will pursue team goals and ensure quality outcomes.

Autonomous teams have gone by various names over the years: tiger teams, skunkworks, self-directed work groups, self-managed teams, and new-venture units to name a few. These teams are commonly composed of people with diverse skill sets who are working on a whole task or encapsulated problem and who have control over the management of the work, methods, task scheduling, and assignment of group members.[18] A team lead or project manager controls internal resources and oversees team members' assignments and performance, keeping the unit at arm's length from the mother ship. The makeup of the group will vary with the size and nature of the initiative, sometimes only having members from specific disciplines, such as research, and sometimes including a cross-section of the enterprise.

These teams are most effective when the initiative involves a high degree of technological novelty or radical innovation in which exploratory learning is needed; that is, there is insufficient prior knowledge and the group needs to generate solutions to novel problems through innovative practices and experimentation. In these situations, teams that are loosely associated with the larger organization are more behaviorally plastic and flexible, have greater internal information-processing capacity, are better equipped to deal with uncertainty and ambiguity, and are more adept at identifying pertinent metrics to gauge progress and evaluate outcomes. In fact, the autonomy of these groups is one essential feature of long-term organizational renewal, because autonomy is a precondition for change. Autonomy permits discoveries and the generation of new ideas and knowledge. It also fosters greater flexibility in acquiring, relating, sharing, and interpreting information with minimal critical specification. The openness to new knowledge and ideas and the enlargement of the knowledge base is a key aspect of corporate entrepreneurship. Researchers have noted the many growth-related advantages of autonomous teams:[19]

- Increased organizational exposure to new technologies and methods
- Greater awareness of marketplace trends and market possibilities
- Enhanced leverage of existing strengths
- Extended identification of opportunities beyond the organization's capabilities
- More pronounced use of new and improved business practices
- More effective creation, transfer, and application of knowledge

Since true innovation implies use, or the commercialization of ideas, a major aim of the team is to fold work back into the corporate mainstream once the team's work is complete. It is imperative then for the project manager to work within broadly defined constraints if the finished product is to have recognized organizational value and applicability.[20,21]

The paradigm case for a separate group that failed to commercialize was the old Bell Labs. Made up of world-renowned talent, the group's basic research was spellbinding. It brought us the transistor, laser technology, touchtone phones, solar cells, and evidence of the Big Bang—along with much more. However, as described to us while on assignment there, the group's contributions to AT&T's annual revenues were lackluster, so the company asked us to come up with ways to better integrate Bell Labs into the commercial enterprises. The Bell Labs group ran outside the usual hierarchy with its own authority structure and self-defined direction. Since the group's contributions to the business were negligible in the near term, we recommended a new integrated oversight structure that would intertwine the needs of the businesses more closely with the areas within Bell Labs. It was a solution that structure alone could not immediately resolve, and ultimately Bell Labs along with most of its equipment manufacturing businesses were spun off as Lucent Technologies (today they are tucked under the Nokia umbrella).

SAS uses approaches that approximate the suggestions we made to AT&T. SAS creates "white space" projects that ask employees to experiment with new methods and technologies, with the settled purpose of folding inventions back into SAS's focal areas for execution. Importantly, "autonomous" in SAS does not mean totally separate from the organization. Autonomous groups are "loosely coupled" to the organization. For example, teams at SAS may remain physically embedded within the parent organization, working part-time on a novel project and staying engaged in current work the rest of the time.

Many companies in our sample were growing rapidly. Several were wary that their entrepreneurial organizations would falter from the weight of their own success. However, these companies are taking precautions and are confident that organizational rejuvenation has been built into their operations. Making employee autonomy an operational fixture is central to that plan. The ability to make decisions outside of organizational pressures allows employees to leverage the company's strengths and current capabilities in pursuit of innovation and entrepreneurial ventures.[22,23] Further, these companies complement autonomy by broadcasting their desire for creative thinking, for a willingness to try out new ideas, and for acceptance of the potential downside of risk-taking.

The companies we visited give their employees the best chance to do their best work. Employees are surrounded by talented peers and given ample room to execute on goals that are of significance to them. They are supplied with the most advanced resources necessary and are able to express their inner, creative thoughts without fear of being mocked or having their ideas confiscated by others. They have license and opportunity to create. And they do.

CHAPTER 10

SELF-ACCEPTANCE

Mind the integrity and dignity of the individual

Self-acceptance is a complex topic in the social sciences because it has many terminology cousins that although closely related are defined in slightly different ways. These cousins include self-worth, self-respect, and self-esteem. All terms share a common motif of approval, value, and worth. Although we use the terms interchangeably in this chapter, "self-acceptance" comes closest to conveying two essential attributes for optimal functioning. The first is an affirmation of one's worth, and the second is ownership of all that one is— both excellences and faults. Genuine self-acceptance thus entails a conviction in one's personal value while admitting to imperfections and shortcomings.

Pathways to Self-Acceptance

Self-acceptance follows a predictable and relatively stable developmental pathway from childhood through adolescence and young adulthood and into old age.[1,2,3,4,5] Our conceptions of ourselves become clearer and more favorable over time as we meet the developmental challenges of forming meaningful friendships, becoming more physically and mentally adept, securing scholastic successes, finding a romantic partner, obtaining a job, and making continuous professional strides. The usual trend is for self-acceptance to increase through adolescence and young adulthood, and to level off between the ages of 50 and 60 before modestly declining at advanced ages, roughly paralleling the timing of age-specific challenges. However, not everyone is equally successful in solving life's developmental riddles, and the height and shape of these growth curves will differ from person to person.

Developmental progress is contingent on a complicated web of factors involving genetics, parenting styles, and the myriad social interactions and events that shape our temperaments. For the fortunate, whose predispositions, interactions, and life experiences combine in the right ways, self-acceptance has its rewards in greater satisfaction in life, work, and relationships. Those who have higher self-acceptance also have greater occupational prestige, income, and job performance. For example, researchers found that higher self-perceptions of worthiness, competence, and capabilities were related to higher independent ratings of performance and, among scientists and engineers, a greater number of patents.[6]

What the Organization Thinks about You

High-stress, high-performance settings such as those found in some organizations can disrupt an individual's self-concept. Situational disturbances can enhance or diminish relatively stable traits of self-acceptance, especially in areas that are of personal significance to people.[7,8] For example, a grievous error or mistake can weigh heavily on a person's self-evaluation as an effective, valuable member of the organization. The way organizations respond to both positive and negative circumstances can boost or diminish employees' self-regard. Overall, the way employees are treated by organizations—referred to as organization-based self-esteem (OBSE)—affects employees' sense of importance and worth and has significant organizational consequences. OBSE positively relates to job satisfaction, organizational commitment, citizenship behaviors (e.g., extra-role behaviors such as helping a coworker), and performance.[9]

Organizations communicate the degree to which they value employees through the care and support they provide. As usual, the quality of supervision is a key factor. Not surprisingly, demeaning, abusive, and eviscerating supervision undermines self-acceptance.[10] When researchers ask people to imagine themselves in the role of an employee and read scenarios in which a boss either abusively condemns the ideas of the employee (and later presents the ideas as his own) or gains approval for the employee's ideas, those in the abusive-supervisor condition rate themselves lower on self-esteem than controls, even though there were no differences between groups on an assessment of self-esteem taken two weeks prior. If the people in this experiment can imagine how their feelings would affect their self-esteem, think what the real thing can do.

Thankfully, the opposite effects occur in organizations as well. Managers who treat employees kindly and considerately instill higher levels of self-worth and greater interpersonal cooperation. One study showed that all it takes to make people feel good about themselves and important in a work setting is to display basic courtesies (e.g., smiling, using people's names), show an interest in employees' lives, inquire about their needs, and compliment them on the work they do. For example, although SAS is popularly known for its preeminent benefits, these were never cited by employees in our focus groups as reasons for liking SAS. Employees highlighted the interest people show to one another. One employee told us how energized he felt following a brief interaction with Jim Goodnight, the CEO, in the elevator. "Hello. How are you doing? What are you working on?" Employees cited all the things that make them feel good about themselves and valued.

At Quality Bicycle Products (QBP), employees are not stereotyped: no one is an accountant, is careless, is a so-so performer, is too young. The company doesn't pigeon-hole or typecast people, consigning them to a life of mediocrity in dead-end roles just because they seem to be good at what they do. At QBP, people are what they are capable of becoming. QBP sees through the superficial to the human core and allows people to experience the supreme joy of knowing that others believe in them and accept them for who they are.

We met Angie, the head of human resources at QBP, when we first arrived. She walked us down the hallway to the aptly named Spokes Café where we treated our bodies to second blasts of caffeine. "Oh, this is Rich," Angie introduced. Rich was clicking through the café in cycling shoes when Angie stopped him. He was wearing bicycle shorts and a tightly fit jersey. He was heated and sweating but not out of breath. He was able to offer a calm and steady "Hi." "You will be talking to Rich later," Angie added, as if to pardon the brief exchange. We waited for Amber to meet us in the café. Amber is a manager in human resources and she would be giving us a tour of the offices and the distribution center. QBP is proud of its distribution center. It was the first LEED gold-certified building in Minnesota. A nearby pond formed through water-efficient landscaping provided a nice backdrop for a couple of our interviews as well as a natural habitat for several species of birds and a convenient landing pad for peripatetic ducks. QBP is fortunate to have a relatively unchiseled wild-life park next to its offices where people can engage in mind-clearing "walking meetings." Amber's arms are covered with tattoos. The tattoos are colorful, but too intricately drawn to make out. As the tour started, we saw flashes of color as Amber pointed out and explained vintage and contemporary bicycles, bicycle paraphernalia, original bicycle-themed murals, and photographs and sculptures that decorated walls and stairwells.

As it happened, the approachable person in tights in the café turned out to be the CEO, who was in training for a grueling high-altitude bike race. Amber gave one of the most professional, crisp, proficient, and information-laden tours we have ever had—truly the work of a remarkable high-performer. QBP is made up of an eclectic bunch who are serious about their mission and dedicated to their work. The company fervently believes in people and does not give up on them. Sports attire, tattoos and piercings, and human foibles are transitory coverings that loosely fit over real people with devotion and heart. When QBP hires, it wants the whole person to show up, body art included. It is all a part of creative expression and the natural embodiment of what it means to be human.

Feedback

The most common way supervisors communicate their attitudes about employees' worth is through performance feedback, most often summarily articulated in an end-of-year ritual loathed by all: the annual performance appraisal. This delicate, time-consuming expression of value often does more harm than good, and the negative consequences are why several companies have decided to abandon formal performance evaluations in favor of more constructive, more frequent conversations prospectively framed to improve performance. Few companies in our sample use traditional methods of performance management. Those companies that have kept end-of-year summaries tend to position employees in a "performance x potential" grid, which they in turn use to contemplate future developmental requirements.

We are not conceptually opposed to end-of-year assessments and reviews. Managers invariably evaluate employees one way or another, whether at the end of the year or not. What we are opposed to are poorly done annual reviews and those conducted in the absence of critical supporting processes.

Regardless of the exact form they may take, effective performance management plans have three essential components: the plans encourage more frequent conversations between managers and employees; they contain robust recognition plans to tabulate the positive actions of individuals throughout the year (catching them in the act of doing the right thing); and they seriously gauge employees' needs for development. At Insomniac Games, managers and employees formally review progress toward goals during 20-minute discussions held quarterly in a program fittingly called 4-20. The Motley Fool's recognition program, YouEarnedIt (named after a vendor), is representative of the types of recognition programs we saw on our tour of companies. The program allows people to acknowledge and thank others for their helpfulness and good works. Each employee starts the year with one thousand points of "Fool's Gold" and distributes those points over a public feed to others throughout the year as symbols of appreciation. Those points in turn are exchangeable for gifts. The volitional aspect of the program does not deter participation: the company's roughly 350 employees post over 15,000 notes of appreciation per year.

Similarly, Edmunds created a program that allows fellow employees to recognize one another for behaviors that are instrumental to job success (and to allocate $1–$5 of cashable or exchangeable "Ed Bucks" per acknowledgment). These behaviors are appropriately called Top Drivers. Examples of Top Drivers include the "cool cucumber" (confident enough to hit the gas on projects, even when the road ahead is uncharted; learns from mistakes; always focuses on the solution) and the "curious cat" (always asks questions; seeks answers everywhere; is forever learning and applying lessons; works outside the comfort zone).

At FONA, people have "Hero Cards" conspicuously displayed on their desks. The cards allow employees to spontaneously recognize one another for extraordinary accomplishments that support the core values of the organization, by attaching stickers of different colors to the cards—the color representing a beneficial action illustrative of various values.

If managers and employees have established solid relations of trust and respect, then there is a wide berth for easy, honest, ongoing feedback, assuming managers give feedback in a nonthreatening, considerate manner. On the other hand, feedback given poorly—in a way that is a direct affront to an employee's character and capabilities—lowers self-worth and self-confidence and damages the quality of the manager-employee relationship. Few people are especially keen to be evaluated, and most are generally sensitive to feedback that can both refresh as well as devastate.

No perfect recipe exists for giving feedback. In general, we deemphasize formulaic feedback, such as mixing good news with bad news. Rather, we endorse open dialog and mutual goodwill, which together can temper negative reactions to words that may at times be clumsily misspoken. We also support feedback cultures, where advice is readily invited and received.

Arkadium has such a culture. When we arrived, Tom in the "Content Reinvention" (or CoRe) team was about to update staff on a new product line currently in beta testing at select client sites. The product, under trademark protection as "Factives," consists of facts that are pulled from comprehensive data sources using artificial intelligence and presented to readers of digital publications in engaging, interactive ways.

Members of the organization huddle together for the presentation in a large conference room called "The Fortress." The name is a holdover from the company's beginnings when it was located in a steel-clad industrial building (its current location is in the trendy Flatiron district in New York City). As the presentation proceeds, people in attendance scribble on two-by-two Post-it notes and flip these miniature sheets onto the conference table beside one of three tent cards that have been set up. The tent cards are spaced to mimic the flow of the presentation and to reflect specific issues the CoRe team is contemplating and seeking thoughts on. There is conversation, but comments are succinct and reserved for matters of clarification or for big questions with straightforward answers. The ingenious use of these notes preserves the momentum of the meeting by averting costly digressions and tiresome pontifications. The notes also attenuate the affective quality of feedback by converting unintended oral inflection and innuendo into three piles of neutral sticky notes by the end of the session. Here is an effective means to disburse and accept feedback.

Arkadium refers to the comments on these notes as "considerations," part 1 of a two-part feedback process that it uses regularly in meetings. Considerations are things to think about or ideas for improvements. Every meeting concludes (part 2) on an upbeat note with attendees saying something positive. Tom thanked the specific people who contributed to the development of the product. Jessica, a cofounder of Arkadium, and others commended the development team for the speed and quality with which the Factives were being produced.

Many things were evident about Arkadium's culture in the 45-minute presentation and later corroborated by other information. First, giving and asking for feedback is well practiced and habitual at Arkadium; this works well because people invest in one another's successes and recognize that feedback is instrumental to their collective welfare—if given and received judiciously as opposed to as a weapon of mass destruction. Every employee meets with every supervising manager every week, no exceptions. The co-CEOs *never* miss a meeting with their direct reports. Conversations are guided by three questions, about team wins, decisions made, and the need for support. The notes and plans that arise from these meetings are recorded by managers and employees in elegant third-party software that allows all members of the organization to see one another's goals and to spontaneously recognize one another for meritorious work. Weekly discussions roll up into monthly reviews that describe what is working and what is not, and what should start, stop, or stay on track.

Second, even though Arkadium is a technology company that works comfortably in the digi-sphere, it is a remarkably tactile organization. Arkadium is high-touch, keeping what is important in front of people. Three nearby conference rooms display the company's core values in large letters of frosted glass: Fierce Drive, Positive Energy, Full Life. Disguised structural pillars are thematically wrapped in the seasonal wear of a "Spring Up" motif with each side of the pillars showing the company's second-quarter goals. Arkadium updates the motifs and goals each quarter, and each side of the pillars displays an objective related to one of four scorecard dimensions the company tracks: People, Product, Revenue, and Improvement.

In the kitchen area, secured to the side of a wall, there is an architecturally distinct, lighted piece of industrial art that spells out the words "Lil Wins." Below the piece are hundreds of "lil wins" stickers, placed there by employees to celebrate business victories and remark on the work that is being done. "Six straight quarters of growth!" "Quiz engine is looking great." Together these tiny scripts form an impressive tapestry of success and goodwill.

Arkadium has a staff meeting every Monday. Without fail. A short period of the meeting is reserved for "Lil Wins and Big Thank Yous" in which people are able to recognize individuals and teams for special efforts and results. It is a period patterned after a Quaker tradition. In that tradition, Friends sit silently together and when moved to share thoughts inspired by a spiritual connection, they stand and do so. The practice gives people a way to be mindful of the efforts of others and to publicly appreciate their good works.

Organizational Support

Apart from feedback and benign supervisory and coworker support, organizations also underscore the significance of their people through robust training and development programs, fair compensation and benefits, advocacy for a healthy home and work life, and job security. In general, organizations that actively strive to be fair and encourage employee involvement, autonomy, discretion, and responsibility have workforces with higher degrees of self-esteem.

The best intentions concerning employee support can sometimes backfire in practice, however. We once worked with a prominent software company that had excellent developmental programs for employees: well-thought-out trainings, money for off-site learning experiences, and a minimum number of annual hours set aside for development. The problem was that the culture inhibited the use of the programs. Employees viewed development as something they did when they were not busy on the job. They saw it as a form of punishment for inactivity. If you had something valuable to do, you would not need to go. Employees interpreted the training roster like a list of condemned prisoners who, on a scheduled date, would march to the public stockade. Employees tried hard to stay off that list—to always be "too busy" for development.

Creating a culture where people feel accepted and valued is a critical aspect of organizational performance. However, people come to institutions with different predispositions for self-acceptance. People who are high in self-esteem have sturdy self-conceptions that can withstand setbacks and negative feedback without undue duress; they are able to press on when tasks get difficult. High self-esteem has protective or stress-buffering features. Conversely, people who are lower in self-esteem are more brittle and susceptible to events that threaten further damage to their sense of worth.[11] They may then avoid tasks in which they might fail, and become exceptionally critical of themselves and feel defeated if they do fail. Because those who are low in self-esteem become socially withdrawn following setbacks, they do not seek the support and affirmation of colleagues (as people with high self-esteem do). Their plummeting self-valuation interferes with their ability to effectively cope with disappointments and restore their sense of importance and value.

One intervention that has been particularly effective with those low in self-esteem (whether chronically or situationally, as through a failure) concerns practices in self-compassion.[12] Based on Eastern philosophies, the practices have a sound therapeutic basis and are sensibly grounded in the wholesome ideal of being kind to oneself; specifically, not being so critical of oneself when having failed to live up to high personal standards. Self-compassion interventions have three components:[13,14,15,16,17]

- Self-kindness: To be kind toward oneself when considering weaknesses; to be caring and compassionate toward oneself in the face of setbacks
- Common humanity: To accept that adversity is part of life and that being human means being imperfect—and that imperfections may be the impetus for growth
- Mindfulness: To attend to and experience negative emotions in the present moment as normal, and to accept emotions with mindful, non-judgmental objectivity in order to react effectively

Studies exemplify what being kind to oneself can do.[18] People were asked to recall an incident such as a failure, rejection, or loss that made them feel badly. Those in the self-compassion condition were asked to write responses that parallel the three components of self-compassion. (This induction of self-compassion was highly structured for experimental purposes, but managers can easily convey each of these components in plain English.) Participants were asked to express kindness and understanding toward themselves as they would sympathize with a friend (self-kindness). They were asked to write about how others have gone through the same sorts of things and have shared their experiences (common humanity). And they were asked to step back and write about the event in an objective, emotionally neutral way (mindfulness). Results show that heightened self-compassion reduces negative affect as well as defensiveness, and increases more-accepting thoughts and creative performance.

Research repeatedly shows the effectiveness of self-compassion interventions, inside and outside the workplace.[19] People who exhibit self-compassion are happier, more optimistic, less depressed and self-critical, and more adventuresome, and they feel more connected than those who are low in self-compassion. Behaviorally, those with high levels of self-compassion admit mistakes, modify unproductive behaviors, take on new challenges, and take initiative to learn and grow. In the end, those who give themselves the benefit of being kind to themselves experience greater satisfaction in life.

Organizations that are afflicted by unforgiving and unsupportive management miss out on all the things that a healthier outlook on employees' value would bring. They miss out on the benefits of having people who feel liked and accepted; are more accepting of their shortcomings; take greater responsibility for the consequences of their actions; worry less about rejection and feel less emotionally disturbed by negative feedback; take more risks and engage in more experimentation; persist with projects; and can fail without feeling badly about themselves.

Unfortunately, there is a type of person with way too much self-love. Researchers identified the type when results of studies showed that people with high self-esteem often acted in dramatically different ways. A collection of studies showed that both a healthy and an unhealthy brand of high self-esteem exist.[20,21] The latter, variously called hubristic or inauthentic self-esteem, contains shards of narcissism.[22,23]

Self-esteem moderately correlates with narcissism. This means that there is a subset of people who think way more highly of themselves than they should. Whereas self-compassion makes people better (and is also moderately correlated with self-esteem), narcissism makes people worse. Both self-esteem and narcissism involve positive self-evaluations; however, healthy self-esteem does not include self-centeredness, entitlement, and superiority—as it does for narcissists. In extreme cases, narcissism can obliterate all the advantages of self-acceptance and self-compassion. The responsible and unperturbed individual transforms into a defensive and churlish know-it-all. To protect their grandiose sense of self from injury, narcissists resort to all sorts of organizationally destructive ploys. They aggress against people who have challenged their authority, dismiss negative feedback as biased and unreliable, discredit the opinions of others, trivialize their failures, blame others for their own mistakes, take credit for others' work, inflate their abilities, cheat and lie, and undermine their relationships. Because they think they are more important, funnier, smarter, and more attractive than everyone else, their point of view is the only one that counts. In a nice review, Lubit elegantly describes how envious narcissists chase out the best people, fall well short of their business objectives, and wreck organizations.[24] The companies in our sample promptly remove these contaminating personalities from their midst.

Acceptance of the Right Things

Good companies ask their employees to meet extraordinarily high standards of conduct in addition to high standards of performance. In particular, they ask employees to think about themselves holistically as humans versus employees (a term that obscures the thrust of what it means to be human). They want people to look at themselves from a broader perspective as members of a wider moral community. Here is why that matters.

We suspect that most Nazis never lost much sleep. Nor, we suspect, has any other member of a hate group lost sleep for reasons pertaining to their membership. This is because they all act on principles; according to the internal logic of their organizations, these are good principles, noble principles (and to be clear, these are not principles we agree with). Consider the Mafia organization.[25] Like corporations, the Mafia is a for-profit business enterprise that has a hierarchy of authority. Also like corporations, the differences between legal and illegal can be blurred. The Mafia uses illegal money for legal purposes, and corporations outwardly operate legally, although some of their money may be earned through bribes, kickbacks, and other nefarious means. Like corporations, the Mafia has a strong, unique identity with an aggressive focus on profit maximization. It has a code of conduct—an unwritten values statement—that everyone knows. One rule, of course, is allegiance to the organization and submission to the larger interests of the organization. Another is fidelity to one another. A third rule is *omertà*, which mandates silence about the organization to anyone outside of it. These rules are strictly enforced through compelling rewards and punishments. Severe consequences await a snitch who betrays the trust of the organization.

Mafiosi (or Nazis, supremacists, Klan members) would all say they act with honor and integrity within their system, although with profit as the primary goal, the temptation to deceive and swindle engulfs the Mafia like a fog. Corporations too can have a strong ethos of loyalty that the corporate community jointly enforces by zealous devotion to the group and associated fear of reprisal for being a snitch, tattletale, stool pigeon, backstabber, ratfink, squealer, bigmouth, turncoat, informer, or whistleblower. There are times when what goes on inside organizations, albeit colorfully shrouded in moral decorum, would fail ethics tests in the outside world. Those who have worldly consciences and point out malfeasance within the organization are ignored, dispatched to the basement office, quietly retired, or terminated. *Omertà*. This is not universally true; however, the percentages for some form of retaliation against whistleblowers is alarmingly high (about one in four, although some estimates have been twice that).[26] In fact, people who have reported bad behavior or unsafe practices have in some instances been physically victimized, a fist being the number one weapon of choice and a stapler the runner-up.[27]

If people believe that the financial interests of the company must be protected at all costs, then blowing the whistle is the dishonorable, versus honorable, thing to do in the eyes of insiders. Whistleblowers are disrupters of the company's economic welfare. (Bill and I dislike the word "whistleblower" because like a police officer blowing his whistle, the connotation is to stop bad behavior, when we should be stressing the commencement of ethical behavior.) Whistleblowers also are threats to the accepted moral order. Studies show that moral rebels (as confederates in experiments) who refuse to collaborate on a racist-tinged task, or to write a deceitful speech, are liked significantly less by participants who previously had performed those tasks. Basically, people do not like to be questioned about something they already have done—and dislike those who do.[28]

In 2002, the Persons of the Year in *Time* magazine were Cynthia Cooper of WorldCom, Coleen Rowley of the Federal Bureau of Investigation, and Sharon Watkins of Enron. Cooper and Watkins notably spotted egregious accounting practices worth billions at their institutions, and Rowley reported how data collection and integration at federal agencies may have contributed to a failure to foresee the 9/11 attacks. We think they likely would call out flawed and disreputable practices again if they had to do it all over, but clearly their ethical heroism was not universally beloved before or after their revelations.[29]

Great leaders must do more than help people feel good about themselves. They must help followers feel good about themselves in the right ways. The best companies do this by asking employees to think about themselves from the perspective of the kind of person they would like to be. It may be too late for some employees who have been thoroughly seduced by all the goodies that organizational membership provides. Others might not care. Nevertheless, the best way to create a company with a conscience is for leadership to present the organization and its people in the proper context—as responsible citizens of a broader community that incorporates universal laws.

Experts have written about the importance of self-awareness for leadership. However, we think it is more important for leaders to make other people—employees—self-aware so that they can tune into their principles, attitudes, and beliefs. For much of the time, we see the world from our points of view without a whole lot of nuance and reflection. We see and act from the inside looking out. But there are times when our brains need to tell us to stop and look and think about ourselves in a different way—to see ourselves as others might, or to figuratively step out of our bodies and look at ourselves objectively from the outside in. Rather than allowing others to act on impulse, the leader's chore is to get followers to probe their thoughts and feelings so that they will act deliberately and prudently.

Getting people to focus inwardly on themselves is called objective self-awareness, and this focus can be achieved rather simply in experimental settings.[30] Looking in a mirror does it. So does listening to a recording of one's voice, hearing one's own heartbeat, and writing a story about oneself. Researchers found that simply putting an image of human eyes ("watchful eyes") and recommended pricing (pricing was posted in all conditions) over an honor-system coffee dispenser and collection container produced almost three times the monetary contributions. This effect presumably occurs because the eyes induce people to look inwardly and reflect on the right standard of conduct.[31,32] Art too elicits self-awareness, as in the "museum effect," where studies show that people perusing museums become more self-reflective about who they are, where their lives are going, the way they interact with others, and the future of society and the planet.[33] Reflection on, and group discussion about, works of art have the same effect of increasing participants' (in this case, managers') self-awareness.[34]

Art and associated interventions that raise people's awareness of who they are and who they wish to be combat the unreflective actions of base instincts. The strong leader will sometimes pause the action and get people to contemplate the essence of their identities: "Are you sure about this? Is this what you really believe to be the right thing to do? Would you be able to talk about this event to your family? Is doing this the way you wish to regard yourself years from now?" Appropriately, art has a prominent place in several of the organizations we visited.

PURE Insurance is missing some of the West Coast panache, but privacy is at a premium; the work areas are partitioned and positioned along the windows. This was what the employees themselves had wanted. They participated in the design and choice of amenities and materials of the office build-out. Plus, we said "missing some," not "missing all": the largest public space at PURE is beautiful, essentially doubling as a museum of modern art. Many reclaimed artworks hang in this bright, inviting area as settlements PURE has made with policyholders.

SAS doesn't have a campus museum per se, but there is the natural beauty of the land, plus imposing, magnificent modern sculptures inside and outside; inspirational, museum-quality artworks, some purchased and others created by two artists in residence; and an exquisite and extensive mineral and rock collection (including a piece of a meteorite) elegantly displayed throughout the headquarters building. The latter collection comes courtesy of a lifelong passion of the CEO, Jim Goodnight. We could see how the multi-colored displays with their infinite shapes would fascinate the mathematically minded: the collection reminded us of Benoit Mandelbrot's fractals with their fine jagged edges and repeating contours. We felt like we were observing the essence of geometry.

Instructure views self-awareness as one of three critical attributes that employees need to develop (self-esteem and sound judgment are the other two), and it finds interesting ways to instill this quality in the workforce. Using the artistic form of film as a mirror, one group showed us an example of how this can be done. This year, at the annual all-employee meeting, the marketing department presented video reenactments of employee suggestions and complaints that it had gathered throughout the year. One complaint concerned the bulk ordering of Pop-Tarts, which distributors ship without identifying the flavors on the foil wrappers. This was presented as a problem; apparently, it is difficult to sniff out the flavors through the wrappers. Marketing's video showed the CEO and CFO standing in a dimly lit basement labeling packages of Pop-Tarts. Very funny! More importantly, the company demonstrates the ability to laugh at itself and not take itself too seriously. Instructure also is putting problems in perspective by vividly depicting the triviality of many concerns and thereby suggesting that there are more important matters to worry about and attend to. It is an open invitation for people to look at themselves and see what really matters.

CHAPTER 11

SELF-CONFIDENCE

Believe in people so they believe in themselves

One of us had just been hired into a senior position at a major human resource consulting firm. My first assignment was a big one: to design an annual incentive plan for the top executives of a prominent beverage company. The work was time sensitive and had to be completed quickly. To complicate matters, I was told that the company had been working with another firm that had made little progress on plan development, and from the perspective of the board, time was running out. As I was leaving the office for a first meeting at the company, the head of the practice yelled down the hallway, "Hey, don't f*** it up." It was not the sort of encouragement one looks for before the start of a big assignment. Nor is it consistent with the advice given to us years ago by Richard Parsons, who at that time was the chairman of Time-Warner. He memorably told us that building the confidence of the workforce was the most important element of leadership. It was, he continued, a necessary component for success, especially in ambiguous situations where employees may wonder if they have the skills to meet new challenges, solve novel problems, and effectively adapt to changing circumstances.

Expectations

Unquestionably, the beliefs we hold about our abilities affect whether our goals will be met or not. That is, the expectations we have of ourselves and others influence the results that we, and they, produce.

These self-fulfilling prophecies can move us forward or hold us back. The transformative power of positive expectations is known as the Pygmalion Effect.[1] The legendary Greek Pygmalion is a sculptor who chisels the ideal woman, Galatea. Pygmalion longs for Galatea to be real, and the goddess of love, Aphrodite, obliges by transforming the statue into flesh and blood. George Bernard Shaw picked up on the idea of personal transformation in his play *Pygmalion*, suggesting that the best way to change the flower girl, Eliza Doolittle, into a lady is to believe that she can become someone other than who she is, and to treat her accordingly. Eliza's metamorphosis is partly contingent on the faith others have in her to change. The classic demonstrations of positive expectations on behaviors have been in schools. Students whose teachers have fictitiously designated them as high achievers outperform children in control group classrooms. These results have been replicated many times and extended into the workplace.

Negative expectation about others' abilities is called the Golem Effect. A Golem is from Jewish legend. It is an anthropomorphic creature made of inanimate material such as mud or clay (like the clay people in Flash Gordon that terrified us as children). A Golem often stands for an uncultivated oaf and is therefore used to describe a person from whom little is expected. In the workplace the Golem Effect shows up when supervisors' low expectations of employees degrade their performance—a frequent finding.[2] Low expectations alone are not the reason for the performance declines; opinions do not do the damage. People who have low (or high) expectations of others treat them in certain ways. Perhaps they give simpler assignments, overexplain action steps, step in too quickly and take over the work when problems arise, or deal out more criticism when things do not turn out as planned.

Behavior change is dependent on the conviction that we have control over our affairs, can make things happen, and are able to achieve goals that matter to us. We are not just helpless actors to whom good and bad things happen, but like Pygmalion we are able to carve our own realities based on the skills we possess. If all goes well, our confidence to adeptly execute actions in various social contexts develops. We become increasingly self-assured that we have the ability to reach specific outcomes. This is commonly referred to as "self-efficacy" in the scientific literature, and we will use the word "confidence" interchangeably to describe a self-ascribed ability to generate desired results.[3,4]

Efficacy, or confidence, involves a synthesis of beliefs that influence the initiation of activities, the degree of effort spent, and the persistence needed to see a task through to completion. These beliefs include a person's conviction that he has the capabilities to perform given tasks, optimism about the success of the undertaking, and the psychological wherewithal to beat back obstacles that interfere with progress.

The relationship between self-efficacy and work performance has been demonstrated so often that it qualifies as a psychological law: results are enabled by confidence.[5,6] Confidence is particularly needed in unfamiliar situations where our skills will be tested and the results are uncertain—when the question, "Can I do it?" arises. The sense of efficacy rouses the impetus to act by reminding us that through our efforts we can close the distance between where we stand today and our aspirations. The sense of efficacy mobilizes our resources and keeps us doggedly engaged in our pursuits.

You Can Do It

The reason we try anything new is because we believe that with time we will build it, solve it, create it, repair it. Just to be clear, although we are talking about a state of mind, real abilities must back it up. Still, it is the state of mind that can make the real difference. Two people with the same skill sets will be differentially successful if only one believes he can competently deploy those skills. One of the duties of management then is to persuade people who have the requisite abilities that they can do more. Managers also can help employees to help themselves by encouraging them to reflect on the positive aspects of their performances rather than linger on their failures or exaggerate their shortcomings. Simple self-reflective exercises help. For example, simply asking people to replay in their minds the things they have done that showcase their creativity, or the ways creativity is characteristic of who they are, increases innovativeness on divergent thinking tasks; for example, in an exercise where the subject is asked to produce as many quality uses as possible for a brick or a candle.[7,8] We also have found that high performers tend to set a timer for reflection on negative aspects of their performance: "I will think about what went wrong for one hour, then it is time to move on."

The best way, however, to sustain an efficacious workforce is to continuously boost employees' confidence in their abilities through progressively difficult assignments, timely feedback, and ultimately increased mastery and experiences of success. With the favorable accumulation of experiences, people form new perspectives about their abilities and new opinions about what they can undertake. And good managers and coaches try to deflect poor performance away from judgments that would permanently scar employees' confidence, and instead move toward more ephemeral rationales. Thus, coaches of sports teams often will attribute a loss to a poor game plan (a coaching failure).

One of the key components of efficacy is resilience, which is like a stress ball you squeeze in your hand: when you release your hold, the ball's shape springs back. Resilience keeps confidence intact when things are not going as planned and lesser mortals would give up. People who are resilient have an inner strength to persevere, refuse to be defeated, and believe they can handle the jumble of misfortunes that life throws at them. They reframe setbacks as learning opportunities, shrug off missteps with humor, problem-solve their dilemmas, rework a plan on how they will achieve a goal, and seek out advice, assistance, and support from others. Consequently, although life may be tumultuous, resilient people are able to remain effective. They continue to function effectively at home and at work, engage in social activities with friends and family, and savor the little pleasures that make up a day.

Building new skills, learning how to constructively cope with failure, and steadily increasing confidence in our abilities to initiate progressively extraordinary work all appears straightforward. But a diabolical nemesis cloaked in good intentions returns to undermine confidence. It is the micromanager. This time it is not the arrogant, oppressive control freak, but a good and concerned manager who is attentive to the general welfare of his employees. The micromanager does not tightly oversee work because he believes he is stuck with a bunch of losers, but because he wants to ensure their success: like parents writing a report for a child because they don't want to see their child fail. Actually, it is *exactly* like that even to the extent that these managers, like parents, mute the emergence of leadership abilities in their apprentices.[9] Micromanagers are like helicopter parents who hover overhead, ready to swoop down and rescue their children from danger or failure.[10,11,12] (In some pockets of Europe, these parents are called "curling parents" because—in reference to the sport—they sweep the path clean for their little stones. The recent college admissions-fixing scandal in the United States has revealed a similar path-clearing winter metaphor for adult intervention, albeit of a more invasive and desperate kind, known as snowplow parenting.[13]) These worried and eager saviors are ever-present to protect their wards from harm and their own managerial reputations from damage. They overadvise, oversolve, and in general get in the way of another person's independence and growth. The message of this managerial (parental) activism is that a person is incapable of managing his own life.

The US army worries that its junior officers are unprepared to rise in rank because they have been overprotected.[14] Although the concept of mission command is to decentralize decision-making under the principles of disciplined initiative and prudent risk, certain factors blunt adoption in practice. Senior officers are held accountable for conservation of resources and for zero defects. This creates incentives for senior officers to insert themselves more closely into the affairs of their junior officers to minimize waste and errors, and to keep their military careers aloft. The results are good in the short term, but the fear expressed within the military is that this precautionary mind-set is undermining the confidence and independence of the next generation of leaders. For more than a century, the military motif for action has been that the acceptance of a few mistakes on the field is preferable to hesitancy and indecision. The agility and adaptability of officers in the field is paramount, yet those abilities will not develop until the incentive system changes and the zeal for perfection yields to the messiness needed for personal growth.

The primary way people gain confidence in their abilities is through cumulative successes. Therefore, the enhancement of self-confidence entails achievement of incremental challenges. Some challenges will be easily fulfilled, some delayed and accomplished only after considerable anguish, and some will be put on hold until the requisite skills are acquired. Management has the considerable responsibility of pushing conventional performance boundaries while giving the proper level of support that encourages initiative and exploration. By and large, however, organizations do not promote breakthrough performances. They tend to settle for predictable, achievable performances; in this way, it is easy for everyone to feel good and claim victory. The reward system associates excellence with goal completion, or with adequate demonstration of an aptitude. This produces the parallel to a zero-defects environment where managers consider anything less than goal fulfillment a failure, in a bad way. That is, "meeting expectations" often means that an employee did everything correctly and that there were no egregious mishaps. In a system in which companies go to great lengths to avoid the semblance of imperfection, nothing changes.

To augment development and efficacy, companies can build a number of teaching moments into daily routines through mentoring, coaching, job shadowing, and group problem-solving sessions. Insomniac Games has "dailies," where the entire game development team examines a particular feature of a game and jointly critiques what changes should be made. Arkadium does everything it can to enrich the lives of employees. It has extensive, clearly specified developmental criteria for advancement and spends handsomely in support of employee growth. It also creates safe environments where people can try out new skills; those aforementioned Monday staff meetings have randomly selected "hosts" who start the meetings with ten-minute presentations on assigned topics to provide interesting information and to hone their facility in presenting to others. Presentations cover a broad range of topics, from how paper is made to a brief history of the Flatiron district of New York.

At N2, the company asks employees to present at lunch-and-learns and to preside over the monthly all-hands meeting. We were present for an annual meeting where we watched two employees expertly emcee the festivities and a young woman fresh out of college give a stellar presentation on the nature of kindness and sacrifice. She nailed it. One employee told us that "people rise to the expectations of the culture." The culture supports psychological safety and commends positivity that enables people to get better and better.

We often ask managers who we are coaching how important it is for a decision-maker to be right or wrong in certain circumstances. "What is the worst that could happen if you allowed Person X to make the decision and it is not the one you would have made? Now weigh that against the damage done by wresting the decision authority away." One person at Instructure recounted the story of an employee who went to his manager for help. "What do you think I should do?" The manager replied that he would gladly review the variables involved in the decision, but the decision was his to make. The philosophy at Instructure is that no one learns to make good decisions unless they are permitted to make decisions.

Empowerment

The ideal for many organizations would be to have cohorts of self-confident employees making decisions and taking actions on the frontlines. Under most circumstances, this distributed form of organization yields faster results of higher quality than more hierarchical, bureaucratic structures. When organizations push accountability out to the rank and file and employees are emboldened to act on their own initiative, we think of the workforce as empowered.

More and more companies are now operating under the concept of ROWE, Results Only Work Environment, in which self-management, independent thinking, and collegiality are supreme. Edmunds is a serious practitioner of ROWE. At Edmunds, people have the right to decide when, where, and how to meet their goals. Few prohibitions are placed on employees. The only real constraint comes from another acronym, TRUST—Edmunds's core values of Transparency, Resourcefulness, Urgency, Simplicity, and Togetherness— which describes behavioral expectations at Edmunds. Otherwise, employees have the road to themselves.

The idea behind ROWE is simple. Companies hire people who in other quarters of their lives responsibly raise children, make financial decisions, organize events, solve problems, and contribute to their local communities. These are capable people who effectively manage their lives outside of the workplace. As adults they are given the same latitude in the workplace and empowered to make decisions that are of value to the organization. This was a common theme in our companies, as articulated by an employee from BambooHR: "Bamboo treats us like adults and trusts us to act with integrity and make good decisions." Good companies assume the best about people and allow them to act, "to press the button," as some employees described to us, on behalf of the organization using their knowledge and judgment as guides. While granting people the latitude to think and act like adults might miscarry given human fallibility, these companies recognize that enduring the occasional mishap is far superior to putting a thumb on the entire workforce.

Tom Caporaso, the CEO of Clarus Commerce, is fond of baseball—so fond he serves as a little league coach. Although baseball is not a metaphor that Tom pushed and is admittedly one that has limitations, we noticed the similarities between a championship baseball team and Clarus Commerce. Clarus has a lot of team speed, which they use to quickly respond to customer needs. In just the single day we were on the premises, we saw several customer requests quickly met by what to us sounded like sophisticated coding challenges. We may be wrong about the code, but not about the company's reaction times. Make an error? You correct the mistake and are expected to stay in the game. You also are expected to back up teammates, dedicate yourself to continuous improvement, and accept wins and losses as a team, neither taking undue credit or passing blame. The idea of a team is that success depends on coordinated effort, but it does not remove the need to acknowledge personal achievements. In a lavish ceremony at the end of the year, Clarus recognizes employee distinctions such as rookie of the year and most valuable player through handsome glass trophies with engravings of the company's logo. Perhaps most importantly, however, once play begins there are a limited number of times that the manager will step onto the field. It is up to the players to play. The field of play is set by goals and budgets. Within these few boundaries, the company authorizes employees to play ball. This empowerment enables Clarus to move quickly according to conditions on the ground and to diligently meet changing customer needs.

The advantages of empowerment are illustrated in a simulation that compares a directive management style with one in which managers allow their people to execute more freely and deliberately as their capabilities permit. Multiple teams of five, including the leader, participated in the Leadership Development Simulator (which originally was developed for the Squadron Officer School at Maxwell Air Force Base). The simulation is complex and is carved up into ten rounds corresponding to ten discrete decision-making periods. The teams have to manage a large number of assets to discover targets on a shared task screen. If our reading is correct, the simulation seems to be like a multiplayer game of Battleship on steroids, in which beneficial outcomes are highly dependent on collaboration, information sharing, and information integration. Two types of leaders were selected to run the team: leaders who scored highly on having a directive leadership style (taking charge of a group, giving team members instructions, etc.), and leaders who scored highly on having an empowering leadership style (encouraging team members to assume responsibilities on their own, advising team members to exchange information, etc.). The respective styles were reinforced through videos of either a directive or an empowering leader that were shown to the team leads. The results show that directive teams perform better than empowered teams in the early rounds of play. However, the directed teams' performance plateaus while the empowered teams show consistent improvement over time until they surpass the directive teams' performance in the later rounds of play. In the early rounds, the empowered teams get acclimated to the simulation environment, but as they test and explore, their emergent cognitions and increased information gathering, learning, and coordination pay off.[15]

Similarly, a field study showed that people who feel psychologically empowered generate results. Assessments of 441 nurses within five hospitals taken over three time periods showed that greater empowerment directly related to a higher composite performance score (consisting of general competencies, integrity, and specific measures of clinical practice such as coordination of care). The results also revealed a bidirectional pattern by which higher levels of empowerment increased performance, which in turn increased empowerment at a subsequent time period. This is precisely the finding that would be expected: confidence increases performance which increases confidence.[16] This study also is consistent with many others showing that empowered employees feel more efficacious, are more satisfied with their jobs, are more committed to the organization, and perform better.

Empowerment has a mixed history in organizations. It has been embraced as an organizational liberator and demonized as a management fad. Studies show that empowerment works when properly implemented. Companies experience fewer errors, faster turnaround times, and better customer service, as well as higher job satisfaction, organizational commitment, and team performance. In contrast, a transition from centralized controls and a host of checks and balances to greater distributed authority is a significant change in culture and operations that involves increased information sharing, technological enhancements, participative decision-making, extensive training, quality leadership and sociopolitical support, collaborative problem-solving, and team trust.[17] Often the necessary preparations have not been made and empowerment strategies falter.

Empowerment initiatives also may collapse because managers are reluctant to give up control, or employees are reluctant to accept responsibility, or both. A study within a hotel chain headquartered in Europe (with brands in Eastern and Western Europe, the Middle East, Asia, and Africa) shows how self-confidence may be differentially expressed depending on conditions. Frontline service providers assessed their general efficacy using a standard questionnaire. Supervisors were matched to these respondents and asked to evaluate employees on a seven-item, agree/disagree service performance measure. A sample item was "Takes ownership by following through with the customer interaction and ensures a smooth transition to other service employees." Service providers who rated themselves higher in general efficacy also were rated higher by their supervisors in the quality of service they delivered. However, this was true only if the attitudinal climate at the hotel was perceived as one in which employees were expected to act on their own initiative—that is, where employees had the organization's explicit permission to satisfy customers' needs as they thought best. Therefore, employees can feel confident and be ready to act, but an organization can negate the advantages that self-confidence affords by withholding its consent for employees to act outside set protocols without obtaining the necessary approvals.[18]

Confidence and Overconfidence

People who develop confidence in their abilities frequently have an abundance of it. People are filled with confidence, head to toe, and then some. In a word, people tend to be overconfident. In fact, it is a common bias that we humans generally seem to have. Many people have watched enough courtroom dramas to be familiar with one form of overconfidence illustrated by the notoriously flawed testimonies of eyewitnesses.[19] Eyewitnesses can be off by a long shot, mistaking the race of a suspect and the color and make of the getaway car. Nevertheless, they are supremely confident in their testimony, which they decisively deliver as fact. This form of overconfidence is an overprecision bias in which the accuracy of people's observations or judgments are off target. People also overestimate their performance expectations and abilities compared to a standard (overestimation bias) or to others (overplacement bias). Overall, people have a tendency to think they are better than they really are, better than others when they are not, and more sure of the truth than justified. Overconfidence in general is associated with exaggerated capabilities, greater imagined control over events, and underestimates of risk.[20] Thus, the majority of people believe they would survive a zombie apocalypse.[21]

Business is a spectacular place to exercise overconfidence. We start businesses that we shouldn't, roll out new products with tenuous markets, and engage in value-destroying mergers. Indeed, one study found that overconfident CEOs were more apt to merge their companies with other companies, falsely believing they could make serial mergers work. Overconfidence also has been implicated in miscalculations of R&D performance, misguided diversification strategies, overambitious international strategies, overreliance on growth through acquisition, and excessive debt financing.[22]

Despite the ominous drawbacks of overconfidence, humanity has not survived by rationality alone. In fact, we would not have Hershey's chocolate, Disneyland, or Ford cars had the founders given up after repeated failures and ceased investing in ambiguous futures. Plenty of evidence demonstrates that we are not rational *Homo economicus* but irrational *hominem brutis*. Overconfidence is an asset that provides benefits for individuals and groups.[23] Thus, it may be a bias that has been naturally selected. In game play, overconfident players win at a disproportionate rate; overconfidence may also help underdogs win battles.[24] In a world of uncertainty (e.g., not knowing the exact capabilities of a competitor), overconfidence keeps people from walking away from contests or opportunities in which they might prevail and allows them to claim prizes they would not otherwise win. Confident bluffers also may keep competitors who might be superior players at bay. In one research study, participants were asked if they would be willing to compete against another participant on an intelligence test. The winner would get a cash payout and the loser would get nothing. Alternatively, participants could opt out and receive a nominal guaranteed payment. Before participants made their choice, they exchanged self-estimates of their percentile rank on intelligence. Decisions on whether or not to engage in the competition were primarily driven by a participant's relative ranking of intelligence compared to the other participant. The relatively high estimates of players discouraged others from competing. Whether from hubris or an actual rendering of perceived intellect, self-confident players give others pause.[25]

We are all better off because there are people who confidently believe that they can achieve the improbable, or that they are right and everyone else is wrong; in short, people who never give up. Most people in the lower 48 states have never heard of Tom Marshall, who as we write sits in an unassuming home in Anchorage, Alaska.[26] Alaskans know who he is. Tom was the state geologist when Alaska became a state in 1959. At the time of admission to statehood, the US government pledged 100 million acres of federal land that the state could use for its sole benefit. Alaska just had to say which 100 million acres it wanted. Tom pushed for real estate in the cold and dark Arctic region called Prudhoe Bay. The area reminded him of oil-rich lands he had seen in the state of Wyoming. Alaska hesitantly claimed the land. Skeptics abounded because oil companies had been drilling on the nearby north face of the Brooks Range for years and the total returns did not justify continued drilling. One by one, energy companies abandoned the site. At Tom's urging, the last rig on the Brooks Range was moved to Prudhoe Bay, now—after three years—known by some as Marshall's Folly. Gil Mull, the geologist on site, drilled for weeks, periodically testing the pressure, until one day, as he explains, "it sounded like a jet plane overhead. It's shaking the rig. It's a rumble. It's a roar." It was the sound of 25 billion barrels of oil.

Alaskans can now celebrate Tom Marshall's folly and be thankful that a highly efficacious geologist, perhaps an overconfident one, had persisted in persuading Alaska to purchase the land in Prudhoe Bay and to continue drilling when the prospects of oil dimmed. Interestingly, one study specifically shows that geologists are not immune to the effects of extreme confidence. Researchers presented petroleum geologists with drilling scenarios that asked if they would continue to drill following particular experiences with dry holes described in the vignettes. Geologists who were high in self-efficacy were significantly more likely to continue drilling. They also expressed greater confidence in finding oil.[27] And, as we see, sometimes they really do.

Confidence and Credibility

Given the overwhelming practical value of confidence, we are able to recognize it from an early age. Children as young as 24 months are highly sensitive to verbal and nonverbal confidence cues.[28] Children will modulate their imitation of an adult by how confidently the adult exhibits specific behaviors. In one study, an adult model either confidently or unconfidently picked up and played with familiar and unfamiliar objects. Children were more likely to emulate the actions of the confident player even though the ways the objects were played with were identical. The only difference was that one model seemed to know what she was doing and the other appeared confused and uncertain. The behavior of the confident model was more credible to observers because confident people are perceived—from a very early age—as more competent. For young parents out there, children are very discerning when it comes to statements like, "You might want to wear your boots, your feet could get cold," versus, "You need to wear your boots, your feet will get cold later." One statement is expressed as a possibility, the other as a fact. Which child will wear his boots?[29]

Unlike adults, children are not as capable of knowing when one of two equally confident people does not know what he is talking about. Truth detection requires substantial knowledge and information integration to understand when the data presented are accurate.[30] We once were privy to an in-house executive speech where the executive emphatically claimed that he would actualize the trifecta of business: quick delivery, high quality, and low cost— a highly problematic proposition in consulting. We watched as eyes darted around the room. Within a two-year period, most of the management team had departed in frustration.

Unfortunately, accuracy cannot always be immediately detected. In business, in particular, there often is a sizable time lag between an ardently argued position and the results. The time delay between pronouncement and discovery gives some unsavory leaders the time they need to make an opportune exit. Charismatic leaders, for example, exude confidence; however, not all charismatic leaders are good and effective.[31,32,33] They all have a knack for invigorating employees through their colorful visions of the future; nevertheless, while some are focused on the social good and the welfare of people, others craftily advocate outlooks best suited to their personal interests.

There are two types of charismatic leaders, then: one who self-confidently portrays an ethical, socially responsible vision, and another who presents a seductive, faux vision ostensibly for the good of all but mostly for the benefit of himself. The former's vision includes the needs of people in his formulation. The latter's motive contains none of that; his motive is to exercise power, to control others, and to enrich himself. Without our keen scrutiny, both kinds of leaders initially are believable. But the surety of their positions—and the convictions they instill—does not guarantee equivalency in the moral worth of their visions or result in equally sustainable outcomes. Employees must be aware of the confidence-credibility connection and wary of the farcical visions espoused by the slick, versus the ingenuous visions of the sincere.

Team Efficacy

The research on efficacy extends to groups. The people within a group hold beliefs about its capabilities to fulfill its assigned mission. Research that aggregates analyses from many studies (meta-analyses) has found that collective efficacy consistently relates to performance: the greater the group's confidence in its abilities to be successful, the greater the performance.[34,35] As with individuals, confidence can be enhanced directly by leaders' stated beliefs in the capabilities of the group, and by the group's trail of successes. One study showed how the behavior of team leads affected the performance of teams of teen basketball players. Team leads expressed either confidence ("Great play, team; if we keep playing like this, we will easily outscore the other teams") or no confidence ("This situation is really getting desperate; if we keep playing like this, we will never win the contest; do we really have to keep on playing?"). The results indicated that over the course of ten trials of free-throw shooting, the performance of the confident group significantly increased whereas the performance of the unconfident group significantly decreased. Further, results showed that poor performance was partially due to the erosion of the teams' perceived abilities (collective efficacy).[36]

Unlike individuals, members of groups also have access to a host of other cues that are telling of the group's prospects. For example, the members are able to observe the competence of their colleagues and whether the group has the requisite number of staff and mix of capabilities to execute well. Members also are sensitive to the myriad markers of function or dysfunction within the group: the level of trust within the group; the affinity of group members for one another; the degree to which members identify with the group; the quality of interactions, communications, information sharing, and decision-making within the group; the effectiveness of the group in setting goals and planning; the group's collective understanding of roles and responsibilities; the ability of the group to learn, change, and adapt; and so on. People form opinions about the team's ability to organize and execute as a group, which dictates the level of effort expended and team performance. Healthy teams that believe in themselves have a knack for bringing out the best in everyone and increasing revenues for businesses. A study of service teams (made up, on average, of 20 people each) at a major European bank showed that teams with higher ratings of team (collective) efficacy provided higher-quality service (customers were randomly selected and questioned) and generated greater revenues (measured as gross profit minus returns on equity) than teams lower in self-efficacy.[37]

Summary judgments about the people with whom employees work, the amount of support and resources the team receives, and the effectiveness of group processes affect performance. Performance can go up or down. A sense of futility, especially in larger groups where individual performances are difficult to disaggregate and detect, can depress team results to the point where the whole is less than the sum of the parts. If the team is not seen as adequate to reach desired outcomes, what is the use in trying? The name of the effect in which individual efforts decline in groups below what each person could do on his or her own is called "social loafing."[38]

On the other hand, sometimes working in groups pulls performances up. Teammates can increase the performances of other members, in particular the less capable members. The collective performance that exceeds the sum of what people can do individually is called the "Köhler Effect," named for Otto Köhler, who identified the phenomenon in the 1920s. In a simple example using motor persistence, individuals were asked to hold a bar out in front of them for as long as possible. Those same people were then asked to repeat the task but this time in a group and with their arms stretched out over a rope, so that when the arm of any individual gave out and hit the rope, a timer was stopped and the performance of the group recorded. The greatest increases in times occurred with individuals who had the lowest individual results. The Köhler Effect is readily seen in naturalistic settings. In relay races, for example, inferior swimmers record faster times in the relays than they do in individual contests.[39]

Extrapolating to working groups, we can see several possible reasons for this effect and the principles that leaders may want to keep in mind when managing teams. First, people are interdependent in that they share a common goal. Second, each member is indispensable to goal success. Third, members have a vested interest in each other's success and are depending on one another to do their best. Fourth, the observation of others performing well stimulates healthy internal competition.

CHAPTER 12

GROWTH

Help people to become better, and a little wiser

Employees in many industries experience what we refer to as the two-year itch. This is the time when employees reconsider their relationship with their employers and begin looking for the exit signs. A host of factors impair the employee-employer relationship at this stage, but one troublesome issue that arises for employees is well verbalized through the question, "Now what?" After two years of doing the same thing, inquisitive, energetic people are ready for the next challenge. When substantive change does not appear to be forthcoming, those who can, move on. Think of it in terms of Newton's First Law: *An object at rest stays at rest and an object in motion stays in motion with the same speed and in the same direction unless acted upon by an unbalanced force.* In the case of employees, the inner motivational force for more demanding tasks is opposed by countervailing organizational forces of unpreparedness and complacency. Confronted by forces that bridle movement, employees begin to look for places where they will meet less resistance to resuming forward momentum, which is critical to employees' commitment to their work.[1]

Growth Mind-set

If employees do not want to make the same mistake twice, the next company they find will posit a growth mind-set and foster personal growth. Companies that subscribe to a growth mind-set believe that skills and abilities are not fixed and immutable but can be honed through instruction, hard work, and persistence. The differences between a fixed organizational belief system, in which companies view abilities as natural, unchangeable gifts, and a growth organizational belief system, in which companies view abilities as malleable and subject to modification, have profound implications for the way talent is conceived, recognized, and managed. Individuals who believe that their talents are mostly fixed by the good or bad fortunes of the genetic draw are less likely to persist at difficult tasks, learn from their mistakes, or attribute successes to their abilities.[2] Managers who similarly embrace the theory that talent is a stable asset take on the role of talent scout, looking to discover the next star, in contrast to talent developer, who nurtures abilities from the ground up, as if cultivating talent within a farm system (as in baseball). The manager with a fixed mind-set places less emphasis on employee development and more on hiring and promoting the most gifted.

In an intriguing sequence of studies, Heslin and associates have shown that managers with fixed (versus growth) mind-sets hold more unchangeable views following employees' initial performances.[3] In one study, the research team first assessed managers' beliefs about people's abilities. They then asked these managers to watch a video of a poor performance by an employee, and to rate the performance. In a later video the managers watched the same hypothetical employee perform well, and were then asked once again to evaluate the performance. The performance ratings by managers with fixed mind-sets did not change from their first assessments. The ratings by managers with growth mind-sets evaluatively tracked the actual performances depicted. Once managers with fixed mind-sets have formed strong opinions regarding the abilities of employees, they attribute future positive changes in an employee's performance to factors such as luck that are external to the person—since the person is presumed incapable of changing on her own initiative. Performance improvements therefore do not create cause for celebration since the results are believed to be aberrational departures of middling performers. The result is that these managers quickly give up on poor performers who ostensibly are beyond help.

Using results such as this and the work of Carol Dweck as the springboard, Patagonia jettisoned its old-fashioned retrospective performance review process for one that is more consistent with its outlook on people.[4] The new format relies on ongoing communications, targeted feedback, and quarterly updates on goals. The basic concept is that capabilities, including creativity, are malleable and can be improved given the right environment and the right opportunities and challenges. This seems rather straightforward and in line with oft-held convictions that people can change and grow; however, it is not the philosophical foundation in many companies where people are viewed as bright stars or as white dwarfs: "You either have it or you don't." Such an outlook is counter to a company that depends on the human spirit for its success. Indeed, Patagonia performs quarterly conversations and goal reviews with an eye toward employees' potential and the development of their skills.

Organizations that have a shortage of developmental opportunities do not communicate faithfulness to the possibilities of employee growth. Companies that prematurely choose "winners" through the discovery and promotion of fast-trackers also implicitly assume that the corporate future belongs to a select, precocious few. Companies bereft of employee development planning, meaningful succession, and intelligent feedback systems appear to have made up their collective mind that talent is impervious to change.

Learning, Growing, Thriving

Organizations with fixed mind-sets are typified by an absence of active, tailored, professional development and the associated resources. These companies forego the expenditures that can deepen technical skills, broaden operational exposure, refine leadership abilities, and provide new challenges. On the other hand, companies that promote learning and growth have open, fluid communications, extensive teamwork and knowledge sharing, dedicated physical and financial resources for innovation and personal development, time allowances for practical experimentation, robust cross-functional relationships, low levels of political intrigue and sundry time-wasters, and prominent displays of work samples and historical artifacts that showcase an organization's timeless ingenuity.

Companies that truly believe people make a difference will make heavy investments in employee growth and go to extraordinary lengths to create environments that stimulate curiosity and the desire to learn and share ideas. We can call these learning environments, and they have two constituent pieces. The first is context. Context consists of the myriad cues and routines that announce to the workforce that learning is important and that a central aim of the organization is to open a permissive space for employees to think and act creatively. The second piece of a learning environment involves activities associated with individual development planning. Below, we have selected examples to illustrate a few salient learning programs that showcase companies' commitment to employee development.

Lunch-and-learns. Several of the companies in our sample have weekly or biweekly lunch-and-learns. *INTUITIVE* holds weekly lunch-and-learns on professional, financial (e.g., credit and savings), and health topics (e.g., healthy cooking). At Edmunds, every Thursday is "Thinking Thursday." No meetings are scheduled. The workforce reserves the day for action items about ongoing work as well as learning opportunities on myriad work-related and life skills topics. Think of this as the day for grand rounds. Given that everyone's calendars are clear on Thursdays, everyone will have a chance to attend these presentations. Similarly, we have been to companies in which one day a month is reserved for learning something new; topics can range from how to set up a home lighting system to how to perform basic car maintenance.

In 2008, The Motley Fool launched a dynamic Speaker Series that hosts people who are luminaries in their respective fields. These have included:

- Jack Bogle, founder of Vanguard
- Elon Musk, CEO of Tesla Motors and SpaceX
- Billy Blanks, founder of Tae Bo
- Adam Braun, CEO of Pencils of Promise
- Kate White, former editor in chief of *Cosmopolitan* magazine
- Alexis Ohanian, founder of Reddit
- Kip Tindell, cofounder and CEO of The Container Store
- Amy Simmons, founder of Amy's Ice Cream

In the words of Touchstone, the goal is to help people "ripen": to grow their capabilities and thrive.

In several companies, the lunch *is* the learn. BAF outsources its cafeteria to local vendors who rotate lunches based on various world cuisines.

Sabbaticals. Several companies allow employees to take extended periods to pursue special projects of their liking. The Motley Fool allows paid sabbaticals of eight weeks after an employee has completed ten years of service. For the super-exceptional performer of the year, Arkadium bestows the Infinite Possibilities Prize. Twenty-five thousand dollars are given to an employee to do anything he wants, from going on an extended yoga retreat to working with an established novelist on a first work of fiction. Employees who have been at Patagonia for one year qualify for a fully paid two-month environmental internship, typically as volunteers. Applications are reviewed by an employee review committee. Patagonia grants most reasonable requests, as funding allows, with 125–50 of 2,000 employees taking internships per year.

Special programs. During our stay at FONA, we met several employees who were earning advanced degrees. In addition to supporting formal instruction, the company subscribes to short courses on myriad subjects open to the entire workforce. FONA also recently initiated an innovative nine-week action learning program for employees. Codenamed "FONA Leaps," the program offers professional instruction for employees to complete a project over a defined span of time, alone or in combination with others. Plus, if you have an interest in becoming a Flavorist, you are free to enroll in FONA's daunting seven-year apprenticeship program.

Arts and crafts. Several of the companies we visited reserve space for employees' art or hold internal crafts fairs that showcase the works of employees and family members. QBP dedicates wall space for employee art. A photographic exhibit was on display the day of our visit. The exhibit featured night photography reminiscent of the pre-smartphone age when photographers used light meters, tripods, and long exposures to capture their evening subjects on film. At BAF, we saw a few skillfully engineered lamps made from bourbon bottles on people's desks. One employee explained, "Someone in analytics makes those. We have a Big Ass Bazaar where employees and their families can sell their arts and crafts, like an internal Etsy."

These slices of creativity may not seem like much, as most works presented will not upend the art world. Yet these "small *c*" (everyday creativity) works denote the importance of creative expression no matter how incidental the works may be. Art is important because the process of creation makes people feel happy, active, and alive. Experimenters who gathered random examples of individuals' behaviors throughout the day found that people were happiest and most enlivened when they were engaged in something creative at the time they were contacted.[5] The advice Kurt Vonnegut once gave to a high school class makes perfect sense. The class asked the prolific fiction writer, onetime prisoner of war, and Dresden bombing survivor to come talk to them. He declined the offer due to his age, but gave them one piece of advice: to practice any art regularly, no matter how good or bad, in order to experience "becoming," to discover themselves, and to make their souls grow.[6]

Art, big or small, engages people in a contemplative life and shows creators that they have the capacity to produce something of worth to share. Art is a life-affirming activity for the inquisitive that increases people's sense of purpose and connection with humanity.[7]

Investment in development. Since 2013, companies have spent $440 billion on corporate training initiatives. The secret ingredient to lifelong generativity and employment at places such as KitchenAid is investment in their workers.[8]

TCG does everything within its power to deploy people according to their current skill sets and ambitions and keep them engaged in projects. "I don't ever want to leave this company" is a common refrain at TCG. To help with employee growth, TCG gives each employee $2,500 a year, which they can use to support the career development plan they create in league with their managers. Expenditures can include classes, subscriptions, and conferences. Some companies don't have limits to development dollars, or the limits are so high ($10,000 at Health Catalyst) that they may as well not have them.

A multitude of developmental options exists for those companies so disposed. Ideally, these options will contain a mix of internal and external (contact outside the company) offerings. Continual exposure to the outside world through attendance at conferences, invited guest speakers, visits to noncompetitors, external training programs and coursework, and such is essential to maintaining porous boundaries, which keep organizational ideas fresh—and prevent the insularity of the "that's not how it's done here" syndrome.

Companies that generate a culture of learning commend independent decision-making, calculated risk-taking, and creativity. They laud individual and team achievements and heartily celebrate new services and product rollouts. Corporations make it very clear which among them want employees to think, and which do not. We recently encountered an example of the latter. We were at a meeting (as consultants) where a group of employees was discussing changes to the departmental structure. The vice president had one idea, and an underling had another. The vice president sought to resolve the impasse by making a power play: "I'm a vice president. I think I'm right." We called for an immediate time-out to refresh group process.

One company we consulted to has an interesting way of interceding when arguments are made based on position authority or when discussions insinuate ill intent or affronts to individuals' character. The meeting organizer pulls out a yellow card, as done in soccer. If an offender receives a second yellow card, the acting referee asks the person to leave the meeting. This keeps debate lively but within a permissible range of propriety.

The learning that takes place in our sample companies is decidedly two-way. As a creative enterprise, Insomniac thrives on teamwork, transparency, and truth. It works very hard to encourage the unfettered, unfiltered flow of ideas necessary for innovation and to remove any obstacle that might interfere with honest two-way dialog. "Great ideas can come from anywhere" is the mantra and, appropriately, it is imperative to keep all lines of communication open. Concord's employees are assured of well-trained, trustworthy managers who facilitate employee development through prompt feedback, attention to new opportunities for associate growth, and two-way conversations. As one manager told us, "I ask myself two questions at the end of the day: did I learn something and did I teach something?" The recipe for beneficial exchange is straightforward: talk and listen.

SAS does something interesting that is very telling about the organization. Like many companies, it teaches older generations of employees about millennials. SAS, however, also teaches millennials about Gen-Xers and baby boomers. It works both ways. We think this is a brilliant way to communicate that conversations have two sides and that people can learn from one another regardless of their station.

A Close Eye on Development

The second aspect of a learning environment concerns the amount of effort put into the development planning process. Development largely rests in the hands of supervisors to whom employees look for inspiration and support. In fact, from the employee's perspective, supervisory support for the developmental enterprise is the most real indicator of an organization's commitment to growth. In this regard, supervisors who are philosophically aligned with a growth mind-set and its associated imperatives are more likely to motivate the development and performance of their employees.[9] These supervisors work with employees to set learning goals, coach and provide feedback as needed, and ensure in tandem with the organization that employees receive helpful developmental opportunities.

Edmunds has a suite of interconnected programs that foster development. These related initiatives are called Fuel Your Potential, Cascade Development, and Internal Internships. We mention these separately but they work in concert toward the same purpose: to continuously upgrade the abilities of the workforce and to ensure that the work people do is consistent with their passions. This network of programs begins with biannual conversations in which employees look back at their accomplishments and lessons learned, as well as forward toward activities they would like to do more of.

These conversations primarily lead to a cascading of roles and responsibilities or to the delegation of important assignments that will edge employees closer to what they want for themselves. Managers thus delegate substantive assignments to their direct reports that dovetail with their interests and longer-term aims. FONA does this during its annual planning processes. Each manager, from the CEO down, is expected to carve out a significant assignment and pass it down.

BambooHR offers standard training opportunities to employees that are specific to their technical backgrounds; however, they also recognize the limitations of the old fixed-function, upwardly mobile career. The vertical job trajectory confines employees' skill development to a narrow functional band. In reality, work is more fluid and less structured than presumed by traditional career pathways. The needs of the organization can easily accommodate expansive employee development and offer employees opportunities to apply their skills in multiple contexts. Though some moves can seem improbable, they make perfect sense given a person's interests and abilities. At BambooHR, a member of the human resources department upgraded his coding capabilities through self-study and boot camps and was moved into the development department, where he was assigned a mentor and received more training. Now, he says, "I feel like I play in a sandbox every day. I get to hang out with friends and code really cool stuff with them." Similarly, after six months on the job, a recent hire was asked by the company to take on a new assignment, which she thought was outside her range of abilities. The company, though, saw talents in her that would be well suited to the move. Today she happily reports that "they were right."

During peak business periods in May and July, senior managers at QBP can be seen working in distribution, picking and receiving goods. Rich, the person in bike clothing whom we met on our arrival, has risen through the ranks to CEO by performing just about every job at one time or another, starting with work in the warehouse. He has done a yeoman's job of product picking over the years. He became a buyer one day when Steve Flagg, the founder of QBP, asked him to look at some data and figure out how many items of various products the company should order. Many more moves were to come. Steve has a habit of tapping people on the shoulder and asking them to do things above their pay grade or that are different from what they are accustomed to doing. This ideology of personal growth permeates QBP and manifests on the job when employees eagerly and confidently assume greater responsibilities and new challenges.

There is a good chance that whomever Clarus hires for a given position will not be in the same job for very long. There is no penalty if an employee prefers to stay put and develop deeper skills in his current occupation, but most people reach a point in their career when they no longer feel challenged, and strategic moves within or across functional lines are necessary for the person's continued growth. It is all part of the fun, and moves are prompted either by a bit of employee self-reflection ("I think I would be a great product coordinator") or through more deliberate, longer-term development plans based on the employee's aspirations. The goal is the same: to continually renew employees' sense of potency and ensure that they perceive the work they do to be worthwhile.

Michelle, in human resources at Regeneron, offers a succinct summary of what a career means in these times of burgeoning technologies and ideas: "The career goal of Regeneron is to help you find a job where you can be the best you." The company never wants anyone's job to become monotonous. Internal candidates always can apply for open positions for which they qualify, and move to an area they find more appealing. Alternatively, some prepare for their next job through a combination of formal education and training (several employees are working toward advanced degrees) and on-the-job mentoring—all of which Regeneron will accommodate. For example, when Rich, one of the employees we spoke with, joined the company, he wasn't an automation expert. In fact, he knew very little about automation. Today he is an expert because someone took the time to train and mentor him. He currently is paying it forward.

Naturally, helping people articulate what they want for themselves is a big step in the developmental process; however, development is a long journey that calls for much more than periodic access to new opportunities, knowledge acquisition, and skill development. Full engagement and growth occur when an individual's abilities mesh with the demands and challenges of a job: a balance that a skilled manager and coach can cultivate.

Coaching for Success

We recently attended a wedding in rural upstate Vermont, where we learned of a developmental process that reiterates itself every generation. An old army transport vehicle carried guests down a dirt road to a lovely remote piece of land with stream and pond—a onetime meditative retreat for the bride. This hidden place was in Richmond, Vermont, which to most readers will be an unfamiliar speck in a vast and relatively unpopulated domain. However, the world ski community knows the place well as home to the skiing Cochran family who have produced three generations of collegiate and Olympic champions. When we were there, another Cochran family disciple, Robby Kelley, was the reigning national giant slalom champion. Upstart Ryan Cochran-Siegle had just won gold in downhill and combined at the Alpine Junior World Ski Championships in Roccasoro, Italy, and more recently was part of the US ski team at the 2018 Olympics in South Korea.

We tell this story of family excellence because these world-class skiers all learned their craft on a small hill in their backyard—a gentle sloping mound of earth that stretches no longer than a couple hundred feet. The action is enabled by a self-installed towline and makeshift lighting strung from trees. It would be facile to attribute the family's successes to the privilege of genes, for the real explanation is more basic. They owe their success to practice, habit, and astute and sensitive guidance.

First, an expert who truly understands excellence oversees skier development. This person knows what to watch for and attend to. These overseers know the skills that learners must master as prerequisites for success, and they focus on process versus outcomes. The Cochrans have always understood that the fastest down a course at any given time is not necessarily the best equipped to compete on the international stage, where a nanosecond flaw in style and form can be costly. Said differently, the focus of training is on mastering a skill, not on achieving a certain performance outcome. Mastery goals repeatedly have been shown to foster greater interest and persistence in activities.[10]

Second, practice involves isolating skills and correcting performances in gradual increments. The best way for a neophyte Cochran to learn to ski is on a small hill. Skiers will not learn faster by starting on a mountaintop. There would be too much that is wildly wrong to fix, and too little enjoyment derived by the skier from the scary descent to persist in the activity. A mentor must be able to isolate features of performance for the learner to work on, so throwing a person into the proverbial fire would not allow the necessary discriminations to be made. Thus, the best way to learn from practice is in small and steady improvements where the success rate is high, but not perfect. People are happiest when they are learning well and growing despite the occasional fall.

Third, effort and practice need to be applied toward those aspects of performance that are most important, that will make the biggest difference, and that people are best at doing (and are therefore activities that are self-rewarding). It doesn't make sense to spend undue time mitigating weaknesses and closing gaps that may be superfluous to longer-term aims and performance. Yes, fix what has to get fixed, but keep in mind that the goal is greatness versus proficiency. Skiers gravitate to events that use their strengths and where they can truly excel. Artists do the same thing. They work in mediums or with themes that they enjoy and are best at executing. They expand on their expertise by straying from proven abilities and experimenting with new ideas and techniques in adjacent areas. Some strengths naturally bleed into weaknesses, so improvements may be observed in once-troublesome areas. Nevertheless, rather than fixing what is broken in employees, managers should find ways to use and improve the most skilled dimensions of their talents.

The idea of strengths-based development has become fashionable over the past decade in organizations, but well before it caught hold within business, strengths already were a well-discussed topic in social work and mental health circles. It might be fair to trace the origins of strengths-based therapies and development back to the 1960s when theorists worried about stigmatizing people by associating them with disorders—labeling them by what was wrong with them versus tuning into their capabilities. As counterweight, many practitioners believed that people could more readily grow and meet personal goals if they defined themselves by, attended to, and used those features in which they excelled; that is, if they applied their rich array of assets to build on and deploy as circumstances required.[11,12] And as it happens, when people use abilities they want to use, they experience higher levels of life satisfaction, job satisfaction, meaning, and well-being.

Self-Help

Since the publication of Malcolm Gladwell's book *Outliers*, many people we have spoken with have come to believe that they can master anything with ten thousand hours of practice.[13] A couple of things about that: first, to obtain the performance benefits of practice, it has to be deliberate. That means focused, effortful, and goal directed with the specific aim of getting better. Second, there are some things people could practice for the rest of their lives and never become experts at. In fact, studies show that deliberate practice only accounts for up to about one third of performance and, for some tasks, almost nothing. This is because there are things other than performance that matter. One factor is anatomy. Physical features and body composition are important for many bodily endeavors and motor-perceptual activities. A large part of the reason that artists, sports figures, and entertainers run in families is because, as Francis Galton reported over a hundred years ago, physiology is inherited. Second, expertise (and job performance) is highly correlated with cognitive abilities, including metacognitive abilities such as knowing how to learn. Third, personal traits relate to the degree to which people are able to practice and stick with an activity; traits such as grit and emotional control are essential for persistence and the formation of habits.[14]

It is tempting to construe learning and development as passive, consumptive activities. In fact, much of growth is dependent on a person's own regulatory abilities to set standards, exert the necessary effort for improvement, and monitor gains against goals while fending off temptations to work on simpler, more easily achievable objectives. Overcoming the lure of appetizing diversions involves self-discipline and self-control. People who lose weight, eat more healthily, exercise more, and perform better are equipped to regulate their attention, emotions, and behaviors by rigging their environments in helpful ways. People who are able to grow and get things done try to make it as easy as possible to learn and execute so they do not have to rely on exhausting heroic efforts to make progress. To return to the ski analogy, the Cochran children ski promptly at 6 p.m., after finishing their homework. Skis hang by the door; the foot of the towline reaches the back of the house; and the Cochran hill is open to anyone who wants to learn to ski. So at 6 p.m. the neighborhood kids already are frolicking in the backyard. Subtle prompts and cues are established that make it easy for the learners to venture out into the cold even when they do not feel like it. The goal, whether on the slopes or within the corporation, is to set up cues and contingencies that yield beneficial, habitual ways of acting. These cues can be self-imposed or introduced by the organization.

Habits are essential for safety, health, growth, efficiency. The elite in the sciences, arts, and sports have one thing in common: they have developed good habits that allow them to do things even when the probability of a reward is quite low and elements of the task are painful, like going outside in subzero weather to ski. Virtuoso violinists practice at the same time for the same length every day.[15] Habits, then, trigger behaviors that may be unpleasant but that are necessary to meet longer-term aims. This might be the case for salespeople or marketers who must make cold calls, where the rejection rates are quite high. It is not that much fun to call people who do not want to be bothered, but that must be done. Those most likely to succeed will be those who develop the best habits.

For the most part, organizations will want to instill good habits in the workforce for the same reasons, as habits help us to be more efficient and productive in all areas of our lives. At work, they help us to be more organized, safer, more service-centric, and so on. For example, developing safety habits—from washing hands to putting on safety goggles—can lead to less contamination and fewer accidents in manufacturing environments. The formation of habits is essential in eliciting these behaviors.

To illustrate how habits work, let's put mice in a maze that looks like a cross. We teach the mice to turn right at the junction to find cheese. One mouse is trained just a little bit, and the other a whole lot so that it develops a habit. Habits are defined as learned patterns of behavior that automatically (with little conscious deliberation) occur in response to cues from the environment (when you get to the intersection, turn right). Habits are well-ingrained chunks of behavior that our brain has decided should be automated. Because we are doing the same thing over and over, our brains put those sequences on automatic pilot so we can attend to more serious concerns that could use our undivided attention. Certain things just wouldn't get done regularly without habits. You can only brush your teeth so many times at bedtime for the self-reinforcing value of clean teeth; environmental cues and associated routines have to take over the chore.

Researchers know that a habit is formed when a mouse will run for the cheese even if it makes it sick, or the cheese has declined in value, or has been removed from the maze (diminutions in value are often manipulated in labs by allowing mice to gorge themselves prior to presenting a reward, or by injecting mice with a substance that will make them sick when they ingest the reward). With habits, behaviors are under stimulus-response (action) control internalized as a "get cheese" sequence, abbreviated as S > R. When I get to the crossroads (S), I take a right and run to the end (R). Under diminished rewards, the mice who have not yet developed a habit will stop running because the sickening cheese, for example, has lost its value. In contrast to habits, many goal-directed behaviors are under instrumental control: people take actions based on the expected outcomes. These behaviors are sensitive to changes in the value of outcomes and to the contingencies between actions and outcomes. This relationship is represented by an action-outcome formula

(A > O). When a lump of cheese diminishes in value, an experienced mouse will change course to find a more satisfying outcome.

Assume that we have been dropping the mice into the maze from the south side and then decide to switch things up and begin putting them into the maze from the opposite, north side, so that everything is reversed from the mice's point of view. The instrumental mice head down the corridor, pause at the intersection, inspect the area for potentially rewarding moves using their senses, and turn left toward the cheese (which is where it always has been). On the other hand, the mice under S > R control turn right, and right again— again and again. Using more advanced techniques than mazes, researchers have found the same results with people. The very thing that is supposed to help us navigate through life successfully has become our nemesis. The fact that the "cheese" isn't there or makes us sick doesn't matter.[16,17,18,19]

Habits thus persist even when the outcome is no longer the preferred response. For example, as a new security measure, people in one of our spouse's office buildings were asked to refrain from using a side fire exit that henceforth would be armed with an alarm. Facilities placed a big sign on the door: PLEASE DO NOT USE AS EXIT. For weeks, the security alarm sounded multiple times every day, triggered by people using the exit. As a fire exit it could not be barricaded, so a security officer ultimately was stationed to reroute traffic down a different corridor. This example underscores two aspects of habits. First, people are much less attentive while their behavior is under the control of a habit. Exiting employees never noticed the sign on the door. Second, habits are hard to break. We can be certain that people told themselves, "Today, I will not set off the alarm," but did anyway. You can't just make up your mind to do something differently. Nature won't let you. The security guard was needed for several weeks to redirect traffic until the employees' habit was broken and replaced with a new association between cues and behavior (turn *left* at the junction).

Mice that continue to operate under strongly established behavioral protocols can look pathetically stupid and resistant from the perspective of more successful mice who may regard them as loathsome, antiquated creatures for their ineffectual action when there is a hardy brick of cheese within sniffing distance. On the other hand, perhaps we are not very good change agents ourselves. If you do not want your mice nibbling on bad cheese or curiously repeating behaviors that objective observers would regard as ineffective, you will have to change processes, restructure the environment, entrain action to new cues, and spend a lot of time retraining people so they overlearn new behaviors. But sounding warnings, arming employees with facts, and making urgent calls to action will not be enough to instigate change. You want to reengage the thinking, attentive parts of their brains that recognize new realities and behavioral consequences.

Even so, habits are necessities for high performance. We marvel at the raw abilities of skiers on the slopes but lose sight of the abilities that lie beneath the surface—their ability to get themselves onto the slopes after a long day, to come back after painful falls, to listen to and accept feedback, to keep a positive outlook and invasive impulses and emotions in check, to develop supportive, encouraging relationships with others, to remain focused on longer-term goals, and to sustain conviction in their capabilities. They have the personal and social competencies that surround their skills and efforts which enable them to grow.

Wise Counsel

Instructure's CEO, Josh Coates, thinks about development as a game of chess. In chess, everything there is to know is in front of you. Accordingly, at Instructure, there are no secrets. Every quarter the executives provide the entire workforce with unfiltered financial results. Each area of the company routinely updates everyone on their goals and the status of different initiatives. The ultimate goal is to make the best moves possible given what you know and what you observe. Instructure wants everyone in the company to become grand masters by honing their abilities to make good decisions. It encourages development, first by urging people to learn as much as they can—to be selfish in the acquisition of knowledge. Instructure has a pool of development funds available to employees and willingly and frequently reassigns people to new roles so that they are able to gain new skills and perspectives on the business. Second, Instructure provides employees with a great deal of independence. It coaches people to take their fingers off their chess pieces and move them! Then the company can review successes, mistakes, or alternative, more effective moves that might be made in the future. Instructure figures that its hiring process is rigorous, its training and development is second to none, and its technological and informational infrastructures are stellar: it would be a spectacular waste of talent to then insist that employees gain approval for decisions within the purview of their jobs.

In essence, Instructure wants people to accumulate data points that inform their judgments. It wants people who are wise: people who have insight into themselves, others, and the world; who are open to new ideas and experiences; who recognize life's complexities; who flexibly and creatively adapt to circumstances; and who thoughtfully transcend their own self-interests.[20,21] The exceptional advice-giving, decision-making, and problem-solving of wisdom allow people to confront the complexities of life experiences and life challenges in wisdom-enhancing ways, which consider manifold perspectives, values, and reasons, and integrate these into superior solutions.

We are constantly presented with dilemmas in life. Should we let a very good, but messy, friend use our tidy apartment while we are away? What do you say to your teen who has just informed you that he wrecked your car? How do you respond when your spouse misses an event that is important to you? Whatever the dilemma, wise choices ultimately place value on the right things, and imprudent choices place value on the wrong things. Wisdom thus measures aims that are not created equal. Were the people who were party to Harvey Weinstein's reign of terror wise or unwise in their tacit acceptance of his behavior? Were the people who allowed a highly abusive rainmaker wealth manager to remain in their employment wise or unwise?[22] We were people before we were board members, managers, employees, spouses, brothers, sisters, friends, rich, or poor. Wisdom is not possible if we are unable to see past our role and into the eyes of another and the person within.

We find it reasonable to wish for ourselves and others a good life and to ask whether the current, yet unnecessary, capitalist criterion of profit maximization precludes the possibility of wisdom. Putting all our understanding into a meat grinder with the proviso that only one non-nutritional solution comes out the other side seems to be a waste of the human capacity for judgment and a recipe that will fall short of our best. If money is the sole criterion used in our decision-making in organizations, we can be assured that we will be unwise more than a few times. And it will go on like that until capitalism becomes better acquainted with what makes life worth living.

REFERENCE MATTER

APPENDIX

LIST OF COMPANIES

BambooHR	Instructure
Big Ass Fans (BAF)	Intuitive Research and Technology (*INTUITIVE*)
Bi-Rite Family of Businesses	The Motley Fool
Clarus Commerce	N2 Publishing
Concord Hospitality	Patagonia
Edmunds	PURE Insurance
ESL Federal Credit Union	Quality Bicycle Products (QBP)
FONA International	Regeneron
Health Catalyst	SAS Institute
Insomniac Games	TCG

Company-approved descriptions follow:

ARKADIUM

Arkadium has been reinventing interactive content since 2001. Every year its engaging, visual technologies create billions of interactions for partners like Microsoft and leading consumer brands, plus more than 450 of the world's leading publishers, including CNN, the *Washington Post*, Time Inc., Gannett, Tribune Publishing, and more. Based in New York City with an additional office in Russia, in 2017 Arkadium received "Best Workplace" awards from Crain's, *Inc.* magazine, *Digiday*, and *Ad Age*. For more information about Arkadium, visit www.arkadium.com.

BAMBOOHR

Serving more than ten thousand customers and supporting one million employees in over one hundred countries, BambooHR is the leading provider of tools that power the strategic evolution of human resources (HR) in small and medium businesses. BambooHR's cloud-based system is an intuitive, affordable way for growing companies to track and manage essential employee information in a personalized Human Resources Information System. Now HR managers have more time for meaningful work; executives get accurate, timely reports; and employees can self-service their time off using a convenient mobile app. BambooHR's clients include innovators like SoundCloud, Foursquare, Freshbooks, Stance, Reddit, and Magnolia Homes, among thousands of others worldwide.

BIG ASS FANS (BAF)

Big Ass Fan Company: the name says it all. Delta T Corporation, doing business as Big Ass Fans, makes 6–24-foot-diameter ceiling fans. The size of the fans allows them to move massive amounts of air over large spaces while the foils (or blades) move at a slow-to-moderate speed. Applications for the company's oversized products include environmental control (circulating hot or cold air) in immense spaces such as warehouses, manufacturing facilities, retail spaces, institutional buildings, and athletic stadiums.

BI-RITE FAMILY OF BUSINESSES

Bi-Rite has been a San Francisco institution for decades and sets the standard for businesses that champion locally sourced products grown by small producers. It offers all staffers, including part-timers, health insurance, a 401(k) with a 4 percent match, and profit-sharing. Sam Mogannam's father and uncle ran the original store in San Francisco's Mission District. Trained as a chef, Sam and his brother Raphael took over the market in 1997 and embarked on a mission of "Creating Community through Food." Installing a kitchen in the center of the market was key to Bi-Rite's evolution and served as a way for Sam to share his passion for cooking and bring delicious, fresh food to the neighborhood. Today Bi-Rite's prepared foods continue to be cooked in-house by Bi-Rite's chefs and are a cornerstone of the markets. The company smokes its own salmon, mixes hummus from Sam and Raphael's mother's recipe, and showcases a different dinner menu every night. Committed to pushing the boundaries of responsible sourcing, Bi-Rite rid its shelves of two bestsellers, farmed salmon and yellowfin tuna, when it became clear both were being overfished. Today the Bi-Rite Family of Businesses has grown to include two neighborhood markets, a world-renowned creamery, a full-service catering operation, a small farm in Sonoma, and a café in San Francisco's Civic Center Plaza. The Bi-Rite family also includes "18 Reasons," a nonprofit community cooking school which teaches more than seven thousand Bay Area residents every year how to shop, cook, and enjoy good food. Bi-Rite is a Certified B Corp.

CLARUS COMMERCE

Clarus Commerce specializes in the design, development, and implementation of fully customized premium loyalty programs for retailers. Clarus Commerce, LLC, develops and markets subscription websites to save consumers time and money. The company offers FreeShipping.com, an e-commerce shopping solution that gives members instant free shipping at online retailers, cash-back deals at retail sites, price protection, and rebates on return shipping costs. It provides its shipping and subscription-based solutions for e-commerce businesses. The company was formerly known as Clarus Marketing Group, LLC, and changed its name to Clarus Commerce, LLC, in June 2015.

CONCORD HOSPITALITY

Concord Hospitality Enterprises Company operates as a hotel development, ownership, and management company in the United States and Canada. The company develops, acquires, and operates its own hotel properties and provides hotel management services to full-service and upscale select-service hotel properties. It offers fee-based management services for various hotel ownerships, including joint ventures, REITs, private equity funds, private entities, and individuals. Concord Hospitality Enterprises Company was founded in 1985 and is based in Raleigh, North Carolina.

EDMUNDS

Edmunds.com is devoted to all things auto-related. The company's namesake site offers tools that help viewers shop for and compare new and used cars, search for deals, read car reviews, find dealers, and get advice on topics like how to buy a car, buying versus leasing, safety, financing, and insurance. It also publishes a "What's Hot" section for car news, photos, videos, and forums. Its "True Cost to Own" pricing system provides ownership costs (taxes and fees, insurance, repairs, fuel costs, maintenance) for new and used vehicles. The Edmunds.com car-shopping app for mobile devices includes the company's pricing, research, and inventory search tools.

ESL FEDERAL CREDIT UNION

ESL Federal Credit Union, once called Eastman Savings and Loan after its original founder, provides deposit accounts, credit cards, loans, insurance, business banking, and wealth management services through its 21 branches in upstate New York. Boasting $6.1 billion in total assets and 348,000 members, the credit union extends membership eligibility to much of the Rochester community, including Rochester residents, select outside employer groups, and employees and retirees of Eastman Kodak. Founded in 1920 by George Eastman (also the founder of Eastman Kodak), it was known as Eastman Savings and Loan until it changed its charter from a thrift to a credit union in 1996.

FONA INTERNATIONAL

FONA International, Inc., develops and produces flavors for food, beverage, nutraceutical, and pharmaceutical companies worldwide. It offers flavor solutions for beverages such as ready-to-drink, dry mix beverage, and shots categories; confections, including sugar-free gums, panned confections, pressed mints, candies, and deposited gummies; grain applications specializing in cereals, bars, snacks, and baked goods; savory systems, such as prepared foods, soups, side-of-plate products, sauces and dressings, and culinary products; healthcare products, including over-the-counter products, supplements, liquid and solid doses, and alternative delivery systems; and sweet products, comprising yogurt desserts, gelatins, puddings, frozen treats, and ice creams. The company was formerly known as Flavors of North America, Inc., and changed its name to FONA International, Inc., in May 2005. It was incorporated in 1986 and is based in Geneva, Illinois, with locations in the United States, Canada, the United Kingdom, Australia, India, and China.

HEALTH CATALYST

Health Catalyst Inc. develops and delivers a data warehousing architecture that uses a just-in-time approach to integrate information from healthcare organizations into source data marts for improving clinical, financial, and operational outcomes for improved population health. The company's products include the Late-Binding data warehouse platform for healthcare analytics; the Health Catalyst Analytics Platform, which extracts data from a healthcare organization's various source systems and gathers them into its Late-Binding data warehouse; the Health Catalyst Data Operating System; the Health Catalyst Cloud Services, which positions organizations to avoid the distractions of internal hosting, allowing them to focus on patient care and outcomes improvement; the Health Catalyst CORUS Suite, which is an activity-based costing solution that focuses on using patient-level clinical and operational data to deliver the first comprehensive and scalable view of the true cost of patient care; and healthcare analytics applications. In addition, it sponsors Health Catalyst University, which provides knowledge, practical skills, and take-home tools for the teams. The company also provides professional services, such as strategic advisory, outcomes improvement, Health Catalyst University educational services, and cloud services. The company serves hospitals, clinics payers, and self-insured employers. The company was formerly known as Healthcare Quality Catalyst, LLC, and changed its name to Health Catalyst Inc. in December 2012. Health Catalyst Inc. was founded in 2008 and is based in Salt Lake City, Utah.

INSOMNIAC GAMES

Insomniac Games, Inc., develops various games for PlayStations. The company also develops social games. It serves customers in the United States and internationally. The company was founded in 1994 and is based in Burbank, California, with studios in Burbank and Durham, North Carolina. Insomniac Games is an AAA independent game development studio that has released award-winning blockbuster hits on console, mobile, PC, and virtual reality platforms for nearly 25 years. The studio is best known for creating an astonishing array of new intellectual properties, such as *Spyro the Dragon*, *Ratchet & Clank*, *Resistance*, and *Sunset Overdrive*, among several others. *Spyro the Dragon* and *Ratchet & Clank* have especially crossed over into mainstream culture via movies, toys, and more—helping Insomniac exceed 50 million games sold worldwide. Insomniac recently developed Marvel's *Spider-Man* for PlayStation 4, perhaps the most anticipated game of the year.

INSTRUCTURE

Instructure, Inc., a software-as-a-service technology company, provides applications for learning, assessment, and performance management worldwide. The company offers its platform through a software-as-a-service business model. It develops Canvas, a learning management system for K–12 and higher education; Bridge, a learning and performance management suite for businesses; Arc, a next-generation online video learning platform for academic and corporate learning; and Gauge, an assessment management system for K–12 schools. The company's applications enhance academic and corporate learning by providing a system of engagement for teachers and learners, enabling frequent and open interactions, a streamlined workflow, and the creation and sharing of content with anytime, anywhere access to information. Its platform also provides data analytics that enable real-time reaction to information and benchmarking in order to personalize curricula and goal setting; and that enhance the efficacy of the learning, assessment, and performance management processes. Instructure, Inc., was founded in 2008 and is headquartered in Salt Lake City, Utah.

INTUITIVE RESEARCH AND TECHNOLOGY *(INTUITIVE)*

Intuitive Research and Technology Corporation, an aerospace engineering and analysis company, provides technical solutions and program management services throughout various phases of a product's life cycle. Its program support services include project and technology management, acquisition support, quality management and assurance, cost estimating and analysis, strategic planning, training support and fielding, production management, and integrated logistics support; its technical solutions comprise software engineering, products and services for unmanned air systems, immersive virtual learning environment, mechanical design, systems analysis and integration, engineering services, assurance, technical services, technical data management, simulation analysis and modeling, quality and reliability support, production systems analysis and support, information technology services, rapid prototyping, electronics and FPGA services, and electronic systems support laboratory. The company also boasts an extensive and diverse portfolio of contract vehicles to provide management, technical, and engineering solutions to the Department of Defense, government agencies, and commercial companies. *INTUITIVE* was founded in 1999 and is based in Huntsville, Alabama.

THE MOTLEY FOOL

To some, this Fool is the king of personal investing tips. The Motley Fool distributes investment information and advice through its Fool.com website. It also publishes about a dozen books (in partnership with Simon & Schuster), a syndicated newspaper column (appearing in more than 125 newspapers), and a handful of subscription-based investment newsletters. Its website offers Fool followers stock quotes, company research reports, personal finance information, news, online seminars, and message boards. The company also operates in England through its Fool UK site (www.fool.co.uk). Brothers David (co-chairman) and Tom Gardner (co-chairman and CEO), often found adorned with jester hats, started the firm in 1993.

N2 PUBLISHING

N2 Publishing partners with affluent neighborhoods to create private, hyperlocal publications. Each publication is as unique as the community it serves—an approach that has generated exceptional readership and audience engagement. As a result, N2 publications provide business owners a unique way to effectively reach local homeowners. And with nearly one thousand publications and counting, N2 proves that given the right niche, print media can defy the odds in the digital age. N2's substantial growth in revenue year over year has landed the publisher on the Inc. 5000 list for seven consecutive years. In 2017 the company reached $137 million in revenue, and for the second year in a row it donated 2 percent ($2.5 million) to the fight against human trafficking via its charitable initiative, N2GIVES.

PATAGONIA

Founded by legendary climber and adventurist Yvon Chouinard, Patagonia has scaled the peak of the outdoor apparel and accessories business. The company designs and markets rugged clothing and accessories to mountain climbers, skiers, surfers, and other extreme sports enthusiasts and environmentalists, with one very serious goal (and the company's mission): "We are in Business to Save Our Home Planet." Besides its signature Patagonia line, the company also supports a growing food business through Patagonia Provisions (which is dedicated to saving the planet through sustainable and regenerative agriculture practices); Tin Shed Ventures (an investment fund for like-minded companies working to save the planet); and Worn Wear (an upcycling division that purchases, repairs, and resells previously worn Patagonia gear—to ensure that no Patagonia products make it to a landfill). While the company may get a lot of attention for its products, it is just as well known for its unconventional culture, outlined in Chouinard's best-selling book, *Let My People Go Surfing*. In 2018 Patagonia was recognized by *Inc.* magazine as one of the top five Most Innovative Companies on the planet.

PURE INSURANCE

PURE Risk Management, LLC, offers property and casualty insurance for high-net-worth individuals. The company offers high-value homeowners insurance; coverage for fraud and cyber fraud; automobile insurance; watercraft insurance; jewelry, art, and collections insurance; personal excess liability insurance; and flood solutions coverage. Further, it offers condo and co-op insurance, home systems protection, and PURE Programs, which is an excess and surplus (E&S) lines solution designed for high-net-worth individuals and families with higher-risk homes that are not accepted by the admitted insurance market. Additionally, the company offers PURE Member Advocates, who are dedicated professionals for claims; PURE Risk Managers to help prevent loss; claims services; PURE 360 risk management consultation; the PURE Situation Room with analysis and advice on many of the risks; PURE Cybersafe Solutions; and a wildfire mitigation program to protect property from the threat of wildfire. It also offers a PURE member portal, which provides 24/7 access to account information, a claims tracker, and a member's guide. PURE Risk Management, LLC, was founded in 2006 and is based in White Plains, New York.

QUALITY BICYCLE PRODUCTS (QBP)

QBP is a bicycle company that builds innovative, world-class brands and distributes bicycle products from the best vendors in the industry to over five thousand bike shops. It puts purpose before profit and strives to be an extraordinary business to partner with and to work for. It aspires to make the world a better place, and get more butts on bikes, and it has made good on that goal for over 30 years. Quality Bicycle Products, Inc., was founded in 1981 and is based in Bloomington, Minnesota. It also has locations in Lancaster, Pennsylvania; Aurora, Colorado; Reno, Nevada; and Taichung, Taiwan.

REGENERON

Regeneron is fighting some serious enemies. Regeneron Pharmaceuticals develops protein-based drugs used to battle a variety of diseases and conditions, including cancer, high cholesterol, inflammatory ailments, and eye diseases. The biotechnology company's first commercialized product was ARCALYST® (rilonacept), a treatment for rare inflammatory diseases including Muckle-Wells Syndrome. Regeneron developed EYLEA® (aflibercept), which is commercialized outside the U.S. with Bayer HealthCare, to treat blindness-causing eye diseases such as wet age-related macular degeneration. Regeneron collaborates with Sanofi to develop antibody treatments, including the FDA-approved medicines Praluent® (alirocumab), Kevzara® (sarilumab), and Dupixent® (dupilumab), and the investigational candidate cemiplimab (a PD-1 inhibitor) for certain types of cancer. It is deeply committed to scientific research and has recently built one of the largest human genetics databases in the world through its Regeneron Genetics Center.

SAS INSTITUTE

SAS Institute was digging into big data and analytics before they were buzzwords du jour. The privately held company's software is used for business intelligence, data warehousing, and data mining by corporations to gather, manage, and analyze enormous amounts of information. Clients, mainly financial services firms, government agencies, and telecom carriers, use its applications to find patterns in customer data, manage resources, and target new business. Cloud-based apps are the company's fastest-growing business. SAS also offers software and support packages for other segments, such as leisure, manufacturing, and retail. It has more than four hundred offices in about 60 countries.

TCG

TCG, Inc., provides the federal government with positively distinct IT and management advisory services in Agile development, Technology Business Management, federal shared services, budget formulation and execution, and health science analytics to help government programs and America succeed. The firm was founded by president Daniel Turner in 1994. Its clients include the National Institutes of Health, the U.S. Securities and Exchange Commission, the U.S. Department of the Treasury, and other major government agencies who prefer not to be named. TCG's offices are in the District of Columbia.

NOTES

INTRODUCTION

1. Jiang K, Lepak DP, Hu J, Baer JC. 2012. How does human resource management influence organizational outcomes? A meta-analytic investigation of mediating mechanisms. *Academy of Management Journal* 55(6): 1264–94.

2. Ryff CD, Singer BH. 2013. Know thyself and become what you are: A eudaimonic approach to psychological well-being. In Delle Fave A, ed., *The Exploration of Happiness: Present and Future Perspectives*, 97–116. Happiness Studies Book Series. New York: Springer.

3. Ryff CD. 2018. Well-being with soul: Science in pursuit of human potential. *Perspectives on Psychological Science* 13(2): 242–48.

4. Deci EL, Olafsen AH, Ryan RM. 2017. Self-Determination theory in work organizations: The state of a science. *Annual Review of Organizational Psychology and Organizational Behavior* 4: 19–43.

5. Seligman MEP. 2011. *Flourish: A Visionary New Understanding of Happiness and Well-Being*. New York: Free Press.

6. Gomez-Baya D, Lucia-Casademunt AM. 2018. A self-determination theory approach to health and well-being in the workplace: Results from the sixth European working conditions survey in Spain. *Journal of Applied Social Psychology* 48(5): 269–83.

7. Maslow AH. 1968. *Toward a Psychology of Being*. 2nd ed. Oxford: D. Van Nostrand.

CHAPTER 1: *MO*

1. Sen A. 2000. A decade of human development. *Journal of Human Development* 1(1): 17–23.

2. Giberson TR, Resick CJ, Dickson MW. 2005. Embedding leader characteristics: An examination of homogeneity of personality and values in organizations. *Journal of Applied Psychology* 90(5): 1002–10.

3. Chatman JA, Eunyoung Cha S. 2003. Leading by leveraging culture. *California Management Review* 45(4): 20–34.

4. Narvaez D. 2015. Understanding flourishing: Evolutionary baselines and morality. *Journal of Moral Education* 44(3): 253–62.

5. Keyes CLM. 2007. Promoting and protecting mental health as flourishing: A complementary strategy for improving national mental health. *American Psychologist* 62(2): 95–108.

6. Cappelli P. 2015. Why we love to hate HR . . . and what HR can do about it (cover story). *Harvard Business Review* 93(7/8): 54–61.

7. Olberding A. 2015. From corpses to courtesy: Xunzi's defense of etiquette. *Journal of Value Inquiry* 49(1/2): 145–59.

8. Olberding A. 2016. Etiquette: A Confucian contribution to moral philosophy. *Ethics* 126(2): 422–46.

9. Bacon TR, Pugh DG. 2004. Ritz-Carlton and EMC: The gold standards in operational behavioral differentiation. *Journal of Organizational Excellence* 23(2): 61.

10. Yeung A. 2006. Setting people up for success: How the Portman Ritz-Carlton hotel gets the best from its people. *Human Resource Management* 45(2): 267–75.

11. Bennis W. 2014. Respect and trust. *Leadership Excellence Essentials* 31(1): 11–12.

12. Porath C. 2014. Half of employees don't feel respected by their bosses. *Harvard Business Review Digital Articles,* November 19, 2-5.

13. Ullmann-Margalit E. 2011. Considerateness. *Iyyun: The Jerusalem Philosophical Quarterly* 60: 205–44.

14. Velleman JD. 2008. Beyond price. *Ethics: An International Journal of Social, Political, and Legal Philosophy* 118(2): 191–212.

15. Fuhrmans V, Steinberg J. 2018. When the client is a harasser—Companies struggle to confront misbehaving customers; a difficult position for sales staff. Exchange section. *Wall Street Journal,* July 7.

16. Buss S. 1999. Appearing respectful: The moral significance of manners. *Ethics: An International Journal of Social, Political, and Legal Philosophy* 109(4): 795–826.

17. Thornberg R. 2008. Values education as the daily fostering of school rules. *Research in Education* 80(1): 52–62.

18. Besser-Jones L. 2008. Personal integrity, morality and psychological well-being: Justifying the demands of morality. *Journal of Moral Philosophy: An International Journal of Moral, Political and Legal Philosophy* 5(3): 361–83.

19. Rosen CC, Koopman J, Gabriel AS, Johnson RE. 2016. Who strikes back? A daily investigation of when and why incivility begets incivility. *Journal of Applied Psychology* 101(11): 1620–34.

20. Woolum A, Foulk T, Lanaj K, Erez A. 2017. Rude color glasses: The contaminating effects of witnessed morning rudeness on perceptions and behaviors throughout the workday. *Journal of Applied Psychology* 102(12): 1658–72.

21. MacCormick N. 1998. Norms, institutions, and institutional facts. *Law and Philosophy: An International Journal for Jurisprudence and Legal Philosophy* 17(3): 301–45.

22. Schmitt BH, Dubé L, Leclerc F. 1992. Intrusions into waiting lines: Does the queue constitute a social system? *Journal of Personality and Social Psychology* 63(5): 806–15.

CHAPTER 2: *VERGONNEN*

1. Hardin G. 1998. Extensions of "the tragedy of the commons." *Science* 280(5364): 682–83.

2. Roux C, Goldsmith K, Bonezzi A. 2015. On the psychology of scarcity: When reminders of resource scarcity promote selfish (and generous) behavior. *Journal of Consumer Research* 42(4): 615–31.

3. Kilduff GJ, Galinsky AD, Gallo E, Reade JJ. 2016. Whatever it takes to win: Rivalry increases unethical behavior. *Academy of Management Journal* 59(5): 1508–34.

4. Shellenbarger S. 2018. When a co-worker is your top competitor. Life & Arts—Work & Family section. *Wall Street Journal*, October 18.

5. Stapel DA, Koomen W. 2005. Competition, cooperation, and the effects of others on me. *Journal of Personality and Social Psychology* 88(6): 1029–38.

6. Kristofferson K, McFerran B, Morales AC, Dahl DW. 2017. The dark side of scarcity promotions: How exposure to limited-quantity promotions can induce aggression. *Journal of Consumer Research* 43(5): 683–706.

7. Cappelli P. 2019. The biggest mistakes companies make with hiring: The most highly qualified and enthusiastic candidates too often get ignored. *Wall Street Journal*, February 21.

8. Inkson K, Amundson NE. 2002. Career metaphors and their application in theory and counseling practice. *Journal of Employment Counseling* 39(3): 98.

9. Campbell J. 2008. *The Hero with a Thousand Faces*. 3rd ed. Novato, CA: New World Library; San Anselmo, CA: Joseph Campbell Foundation.

10. Adler JM. 2012. Living into the story: Agency and coherence in a longitudinal study of narrative identity development and mental health over the course of psychotherapy. *Journal of Personality and Social Psychology* 102(2): 367–89.

11. Adler JM, Turner AF, Brookshier KM, et al. 2015. Variation in narrative identity is associated with trajectories of mental health over several years. *Journal of Personality and Social Psychology* 108(3): 476–96.

12. Lyons D. 2016. Congratulations! You've been fired. *New York Times*, April 10.

13. www.sportingcharts.com/dictionary/mlb/run-or-runs-scored-r.aspx

14. Shellenbarger S. 2018. Why perks no longer cut it for workers: The most successful companies give employees a sense of belonging. The Year Ahead (A Special Report): Work & Family section. *Wall Street Journal*, December 3.

15. Nelson SK, Layous K, Cole SW, Lyubomirsky S. 2016. Do unto others or treat yourself? The effects of prosocial and self-focused behavior on psychological flourishing. *Emotion* 16(6): 850–61.

16. Weinstein N, Ryan RM. 2010. When helping helps: Autonomous motivation for prosocial behavior and its influence on well-being for the helper and recipient. *Journal of Personality and Social Psychology* 98(2): 222–44.

17. Thoits PA, Hewitt LN. 2001. Volunteer work and well-being. *Journal of Health and Social Behavior* 42(2): 115–31.

18. Son J, Wilson J. 2012. Volunteer work and hedonic, eudemonic, and social well-being. *Sociological Forum* 27(3): 658–81.

19. Kawachi I, Berkman LF. 2001. Social ties and mental health. *Journal of Urban Health: Bulletin of the New York Academy of Medicine* 78(3): 458–67.

20. Muthuri JN, Matten D, Moon J. 2009. Employee volunteering and social capital: Contributions to corporate social responsibility. *British Journal of Management* 20(1): 75–89.

21. Pohling R, Diessner R. 2016. Moral elevation and moral beauty: A review of the empirical literature. *Review of General Psychology* 20(4): 412–25.

22. Piff PK, Dietze P, Feinberg M, Stancato DM, Keltner D. 2015. Awe, the small self, and prosocial behavior. *Journal of Personality and Social Psychology* 108(6): 883–99.

23. Yaden DB, Haidt J, Hood RW, Jr., Vago DR, Newberg AB. 2017. The varieties of self-transcendent experience. *Review of General Psychology* 21(2): 143–60.

24. Bai Y, Maruskin LA, Chen S, et al. 2017. Awe, the diminished self, and collective engagement: Universals and cultural variations in the small self. *Journal of Personality and Social Psychology* 113(2): 185–209.

25. Flora C. 2016. It's not all about you. *Psychology Today* 49(2): 48–56.

26. Keltner D, Haidt J. 2003. Approaching awe, a moral, spiritual, and aesthetic emotion. *Cognition and Emotion* 17(2): 297.

27. Haidt J, Morris JP. 2009. Finding the self in self-transcendent emotions. *Proceedings of the National Academy of Sciences* 106(19): 7687–88.

28. Marchant J. 2017. Awesome awe: The overused superlative is truly apt for an emotion that gives us superpowers. *New Scientist* 235(3136): 32–35.

CHAPTER 3: KINDNESS

1. Cann A. 2004. Rated importance of personal qualities across four relationships. *Journal of Social Psychology* 144(3): 322–34.

2. Dahlsgaard K, Peterson C, Seligman MEP. 2005. Shared virtue: The convergence of valued human strengths across culture and history. *Review of General Psychology* 9(3): 203–13.

3. Brooks AC. 2016. Nice people really do have more fun. *Wall Street Journal, Online Edition,* October 19, 1.

4. Porath C. 2017. The hidden toll of workplace incivility. *McKinsey Quarterly* (1): 12–15.

5. Schat ACH, Frone MR, Kelloway EK. 2006. Prevalence of workplace aggression in the U.S. workforce: Findings from a national study. *Handbook of workplace violence,* 47–89. Thousand Oaks, CA: Sage.

6. Lutgen-Sandvik P, Tracy SJ, Alberts JK. 2007. Burned by bullying in the American workplace: Prevalence, perception, degree and impact. *Journal of Management Studies* 44(6): 837–62.

7. Schat ACH, Frone MR. 2011. Exposure to psychological aggression at work and job performance: The mediating role of job attitudes and personal health. *Work and Stress* 25(1): 23–40.

8. Caza BB, Cortina LM. 2007. From insult to injury: Explaining the impact of incivility. *Basic and Applied Social Psychology* 29(4): 335–50.

9. Porath C, Pearson C. 2013. The price of incivility. *Harvard Business Review* 91: 114–21.

10. Riskin A, Erez A, Foulk TA, et al. 2015. The impact of rudeness on medical team performance: A randomized trial. *Pediatrics* 136(3): 487–95.

11. Priesemuth M, Schminke M, Ambrose ML, Folger R. 2014. Abusive supervision climate: A multiple-mediation model of its impact on group outcomes. *Academy of Management Journal* 57(5): 1513–34.

12. Foulk T, Woolum A, Erez A. 2016. Catching rudeness is like catching a cold: The contagion effects of low-intensity negative behaviors. *Journal of Applied Psychology* 101(1): 50–67.

13. Yang L-Q, Caughlin DE, Gazica MW, Truxillo DM, Spector PE. 2014. Workplace mistreatment climate and potential employee and organizational outcomes: A meta-analytic review from the target's perspective. *Journal of Occupational Health Psychology* 19(3): 315–35.

14. Vickers M. 2014. Towards reducing the harm: Workplace bullying as workplace corruption—a critical review. *Employee Responsibilities and Rights Journal* 26(2): 95–113.

15. Reich TC, Hershcovis MS. 2015. Observing workplace incivility. *Journal of Applied Psychology* 100(1): 203–15.

16. Porath CL, Erez A. 2007. Does rudeness really matter? The effects of rudeness on task performance and helpfulness. *Academy of Management Journal* 50(5): 1181–97.

17. Lim S, Cortina LM, Magley VJ. 2008. Personal and workgroup incivility: Impact on work and health outcomes. *Journal of Applied Psychology* 93(1): 95–107.

18. Paulin D, Griffin B. 2016. The relationships between incivility, team climate for incivility and job-related employee well-being: A multilevel analysis. *Work and Stress* 30(2): 132–51.

19. Farh CIC, Chen Z. 2014. Beyond the individual victim: Multilevel consequences of abusive supervision in teams. *Journal of Applied Psychology* 99(6): 1074–95.

20. Andersson LM, Pearson CM. 1999. Tit for tat? The spiraling effect of incivility in the workplace. *Academy of Management Review* 24(3): 452–71.

21. Tepper BJ. 2007. Abusive supervision in work organizations: Review, synthesis, and research agenda. *Journal of Management* 33(3): 261–89.

22. Pollock LA. 2011. The practice of kindness in early modern elite society. *Past and Present* 211(1): 121–58.

23. Rowland S. 2009. Kindness. *London Review of Education* 7(3): 207–10.

24. Curry OS, Rowland LA, Van Lissa CJ, Zlotowitz S, McAlaney J, Whitehouse H. 2018. Happy to help? A systematic review and meta-analysis of the effects of performing acts of kindness on the well-being of the actor. *Journal of Experimental Social Psychology* 76: 320–29.

25. Rowland L, Curry OS. 2018. A range of kindness activities boost happiness. *Journal of Social Psychology* 1–4.

26. Alden LE, Trew JL. 2013. If it makes you happy: Engaging in kind acts increases positive affect in socially anxious individuals. *Emotion* 13(1): 64–75.

27. Andersen SM, Saribay A, Thorpe JS. 2008. Simple kindness can go a long way: Relationships, social identity, and engagement. *Social Psychology* 39(1): 59–69.

28. Hutcherson CA, Seppala EM, Gross JJ. 2008. Loving-kindness meditation increases social connectedness. *Emotion* 8(5): 720–24.

29. Otake K, Shimai S, Tanaka-Matsumi J, Otsui K, Fredrickson BL. 2006. Happy people become happier through kindness: A counting kindnesses intervention. *Journal of Happiness Studies* 7(3): 361–75.

30. Thielmann I, Hilbig BE. 2015. The traits one can trust: Dissecting reciprocity and kindness as determinants of trustworthy behavior. *Personality and Social Psychology Bulletin* 41(11): 1523–36.

31. Trew J, Alden L. 2015. Kindness reduces avoidance goals in socially anxious individuals. *Motivation and Emotion* 39(6): 892–907.

32. Galante J, Galante I, Bekkers M-J, Gallacher J. 2014. Effect of kindness-based meditation on health and well-being: A systematic review and meta-analysis. *Journal of Consulting and Clinical Psychology* 82(6): 1101–14.

33. Raila H, Scholl BJ, Gruber J. 2015. Seeing the world through rose-colored glasses: People who are happy and satisfied with life preferentially attend to positive stimuli. *Emotion* 15(4): 449–62.

34. Fredrickson BL. 2006. The broaden-and-build theory of positive emotions. In Csikszentmihalyi M, Csikszentmihalyi IS, Csikszentmihalyi M, Csikszentmihalyi IS, eds., *A Life Worth Living: Contributions to Positive Psychology*, 85–103. New York: Oxford University Press.

35. Fredrickson BL, Cohn MA, Coffey KA, Pek J, Finkel SM. 2008. Open hearts build lives: Positive emotions, induced through loving-kindness meditation, build consequential personal resources. *Journal of Personality and Social Psychology* 95(5): 1045–62.

36. Fredrickson BL, Joiner T. 2018. Reflections on positive emotions and upward spirals. *Perspectives on Psychological Science* 13(2): 194–99.

37. Catalino LI, Fredrickson BL. 2011. A Tuesday in the life of a flourisher: The role of positive emotional reactivity in optimal mental health. *Emotion* 11(4): 938–50.

38. Kteily N, Bruneau E, Waytz A, Cotterill S. 2015. The ascent of man: Theoretical and empirical evidence for blatant dehumanization. *Journal of Personality and Social Psychology* 109(5): 901–31.

39. Tierney J. 2016. An offstage debate: Whether empathy matters. *New York Times*, March 21, 165(57179): D3.

40. Ferguson ED, Hagaman J, Grice JW, Peng K. 2006. From leadership to parenthood: The applicability of leadership styles to parenting styles. *Group Dynamics: Theory, Research, and Practice* 10(1): 43–55.

41. Chemers MM. 2000. Leadership research and theory: A functional integration. *Group Dynamics: Theory, Research, and Practice* 4(1): 27–43.

42. Baumrind D. 1971. Current patterns of parental authority. *Developmental Psychology* 4(1, pt. 2): 1–103.

43. Cablova L, Csemy L, Belacek J, Miovsky M. 2016. Parenting styles and typology of drinking among children and adolescents. *Journal of Substance Use* 21(4): 381–89.

44. Darling N, Steinberg L. 1993. Parenting style as context: An integrative model. *Psychological Bulletin* 113(3): 487–96.

45. Bagnoli C. 2007. Respect and membership in the moral community. *Ethical Theory and Moral Practice: An International Forum* 10(2): 113–28.

46. Jaworska A. 2007. Caring and full moral standing. *Ethics: An International Journal of Social, Political, and Legal Philosophy* 117(3): 460–97.

47. Van Ogtrop K. 2015. Everyone's the boss. *Time* 185(21): 62.

48. Reingold J. 2016. The Zappos experiment. *Fortune* 173(4): 206–14.

49. Zlatev JJ, Halevy N, Tiedens LZ. 2016. Roles and ranks: The importance of hierarchy for group functioning. *Behavioral and Brain Sciences* 39: e166.

50. Lewin K, Lippitt R, White RK. 1939. Patterns of aggressive behavior in experimentally created "social climates." *Journal of Social Psychology* 10(2): 271–99.

51. Bryant A. 2017. A Leader Who Encourages Dissent. *New York Times*, April 8.

52. Mishra PS, Mohapatra AKD. 2010. Relevance of emotional intelligence for effective job performance: An empirical study. *Vikalpa: The Journal for Decision Makers* 35(1): 53–61.

53. O'Boyle EH, Jr., Humphrey RH, Pollack JM, Hawver TH, Story PA. 2011. The relation between emotional intelligence and job performance: A meta-analysis. *Journal of Organizational Behavior* 32(5): 788–818.

54. Matthew S. 2016. How to curb your ego—and get ahead. *London Times*, January 7.

55. Malone TW. 2018. How human-computer "superminds" are redefining the future of work. *MIT Sloan Management Review* 59(4): 34–41.

CHAPTER 4: UNRULY

1. Gardner A, Dawsey J, Seung M K. 2018. Frustrated VA nominee considers withdrawing. *Washington Post*, April 26, A1.

2. White MC. 2015. If you think your boss is horrible, you're probably right. *Timecom,* February 3.

3. Leary TG, Green R, Denson K, Schoenfeld G, Henley T, Langford H. 2013. The relationship among dysfunctional leadership dispositions, employee engagement, job satisfaction, and burnout. *Psychologist-Manager Journal* 16(2): 112–30.

4. Smith R. 2014. Over 65 million workers affected by bullying; employer response inadequate. *HR Focus* 91(5): 9–10.

5. Lerner MJ, Miller DT. 1978. Just world research and the attribution process: Looking back and ahead. *Psychological Bulletin* 85(5): 1030–51.

6. Cortina LM, Magley VJ. 2009. Patterns and profiles of response to incivility in the workplace. *Journal of Occupational Health Psychology* 14(3): 272–88.

7. Porath C. 2016. An antidote to incivility. *Harvard Business Review* 94(4): 108–11.

8. Alex R. 2017. Decline in productivity "down to bad managers." *London Times*, 35.

9. Nielsen MB. 2013. Bullying in work groups: The impact of leadership. *Scandinavian Journal of Psychology* 54(2): 127–36.

10. Nielsen MB, Einarsen S. 2012. Outcomes of exposure to workplace bullying: A meta-analytic review. *Work and Stress* 26(4): 309–32.

11. Trépanier S-G, Fernet C, Austin S. 2016. Longitudinal relationships between workplace bullying, basic psychological needs, and employee functioning: A simultaneous investigation of psychological need satisfaction and frustration. *European Journal of Work and Organizational Psychology* 25(5): 690–706.

12. Bedeian AG, Armenakis AA. 1998. The cesspool syndrome: How dreck floats to the top of declining organizations. *Academy of Management Executive* 12(1): 58–63.

13. Kim E, Glomb TM. 2010. Get smarty pants: Cognitive ability, personality, and victimization. *Journal of Applied Psychology* 95(5): 889–901.

14. Kim E, Glomb TM. 2014. Victimization of high performers: The roles of envy and work group identification. *Journal of Applied Psychology* 99(4): 619–34.

15. Campbell EM, Liao H, Chuang A, Zhou J, Dong Y. 2017. Hot shots and cool reception? An expanded view of social consequences for high performers. *Journal of Applied Psychology* 102(5): 845–66.

16. The bane of brilliance. 2016. *Economist*, August 18, 420(9003): 55.

17. Jensen JM, Patel PC, Raver JL. 2014. Is it better to be average? High and low performance as predictors of employee victimization. *Journal of Applied Psychology* 99(2): 296–309.

18. Chan ME, McAllister DJ. 2014. Abusive supervision through the lens of employee state paranoia. *Academy of Management Review* 39(1): 44–66.

19. Foa EB, Zinbarg R, Rothbaum BO. 1992. Uncontrollability and unpredictability in post-traumatic stress disorder: An animal model. *Psychological Bulletin* 112(2): 218–38.

20. Boonstra R, Fox C. 2013. Reality as the leading cause of stress: Rethinking the impact of chronic stress in nature. *Functional Ecology* 27(1): 11–23.

21. Jaggi AS, Bhatia N, Kumar N, Singh N, Anand P, Dhawan R. 2011. A review on animal models for screening potential anti-stress agents. *Neurological Sciences* 32(6): 993–1005.

22. Pitman RK, Rasmusson AM, Koenen KC, et al. 2012. Biological studies of post-traumatic stress disorder. *Nature Reviews Neuroscience* 13(11): 769–87.

23. Tehrani N. 2004. Bullying: A source of chronic post traumatic stress? *British Journal of Guidance and Counselling* 32(3): 357–66.

24. Zoladz PR, Conrad CD, Fleshner M, Diamond DM. 2008. Acute episodes of predator exposure in conjunction with chronic social instability as an animal model of post-traumatic stress disorder. *Stress: The International Journal on the Biology of Stress* 11(4): 259–81.

25. Matthiesen SB, Einarsen S. 2004. Psychiatric distress and symptoms of PTSD among victims of bullying at work. *British Journal of Guidance and Counselling* 32(3): 335–56.

26. Nixon AE, Mazzola JJ, Bauer J, Krueger JR, Spector PE. 2011. Can work make you sick? A meta-analysis of the relationships between job stressors and physical symptoms. *Work and Stress* 25(1): 1–22.

27. Tsui B. 2014. Cashing in on kindness. *Newsweek Global* 162(12): 1–5.

28. Fuss and bother. 2016. *Economist*, July 21, 420(8999): 46.

29. Bridge M, Mark B. 2018. Musk: Tesla worker has sabotaged our systems (Scot Region). *London Times*, June 21, 13.

30. The enemy within. 2015. *Economist*, July 23, 416(8948): 53.

31. Hauge LJ, Einarsen S, Knardahl S, Lau B, Notelaers G, Skogstad A. 2011. Leadership and role stressors as departmental level predictors of workplace bullying. *International Journal of Stress Management* 18(4): 305–23.

32. Hauge LJ, Skogstad A, Einarsen S. 2010. The relative impact of workplace bullying as a social stressor at work. *Scandinavian Journal of Psychology* 51(5): 426–33.

33. Salin D. 2015. Risk factors of workplace bullying for men and women: The role of the psychosocial and physical work environment. *Scandinavian Journal of Psychology* 56(1): 69–77.

34. Hodson R, Roscigno VJ, Lopez SH. 2016. Chaos and the abuse of power: Workplace bullying in organizational and interactional context. In Boyle GJ, O'Gorman JG, Fogarty GJ, Boyle GJ, O'Gorman JG, Fogarty GJ, eds., *Work and organisational psychol-*

ogy: Research methodology; Assessment and selection; Organisational change and development; Human resource and performance management; Emerging trends: Innovation/ globalisation/technology, 277–305. Thousand Oaks, CA: Sage.

35. Roscigno VJ, Lopez SH, Hodson R. 2009. Supervisory bullying, status inequalities and organizational context. *Social Forces* 87(3): 1561–89.

36. Zimbardo PG. 2001. *The Pathology of Imprisonment. Down to Earth Sociology: Introductory Readings,* 272–77. New York: Free Press.

37. Castro SA, Zautra AJ. 2016. Humanization of social relations: Nourishing health and resilience through greater humanity. *Journal of Theoretical and Philosophical Psychology* 36(2): 64–80.

38. Postmes T, Spears R. 1998. Deindividuation and antinormative behavior: A meta-analysis. *Psychological Bulletin* 123(3): 238–59.

39. Keltner D. 2016. Don't let power corrupt you (cover story). *Harvard Business Review* 94(10): 112–15.

40. Tuckey MR, Dollard MF, Hosking PJ, Winefield AH. 2009. Workplace bullying: The role of psychosocial work environment factors. *International Journal of Stress Management* 16(3): 215–32.

41. Formanowicz M, Goldenberg A, Saguy T, Pietraszkiewicz A, Walker M, Gross JJ. 2018. Understanding dehumanization: The role of agency and communion. *Journal of Experimental Social Psychology* 77: 102–16.

42. Magee JC, Smith PK. 2013. The social distance theory of power. *Personality and Social Psychology Review* 17: 158–86.

CHAPTER 5: COMMUNITY

1. Northrop E. 2013. The accuracy, market ethic, and individual morality surrounding the profit maximization assumption. *American Economist* 58(2): 111–23.

2. Solomon RC. 1998. The moral psychology of business: Care and compassion in the corporation. *Business Ethics Quarterly* 8(3): 515–33.

3. Moore G. 2005. Humanizing business: A modern virtue ethics approach. *Business Ethics Quarterly* 15(2): 237–55.

4. Sennett R. 2008. Exploring our neglect of craft and love of money: The Craftsman. *RSA Journal* (Spring): 48–49.

5. Choosing plan B; Danone and the rise of B Corporations. 2018. *Economist* 428(9104): 52.

6. Schor EL. 2003. Family pediatrics: Report of the Task Force on the Family. *Pediatrics* 111(6, pt. 2): 1541–71.

7. Wolcott I. 1999. Strong families and satisfying marriages. *Family Matters* (53): 21–30.

8. Wayne JH, Casper WJ, Matthews RA, Allen TD. 2013. Family-supportive organization perceptions and organizational commitment: The mediating role of work–family conflict and enrichment and partner attitudes. *Journal of Applied Psychology* 98(4): 606–22.

9. Boyd NM, Nowell B. 2017. Testing a theory of sense of community and community responsibility in organizations: An empirical assessment of predictive capacity on

employee well-being and organizational citizenship. *Journal of Community Psychology* 45(2): 210–29.

10. Sinclair RR, Cheung JH, Arpin SN, Mohr CP. 2015. Personal benefits of strong organizational and community ties: Health, engagement and retention. *Journal of Community Psychology* 43(6): 778–93.

11. Bashshur MR, Oc B. 2015. When voice matters: A multilevel review of the impact of voice in organizations. *Journal of Management* 41(5): 1530–54.

12. Davis DE, Choe E, Meyers J, et al. 2016. Thankful for the little things: A meta-analysis of gratitude interventions. *Journal of Counseling Psychology* 63(1): 20–31.

13. Kerr S, O'Donovan A, Pepping C. 2015. Can gratitude and kindness interventions enhance well-being in a clinical sample? *Journal of Happiness Studies* 16(1): 17–36.

14. Fehr R, Fulmer A, Awtrey ELI, Miller JA. 2017. The grateful workplace: A multilevel model of gratitude in organizations. *Academy of Management Review* 42(2): 361–81.

15. Emmons RA, McCullough ME. 2003. Counting blessings versus burdens: An experimental investigation of gratitude and subjective well-being in daily life. *Journal of Personality and Social Psychology* 84(2): 377–89.

16. Wallace JB. 2018. How to raise more grateful children. *Wall Street Journal Online Edition,* 1.

17. Ma LK, Tunney RJ, Ferguson E. 2017. Does gratitude enhance prosociality? A meta-analytic review. *Psychological Bulletin* 143(6): 601–35.

18. Algoe SB, Haidt J, Gable SL. 2008. Beyond reciprocity: Gratitude and relationships in everyday life. *Emotion* 8(3): 425–29.

19. Algoe SB, Kurtz LE, Hilaire NM. 2016. Putting the "you" in "thank you": Examining other-praising behavior as the active relational ingredient in expressed gratitude. *Social Psychological and Personality Science* 7(7): 658–66.

20. Grant AM, Gino F. 2010. A little thanks goes a long way: Explaining why gratitude expressions motivate prosocial behavior. *Journal of Personality and Social Psychology* 98(6): 946–55.

21. Chancellor J, Margolis S, Jacobs Bao K, Lyubomirsky S. 2017. Everyday prosociality in the workplace: The reinforcing benefits of giving, getting, and glimpsing. *Emotion* 18: 507–17.

22. Doebeli M, Hauert C, Killingback T. 2004. The evolutionary origin of cooperators and defectors. *Science* 306(5697): 859–62.

23. Fehr E, Gachter S. 2002. Altruistic punishment in humans. *Nature* 415(6868): 137.

24. Gürerk Ö, Irlenbusch B, Rockenbach B. 2006. The competitive advantage of sanctioning institutions. *Science* 312(5770): 108–11.

25. Nowak MA. 2013. Five rules for the evolution of cooperation. In Nowak MA, Coakley S, Nowak MA, Coakley S, eds., *Evolution, Games, and God: The Principle of Cooperation,* 99–114. Cambridge, MA: Harvard University Press.

26. Henrich J, McElreath R, Barr A, et al. 2006. Costly punishment across human societies. *Science* 312(5781): 1767–70.

27. O'Malley MN, Schubarth G. 1984. Fairness and appeasement: Achievement and affiliation motives in interpersonal relations. *Social Psychology Quarterly* 47(4): 364–71.

28. Lange F, Eggert F. 2015. Selective cooperation in the supermarket. *Human Nature* 26(4): 392–400.

29. Bond M. 2009. Be nice to people (cover story). *New Scientist* 203(2726): 32.

30. Bhatnagar N, Manchanda RV. 2013. Understanding why and how individuals choose to help others: Indirect reciprocal considerations and the moderating role of situation severity. *Journal of Applied Social Psychology* 43(11): 2185–94.

31. Benkler Y. 2011. The unselfish gene. *Harvard Business Review* 89(7/8): 76–85.

32. Mikulincer M, Shaver PR, Gillath O, Nitzberg RA. 2005. Attachment, caregiving, and altruism: Boosting attachment security increases compassion and helping. *Journal of Personality and Social Psychology* 89(5): 817–39.

33. From dysfunctional to dream team. 2016. *Finweek*, September 8, 48–49.

34. Lobel O. 2017. Isn't competition a worker's right? *New York Times* 166(57587): A23.

35. Foot P. 1967. The problem of abortion and the doctrine of the double effect. *Oxford Review* (5): 5–15.

36. Bankard J. 2015. Training emotion cultivates morality: How loving-kindness meditation hones compassion and increases prosocial behavior. *Journal of Religion and Health* 54(6): 2324–43.

CHAPTER 6: BASIC NEEDS

1. Rasskazova E, Ivanova T, Sheldon K. 2016. Comparing the effects of low-level and high-level worker need-satisfaction: A synthesis of the self-determination and Maslow need theories. *Motivation and Emotion* 40(4): 541–55.

2. Minimum wage overview: Provisions of the Fair Labor Standards Act (cover story). 2013. *Congressional Digest* 92(5): 3–10.

3. Reich M. 2015. The ups and downs of minimum wage policy: The Fair Labor Standards Act in historical perspective. *Industrial Relations: A Journal of Economy and Society* 54(4): 538–46.

4. The Hamilton Project. www.hamiltonproject.org/

5. Blinder AS. 2014. Petrified paychecks: Seven ways to raise wages. *Washington Monthly* 46(11/12): 29–34.

6. Paquette D. 2017. Wages remain mostly stagnant despite unemployment hitting new lows. *Washington Post*.

7. Russell K, Casselman BEN, Cohen P, Scheiber N. 2018. Why pay is lagging in a tight job market. *New York Times*, February 1, 167(57861): B1.

8. Leonhardt D. 2019. How the upper middle class is really doing. *New York Times*, February 24, A23.

9. Looking for a rise. 2015. *Economist*, November 14, 417(8964): 29–30.

10. Doucouliagos H, Stanley TD. 2009. Publication selection bias in minimum-wage research? A meta-regression analysis. *British Journal of Industrial Relations* 47(2): 406–28.

11. Krueger AB. The history of economic thought on the minimum wage. *Industrial Relations* 2015; 54(4): 533–7.

12. Stewart MB, Swaffield JK. 2008. The other margin: Do minimum wages cause working hours adjustments for low-wage workers? *Economica* 75(297): 148–67.

13. Sturn S. 2018. Do minimum wages lead to job losses? Evidence from OECD countries on low-skilled and youth employment. *ILR Review* 71(3): 647–75.

14. Basker E, Khan MT. 2016. Does the minimum wage bite into fast-food prices? *Journal of Labor Research* 37(2): 129–48.

15. Pollin R, Wicks-Lim J. 2016. A $15 U.S. minimum wage: How the fast-food industry could adjust without shedding jobs. *Journal of Economic Issues* 50(3): 716–44.

16. Allegretto S, Reich M. 2018. Are local minimum wages absorbed by price increases? Estimates from internet-based restaurant menus. *ILR Review* 71(1): 35–63.

17. Kahneman D, Deaton A. 2010. High income improves evaluation of life but not emotional well-being. *Proceedings of the National Academy of Sciences* 107(38): 16489–93.

18. Poppick S. 2014. Does money bring you happiness? (cover story). *Money* 43(5): 78–81.

19. Cummins RA. 2000. Personal income and subjective well-being: A review. *Journal of Happiness Studies* 1(2): 133–58.

20. Coley RL, Lombardi CM. 2014. Low-income women's employment experiences and their financial, personal, and family well-being. *Journal of Family Psychology* 28(1): 88–97.

21. Kiviat B. 2011. Below the line. *Time* 178(21): 34–41.

22. Diener E, Ng W, Harter J, Arora R. 2010. Wealth and happiness across the world: Material prosperity predicts life evaluation, whereas psychosocial prosperity predicts positive feeling. *Journal of Personality and Social Psychology* 99(1): 52–61.

23. Wolfers J. 2018. Winning the lottery beats losing, a study finds. *New York Times*, August 24, sec. 5.

24. Johnson W, Krueger RF. 2006. How money buys happiness: Genetic and environmental processes linking finances and life satisfaction. *Journal of Personality and Social Psychology* 90(4): 680–91.

25. Howell RT, Kurai M, Tam L. 2013. Money buys financial security and psychological need satisfaction: Testing need theory in affluence. *Social Indicators Research* 110(1): 17–29.

26. Howell RT, Howell CJ. 2008. The relation of economic status to subjective well-being in developing countries: A meta-analysis. *Psychological Bulletin* 134(4): 536–60.

27. Berner M, Ozer T, Paynter S. 2008. A portrait of hunger, the social safety net, and the working poor. *Policy Studies Journal* 36(3): 403–20.

28. Rossi MM, Curtis KA. 2013. Aiming at half of the target: An argument to replace poverty thresholds with self-sufficiency, or "living wage" standards. *Journal of Poverty* 17(1): 110–30.

29. Luce S. 2002. "The full fruits of our labor": The rebirth of the living wage movement. *Labor History* 43(4): 401–9.

30. Luce S. 2017. Living wages: A US perspective. *Employee Relations* 39(6): 863–74.

31. Devinatz V. 2013. The significance of the living wage for US workers in the early twenty-first century. *Employee Responsibilities and Rights Journal* 25(2): 125–34.

32. Weed J. 2017. Near Seattle, hotels are rising along with minimum wage. *New York Times* 166(57676): B4.

33. Sosnaud B. 2016. Living wage ordinances and wages, poverty, and unemployment in US cities. *Social Service Review* 90(1): 3–34.

34. Swaffield J, Snell C, Tunstall B, Bradshaw J. 2018. An evaluation of the living wage: Identifying pathways out of in-work poverty. *Social Policy and Society* 17(3): 379–92.

35. Mangum G, Sum A, Fogg N. 2000. Poverty ain't what it used to be. *Challenge* 43(2): 97–130.

36. Fisher GM. 1992. The development and history of the poverty thresholds. *Social Security Bulletin* 55(4): 3–14.

37. Boone G. 2016. Keeping up with basic needs: Spending patterns over the past 30 years. *Monthly Labor Review,* 1–2.

38. Fusaro VA. 2015. Who's left out: Characteristics of households in economic need not receiving public support. *Journal of Sociology and Social Welfare* 42(3): 65–85.

39. Hirsch D. 2018. The "living wage" and low income: Can adequate pay contribute to adequate family living standards? *Critical Social Policy* 38(2): 367–86.

40. Tanner MD, Hughes C. War on poverty turns 50: Are we winning yet? Cato Institute. www.cato.org/publications/policy-analysis/war-poverty-turns-50-are-we-winning-yet

41. Jones K. 2017. The most desirable employee benefits. *Harvard Business Review Digital Articles,* 2–6.

42. Health costs. Henry J. Kaiser Family Foundation. www.kff.org/health-costs/

43. 2016 Health and Voluntary Workplace Benefits Survey (cover story). 2016. *Medical Benefits* 33(21): 1–3.

44. Bishow JL. 2015. The relationship between access to benefits and weekly work hours. *Monthly Labor Review* 136(6): E1–E11.

45. Galinsky E, Sakai K, Wigton T. 2011. Workplace flexibility: From research to action. *Future of Children* 21(2): 141–61.

46. Heinrich CJ. 2014. Parents' employment and children's wellbeing. *Future of Children* 24(1): 121–46.

47. Kossek EE, Thompson RJ, Lautsch BA. 2015. Balanced workplace flexibility: Avoiding the traps. *California Management Review* 57(4): 5–25.

48. Nuwer R. 2016. No workplace like home. *Scientific American Mind* 27(5): 38–43.

49. Spieler I, Scheibe S, Stamov-Roßnagel C, Kappas A. 2017. Help or hindrance? Day-level relationships between flextime use, work–nonwork boundaries, and affective well-being. *Journal of Applied Psychology* 102(1): 67–87.

50. Earle A, Mokomane Z, Heymann J. 2011. International perspectives on work-family policies: Lessons from the world's most competitive economies. *Future of Children* 21(2): 191–210.

51. Covert B. 2018. The wrong fix for family leave(op-ed). *New York Times,* August 12.

52. Kitroeff N, Silver-Greenberg J. 2018. Penalizing pregnancy, from Walmart to Wall St. (cover story). *New York Times* 167(57996): 1–17.

53. Rowe-Finkbeiner K, Martin R, Abrams B, Zuccaro A, Dardari Y. 2016. Why paid family and medical leave matters for the future of America's families, businesses and economy. *Maternal and Child Health Journal* 20: 8–12.

54. Wiese BS, Ritter JO. 2012. Timing matters: Length of leave and working mothers' daily reentry regrets. *Developmental Psychology* 48(6): 1797–807.

55. Miller CC. 2017. The power of day care. *New York Times*, April 20, 166(57575): B1–B3.

56. Heckman JJ. 2013. Lifelines for poor children. *New York Times*.

57. Kristof N. 2018. U.S. is guilty of neglecting kids: Our own (commentary). *New York Times*, June 27.

58. Duncan GJ, Kalil A, Ziol-Guest KM. 2014. Early childhood poverty and adult productivity and health. In Reynolds AJ, Rolnick AJ, Temple JA, Reynolds AJ, Rolnick AJ, Temple JA, eds., *Health and Education in Early Childhood: Predictors, Interventions, and Policies*, 52–65. New York: Cambridge University Press.

59. Hansen MT. 2018. The key to success? Doing less: Talent and hard work are important, but most top performers in business have one thing in common: They accept fewer tasks and then obsess over them (review). *Wall Street Journal*, January 12, C1–C2.

60. Dickey J. 2015. Save our vacation (cover story). *Time* 185(20): 44–49.

61. Fontana F. 2017. Unlimited vacation time is a lot of work. *Wall Street Journal Online Edition*, August 27, 1.

62. Fiksenbaum LM. 2014. Supportive work–family environments: Implications for work–family conflict and well-being. *International Journal of Human Resource Management* 25(5): 653–72.

63. Butts MM, Casper WJ, Yang TS. 2013. How important are work–family support policies? A meta-analytic investigation of their effects on employee outcomes. *Journal of Applied Psychology* 98(1): 1–25.

64. Renaud S, Morin L, Béchard A. 2017. Traditional benefits versus perquisites: A longitudinal test of their differential impact on employee turnover. *Journal of Personnel Psychology* 16(2): 91–103.

CHAPTER 7: BELONGING

1. Easterlin RA. 2013. *Happiness, Growth, and Public Policy*. Hoboken, NJ: Wiley-Blackwell, 1–15.

2. Bartolini S, Bilancini E, Pugno M. 2013. Did the decline in social connections depress Americans' happiness? *Social Indicators Research* 110(3): 1033–59.

3. Colbert AE, Bono JE, Purvanova RK. 2016. Flourishing via workplace relationships: Moving beyond instrumental support. *Academy of Management Journal* 59(4): 1199–223.

4. Demir M, Weitekamp LA. 2007. I am so happy 'cause today I found my friend: Friendship and personality as predictors of happiness. *Journal of Happiness Studies* 8(2): 181–211.

5. Kristof-Brown AL, Zimmerman RD, Johnson EC. 2005. Consequences of individuals' fit at work: A meta-analysis of person-job, person-organization, person-group, and person-supervisor fit. *Personnel Psychology* 8(2): 281–342.

6. Seppala E, Rossomando T, Doty JR. 2013. Social connection and compassion: Important predictors of health and well-being. *Social Research* 80(2): 411–30.

7. Shakespeare-Finch J, Daley E. Workplace belongingness, distress, and resilience in emergency service workers. *Psychological Trauma: Theory, Research, Practice, and Policy* 2017; 9(1): 32–5.

8. Shilling AA, Brown CM. 2016. Goal-driven resource redistribution: An adaptive response to social exclusion. *Evolutionary Behavioral Sciences* 10(3): 149–67.

9. Baumeister RF, Leary MR. 1995. The need to belong: Desire for interpersonal attachments as a fundamental human motivation. *Psychological Bulletin* 117(3): 497–529.

10. Gere J, MacDonald G. 2010. An update of the empirical case for the need to belong. *Journal of Individual Psychology* 66(1): 93–115.

11. Obst PL, White KM. 2007. Choosing to belong: The influence of choice on social identification and psychological sense of community. *Journal of Community Psychology* 35(1): 77–90.

12. Oaklander M. 2015. Why chasing happiness might be making you miserable. *Time* 186(14): 28.

13. Shifron R. 2010. *Adler's Need to Belong as the Key for Mental Health*, 10–29. Austin: University of Texas Press.

14. Begen FM, Turner-Cobb JM. 2015. Benefits of belonging: Experimental manipulation of social inclusion to enhance psychological and physiological health parameters. *Psychology and Health* 30(5): 568–82.

15. Gunther Moor B, Crone EA, van der Molen MW. 2010. The heartbrake of social rejection: Heart rate deceleration in response to unexpected peer rejection. *Psychological Science* 21(9): 1326–33.

16. Schopenhauer A, De Caro A, Janaway C. 2017. *Parerga and Paralipomena: Short Philosophical Essays*, vol. 2. *Tijdschrift voor Filosofie* 79(1): 155–58.

17. Romero-Canyas R, Downey G, Reddy KS, Rodriguez S, Cavanaugh TJ, Pelayo R. 2010. Paying to belong: When does rejection trigger ingratiation? *Journal of Personality and Social Psychology* 99(5): 802–23.

18. Wesselmann ED, Butler FA, Williams KD, Pickett CL. 2010. Adding injury to insult: Unexpected rejection leads to more aggressive responses. *Aggressive Behavior* 36(4): 232–37.

19. Chester DS, DeWall CN. 2017. Combating the sting of rejection with the pleasure of revenge: A new look at how emotion shapes aggression. *Journal of Personality and Social Psychology* 112(3): 413–30.

20. Kouchaki M, Wareham J. 2015. Excluded and behaving unethically: Social exclusion, physiological responses, and unethical behavior. *Journal of Applied Psychology* 100(2): 547–56.

21. Maner JK, DeWall CN, Baumeister RF, Schaller M. 2007. Does social exclusion motivate interpersonal reconnection? Resolving the "porcupine problem." *Journal of Personality and Social Psychology* 92(1): 42–55.

22. Matschke C, Sassenberg K. 2010. Does rejection lead to disidentification? The role of internal motivation and avoidance strategies. *European Journal of Social Psychology* 40(6): 891–900.

23. Asch SE. 1956. Studies of independence and conformity: A minority of one against a unanimous majority. *Psychological Monographs: General and Applied* 70(9): 1–70.

24. Morrison KR, Matthes J. 2011. Socially motivated projection: Need to belong increases perceived opinion consensus on important issues. *European Journal of Social Psychology* 41(6): 707–19.

25. Grossman, CL. 2002. John Paul II is history's champion saintmaker. *USA Today*, October 2.

26. Herbert TT, Estes RW. 1977. Improving executive decisions by formalizing dissent: The corporate devil's advocate. *Academy of Management Review* 2(4): 662–67.

27. Manning K. 2013. How many saints are there? *US Catholic* 78(11): 46.

28. Gerbasi A, Porath CL, Parker A, Spreitzer G, Cross R. 2015. Destructive de-energizing relationships: How thriving buffers their effect on performance. *Journal of Applied Psychology* 100(5): 1423–33.

29. Van Maanen J, Schein EH. 1979. Toward a theory of organizational socialization. *Research in Organizational Behavior* 1: 209.

30. Kammeyer-Mueller J, Wanberg C, Rubenstein A, Song Z. 2013. Support, undermining, and newcomer socialization: Fitting in during the first 90 days. *Academy of Management Journal* 56(4): 1104–24.

31. Korte R. 2010. "First, get to know them": A relational view of organizational socialization. *Human Resource Development International* 13(1): 27–43.

32. Bauer TN, Bodner T, Erdogan B, Truxillo DM, Tucker JS. 2007. Newcomer adjustment during organizational socialization: A meta-analytic review of antecedents, outcomes, and methods. *Journal of Applied Psychology* 92(3): 707–21.

33. Tong C, Kram KE. 2013. The efficacy of mentoring: The benefits for mentees, mentors, and organizations. In Passmore J, Peterson DB, Freire T, eds., *The Wiley-Blackwell Handbook of the Psychology of Coaching and Mentoring*, 217–42. Hoboken, NJ: Wiley-Blackwell.

34. Farnese ML, Bellò B, Livi S, Barbieri B, Gubbiotti P. 2016. Learning the ropes: The protective role of mentoring in correctional police officers' socialization process. *Military Psychology* 28(6): 429–47.

35. Boyatzis RE, Smith ML, Blaize N. 2006. Developing sustainable leaders through coaching and compassion. *Academy of Management Learning and Education* 5(1): 8–24.

36. Lee E-S, Park T-Y, Koo B. 2015. Identifying organizational identification as a basis for attitudes and behaviors: A meta-analytic review. *Psychological Bulletin* 141(5): 1049–80.

37. Slotter EB, Winger L, Soto N. 2015. Lost without each other: The influence of group identity loss on the self-concept. *Group Dynamics: Theory, Research, and Practice* 19(1): 15–30.

38. Kern ML, Della Porta SS, Friedman HS. 2014. Lifelong pathways to longevity: Personality, relationships, flourishing, and health. *Journal of Personality* 82(6): 472–84.

CHAPTER 8: MEANING

1. Kauppinen A. 2013. Meaning and happiness. *Philosophical Topics* 41(1): 161–85.

2. Smith A. 1985. *An Inquiry into the Nature and Causes of the Wealth of Nations.* Indianapolis: Liberty Classics.

3. Kornhauser A. 1965. *Mental Health of the Industrial Worker: A Detroit Study.* Oxford: Wiley.

4. Schwartz A. 1982. Meaningful work. *Ethics: An International Journal of Social, Political, and Legal Philosophy* 92: 634–46.

5. Wolf S. 2014. Happiness and meaning: A plurality of values rather than a conflict of norms. *Proceedings of the American Philosophical Society* 158(1): 18–24.

6. Cascio WF. 2003. Responsible restructuring: Seeing employees as assets, not costs. *Ivey Business Journal* 68(2): 1–5.

7. Burrell T. 2017. Why am I here? *New Scientist* 80–83.

8. George LS, Park CL. 2016. Meaning in life as comprehension, purpose, and mattering: Toward integration and new research questions. *Review of General Psychology* 20(3): 205–20.

9. Hofer J, Busch H, Au A, Poláčková Šolcová I, Tavel P, Tsien Wong T. 2014. For the benefit of others: Generativity and meaning in life in the elderly in four cultures. *Psychology and Aging* 29(4): 764–75.

10. Lips-Wiersma M, Morris L. 2009. Discriminating between "meaningful work" and the "management of meaning." *Journal of Business Ethics* 88(3): 491–511.

11. *The Why of Work*, 46–47. 2012. Adrenalin Publishing.

12. Herman RE, Gioia JL, Chalkley T. 1998. Making work meaningful: Secrets of the future-focused corporation. *Futurist* 32(9): 24–38.

13. Are you stuck in a "bullshit job"? (Bartleby). 2018. *Economist*, March 31, 414(9091).

14. Graeber, D. 2008. *Bullshit Jobs: A Theory.* New York: Simon & Schuster.

15. Bunderson JS, Thompson JA. 2009. The call of the wild: Zookeepers, callings, and the double-edged sword of deeply meaningful work. *Administrative Science Quarterly* 54(1): 32–57.

16. Duffy RD, Allan BA, Autin KL, Bott EM. 2013. Calling and life satisfaction: It's not about having it, it's about living it. *Journal of Counseling Psychology* 60(1): 42–52.

17. Dik BJ, Duffy RD, Eldridge BM. 2009. Calling and vocation in career counseling: Recommendations for promoting meaningful work. *Professional Psychology: Research and Practice* 40(6): 625–32.

18. Frankl VE, Lasch I. 1992. *Man's Search for Meaning: An Introduction to Logotherapy.* 4th ed. Boston: Beacon Press.

19. Das AK. 1998. Frankl and the realm of meaning. *Journal of Humanistic Education and Development* 36(4): 199.

20. Bailey C, Madden A. 2016. What makes work meaningful—or meaningless. *MIT Sloan Management Review* 57(4): 53–61.

21. Amabile T, Kramer S. 2012. How leaders kill meaning at work. *McKinsey Quarterly* (1): 124–31.

22. Omansky R, Eatough EM, Fila MJ. 2016. Illegitimate tasks as an impediment to job satisfaction and intrinsic motivation: Moderated mediation effects of gender and effort-reward imbalance. *Frontiers in Psychology*, 7.

23. Feinberg J. 1973. *Social Philosophy.* Englewood Cliffs, NJ: Prentice Hall.

24. Kube S, Marechal MA, Puppe C. 2012. The currency of reciprocity: Gift exchange in the workplace. *American Economic Review* 102(4): 1644–62.

25. Hackman JR, Oldham G, Janson R, Purdy K. 1975. A new strategy for job enrichment. *California Management Review* 17(4): 57–71.

26. Roberts G. 2016. Honda introduces "flowing cell" production system in Thailand. *Aroq—Just-Autocom (Global News),* April 21, 3.

27. Michaelson C, Pratt MG, Grant AM, Dunn CP. 2014. Meaningful work: Connecting business ethics and organization studies. *Journal of Business Ethics* 121(1): 77–90.

28. Grant AM. 2011. How customers can rally the troops. *Harvard Business Review* 89(6): 96–103.

29. Cameron KS, Spreitzer GM. 2012. *The Oxford Handbook of Positive Organizational Scholarship.* New York: Oxford University Press.

30. Allan BA, Duffy RD, Collisson B. 2018. Helping others increases meaningful work: Evidence from three experiments. *Journal of Counseling Psychology* 65(2): 155–65.

31. Reijseger G, Schaufeli WB, Peeters MCW, Taris TW, van Beek I, Ouweneel E. 2013. Watching the paint dry at work: Psychometric examination of the Dutch Boredom Scale. *Anxiety, Stress and Coping: An International Journal* 26(5): 508–25.

32. McIntyre KP, Mattingly BA, Lewandowski GW, Simpson A. 2014. Workplace self-expansion: Implications for job satisfaction, commitment, self-concept clarity, and self-esteem among the employed and unemployed. *Basic and Applied Social Psychology* 36(1): 59–69.

33. Seifert T, Hedderson C. 2010. Intrinsic motivation and flow in skateboarding: An ethnographic study. *Journal of Happiness Studies* 11(3): 277–92.

34. Van Iddekinge CH, Roth PL, Putka DJ, Lanivich SE. 2011. Are you interested? A meta-analysis of relations between vocational interests and employee performance and turnover. *Journal of Applied Psychology* 96(6): 1167–94.

35. Kowal J, Fortier MS. 1999. Motivational determinants of flow: Contributions from self-determination theory. *Journal of Social Psychology* 139(3): 355–68.

36. Csikszentmihalyi M, Montijo MN, Mouton AR. 2018. Flow theory: Optimizing elite performance in the creative realm. In Pfeiffer SI, Shaunessy-Dedrick E, Foley-Nicpon M, Pfeiffer SI, Shaunessy-Dedrick E, Foley-Nicpon M, eds., *APA Handbook of Giftedness and Talent,* 215–29. Washington, DC: American Psychological Association.

37. Burke R. 1971. "Work" and "Play." *Ethics: An International Journal of Social, Political, and Legal Philosophy* 82: 33–47.

38. O'Brien E, Roney E. 2017. Worth the wait? Leisure can be just as enjoyable with work left undone. *Psychological Science* 28(7): 1000–1015.

39. Plass JL, Homer BD, Kinzer CK. 2015. Foundations of game-based learning. *Educational Psychologist* 50(4): 258–83.

40. Lepper MR, Greene D. 1975. Turning play into work: Effects of adult surveillance and extrinsic rewards on children's intrinsic motivation. *Journal of Personality and Social Psychology* 31(3): 479–86.

41. Cerasoli CP, Nicklin JM, Ford MT. 2014. Intrinsic motivation and extrinsic incentives jointly predict performance: A 40-year meta-analysis. *Psychological Bulletin* 140(4): 980–1008.

42. Byron K, Khazanchi S. 2012. Rewards and creative performance: A meta-analytic test of theoretically derived hypotheses. *Psychological Bulletin* 138(4): 809–30.

43. Klink PC, Jentgens P, Lorteije JAM. 2014. Priority maps explain the roles of value, attention, and salience in goal-oriented behavior. *Journal of Neuroscience* 34(42): 13867–69.

44. Krebs RM, Boehler CN, Egner T, Woldorff MG. 2011. The neural underpinnings of how reward associations can both guide and misguide attention. *Journal of Neuroscience* 31(26): 9752–59.

45. Rowlands M. 2015. The immortal, the intrinsic and the quasi meaning of life. *Journal of Ethics: An International Philosophical Review* 19(3–4): 379–408.

46. Metz T. 2012. The meaningful and the worthwhile: Clarifying the relationships. *Philosophical Forum* 43(4): 435–48.

47. Sayre-Mccord G. 1988. *Essays on Moral Realism.* Ithaca, NY: Cornell University Press.

48. Free exchange. 2015. *Economist* 417(8962): 80.

49. Dittmar H, Bond R, Hurst M, Kasser T. 2014. The relationship between materialism and personal well-being: A meta-analysis. *Journal of Personality and Social Psychology* 107(5): 879–924.

50. Michaelson C. 2008. Work and the most terrible life. *Journal of Business Ethics* 77(3): 335–45.

CHAPTER 9: AUTONOMY

1. Ryan RM, Deci EL. 2017. *Self-Determination Theory: Basic Psychological Needs in Motivation, Development, and Wellness.* New York: Guilford Press.

2. Legault L, Inzlicht M. 2013. Self-Determination, self-regulation, and the brain: Autonomy improves performance by enhancing neuroaffective responsiveness to self-regulation failure. *Journal of Personality and Social Psychology* 105(1): 123–38.

3. Buss S. 2005. Valuing autonomy and respecting persons: Manipulation, seduction, and the basis of moral constraints. *Ethics* 115(2): 195–235.

4. Maslow AH. 1971. *The Farther Reaches of Human Nature.* New York: Arkana/Penguin Books.

5. Lenton AP, Bruder M, Slabu L, Sedikides C. 2013. How does "being real" feel? The experience of state authenticity. *Journal of Personality* 81(3): 276–89.

6. Boyraz G, Waits JB, Felix VA. 2014. Authenticity, life satisfaction, and distress: A longitudinal analysis. *Journal of Counseling Psychology* 61(3): 498–505.

7. Wood AM, Linley PA, Maltby J, Baliousis M, Joseph S. 2008. The authentic personality: A theoretical and empirical conceptualization and the development of the Authenticity Scale. *Journal of Counseling Psychology* 55(3): 385–99.

8. van den Bosch R, Taris TW. 2014. Authenticity at work: Development and validation of an individual authenticity measure at work. *Journal of Happiness Studies* 15(1): 1–18.

9. Oshana MAL. 2007. Autonomy and the question of authenticity. *Social Theory and Practice: An International and Interdisciplinary Journal of Social Philosophy* 33(3): 411–29.

10. Ntoumanis N, Healy LC, Sedikides C, et al. 2014. When the going gets tough: The "why" of goal striving matters. *Journal of Personality* 82(3): 225–36.

11. Knoll M, Lord RG, Petersen LE, Weigelt O. 2016. Examining the moral grey zone: The role of moral disengagement, authenticity, and situational strength in predicting unethical managerial behavior. *Journal of Applied Social Psychology* 46(1): 65–78.

12. Carr MD, Mellizo P. 2013. The relative effect of voice, autonomy, and the wage on satisfaction with work. *International Journal of Human Resource Management* 24(6): 1186–201.

13. Pierce JL, O'Driscoll MP, Coghlan A-M. 2004. Work environment structure and psychological ownership: The mediating effects of control. *Journal of Social Psychology* 144(5): 507–34.

14. Pierce JL, Gardner DG, Cummings LL, Dunham RB. 1989. Organization-based self-esteem: Construct definition, measurement, and validation. *Academy of Management Journal* 32(3): 622–48.

15. Aronson E, Carlsmith JM. 1963. Effect of the severity of threat on the devaluation of forbidden behavior. *Journal of Abnormal and Social Psychology* 66(6): 584–88.

16. Yagil D. 2015. Display rules for kindness: Outcomes of suppressing benevolent emotions. *Motivation and Emotion* 39(1): 156–66.

17. Wagner SH, Parker CP, Christiansen ND. 2003. Employees that think and act like owners: Effects of ownerships beliefs and behaviors on organizational effectiveness. *Personnel Psychology* 56(4): 847–71.

18. Janz BD, Wetherbe JC, Davis GB, Noe RA. 1997. Reengineering the systems development process: The link between autonomous teams and business process outcomes. *Journal of Management Information Systems* 14(1): 41–68.

19. Moreno-Luzón MD, Begoña Lloria M. 2008. The role of non-structural and informal mechanisms of integration and coordination as forces in knowledge creation. *British Journal of Management* 19(3): 250–76.

20. Janz BD, Prasarnphanich P. 2003. Understanding the antecedents of effective knowledge management: The importance of a knowledge-centered culture. *Decision Sciences* 34(2): 351.

21. Patanakul P, Chen J, Lynn GS. 2012. Autonomous teams and new product development. *Journal of Product Innovation Management* 29(5): 734–50.

22. Lumpkin GT, Brigham KH, Moss TW. 2010. Long-term orientation: Implications for the entrepreneurial orientation and performance of family businesses. *Entrepreneurship and Regional Development* 22(3–4): 241–64.

23. Lumpkin GT, Cogliser CC, Schneider DR. 2009. Understanding and measuring autonomy: An entrepreneurial orientation perspective. *Entrepreneurship: Theory and Practice* 33(1): 47–69.

CHAPTER 10: SELF-ACCEPTANCE

1. Huang C. 2010. Mean-level change in self-esteem from childhood through adulthood: Meta-analysis of longitudinal studies. *Review of General Psychology* 14(3): 251–60.

2. Orth U, Robins RW, Widaman KF. 2012. Life-span development of self-esteem and its effects on important life outcomes. *Journal of Personality and Social Psychology* 102(6): 1271–88.

3. von Soest T, Wichstrøm L, Kvalem IL. 2016. The development of global and domain-specific self-esteem from age 13 to 31. *Journal of Personality and Social Psychology* 110(4): 592–608.

4. Wagner J, Lüdtke O, Jonkmann K, Trautwein U. 2013. Cherish yourself: Longitudinal patterns and conditions of self-esteem change in the transition to young adulthood. *Journal of Personality and Social Psychology* 104(1): 148–63.

5. Chung JM, Robins RW, Trzesniewski KH, Noftle EE, Roberts BW, Widaman KF. 2014. Continuity and change in self-esteem during emerging adulthood. *Journal of Personality and Social Psychology* 106(3): 469–83.

6. Keller RT. 2012. Predicting the performance and innovativeness of scientists and engineers. *Journal of Applied Psychology* 97(1): 225–33.

7. Crocker J, Wolfe CT. 2001. Contingencies of self-worth. *Psychological Review* 108(3): 593–623.

8. Crocker J, Brook AT, Niiya Y, Villacorta M. 2006. The pursuit of self-esteem: Contingencies of self-worth and self-regulation. *Journal of Personality* 74(6): 1749–71.

9. Bowling NA, Eschleman KJ, Wang Q. 2010. A meta-analytic examination of the relationship between job satisfaction and subjective well-being. *Journal of Occupational and Organizational Psychology* 83(4): 915–34.

10. Burton JP, Hoobler JM. 2006. Subordinate self-esteem and abusive supervision. *Journal of Managerial Issues* 18(3): 340–55.

11. Brown JD. 2010. High self-esteem buffers negative feedback: Once more with feeling. *Cognition and Emotion* 24(8): 1389–404.

12. Steindl SR, Kirby JN, Tellegan C. 2018. Motivational interviewing in compassion-based interventions: Theory and practical applications. *Clinical Psychologist* 22(3): 265–79.

13. Neff K. 2003. Self-Compassion: An alternative conceptualization of a healthy attitude toward oneself. *Self and Identity* 2(2): 85.

14. Neff K, Germer C. 2017. Self-Compassion and psychological well-being. In Seppälä EM, Simon-Thomas E, Brown SL, et al., eds., *The Oxford Handbook of Compassion Science*, 371–85. New York: Oxford University Press.

15. Neff KD, Vonk R. 2009. Self-Compassion versus global self-esteem: Two different ways of relating to oneself. *Journal of Personality* 77(1): 23–50.

16. Smeets E, Neff K, Alberts H, Peters M. 2014. Meeting suffering with kindness: Effects of a brief self-compassion intervention for female college students. *Journal of Clinical Psychology* 70(9): 794–807.

17. Roeser RW, Peck SC. 2009. An education in awareness: Self, motivation, and self-regulated learning in contemplative perspective. *Educational Psychologist* 44(2): 119–36.

18. Johnson EA, O'Brien KA. 2013. Self-Compassion soothes the savage ego-threat system: Effects on negative affect, shame, rumination, and depressive symptoms. *Journal of Social and Clinical Psychology* 32(9): 939–63.

19. Dutton JE, Workman KM, Hardin AE. 2014. *Compassion at Work*, 277–304. Palo Alto, CA: Annual Reviews.

20. Kernis MH. 2003. Toward a conceptualization of optimal self-esteem. *Psychological Inquiry* 14(1): 1.

21. Harder DW. 1984. Character style of the defensively high self-esteem man. *Journal of Clinical Psychology* 40(1): 26–35.

22. Orth U, Robins RW, Meier LL, Conger RD. 2016. Refining the vulnerability model of low self-esteem and depression: Disentangling the effects of genuine self-esteem and narcissism. *Journal of Personality and Social Psychology* 110(1): 133–49.

23. Tracy JL, Cheng JT, Robins RW, Trzesniewski KH. 2009. Authentic and hubristic pride: The affective core of self-esteem and narcissism. *Self and Identity* 8(2/3): 196–213.

24. Lubit R. 2002. The long-term organizational impact of destructively narcissistic managers. *Academy of Management Executive* 16(1): 127–38.

25. Bagnoli C. 2009. The Mafioso case: Autonomy and self-respect. *Ethical Theory and Moral Practice: An International Forum* 12(5): 477–93.

26. Jackson RA. 2012. The wall of deceit. *Internal Auditor* 69(6): 36–41.

27. Casserly M. 2012. When snitches get stitches: Physical violence as workplace retaliation on the rise. *Forbescom*, September 21, 44.

28. Monin B, Sawyer PJ, Marquez MJ. 2008. The rejection of moral rebels: Resenting those who do the right thing. *Journal of Personality and Social Psychology* 95(1): 76–93.

29. Malmstrom FV, Mullin D. 2014. Why whistleblowing doesn't work. *Skeptic* 19(1): 30–35.

30. Silvia PJ, Duval TS. 2001. Objective self-awareness theory: Recent progress and enduring problems. *Personality and Social Psychology Review* 5(3): 230–41.

31. Bateson M, Nettle D, Roberts G. 2006. Cues of being watched enhance cooperation in a real-world setting. *Biology Letters* 2(3): 412–14.

32. Pfattheicher S, Keller J. 2015. The watching eyes phenomenon: The role of a sense of being seen and public self-awareness. *European Journal of Social Psychology* 45(5): 560–66.

33. Smith JK. 2014. Art as mirror: Creativity and communication in aesthetics. *Psychology of Aesthetics, Creativity, and the Arts* 8(1): 110–18.

34. Romanowska J, Larsson G, Theorell T. 2014. An art-based leadership intervention for enhancement of self-awareness, humility, and leader performance. *Journal of Personnel Psychology* 13(2): 97–106.

CHAPTER 11: SELF-CONFIDENCE

1. McNatt DB. 2000. Ancient Pygmalion joins contemporary management: A meta-analysis of the result. *Journal of Applied Psychology* 85(2): 314–22.

2. Babad EY, Inbar J, Rosenthal R. 1982. Pygmalion, Galatea, and the Golem: Investigations of biased and unbiased teachers. *Journal of Educational Psychology* 74(4): 459–74.

3. Bandura A. 1989. Human agency in social cognitive theory. *American Psychologist* 44(9): 1175–84.

4. Gist ME. 1987. Self-Efficacy: Implications for organizational behavior and human resource management. *Academy of Management Review* 12(3): 472–85.

5. Stajkovic AD, Luthans F. 1998. Self-Efficacy and work-related performance: A meta-analysis. *Psychological Bulletin* 124(2): 240–61.

6. Judge TA, Bono JE. 2001. Relationship of core self-evaluations traits—self-esteem, generalized self-efficacy, locus of control, and emotional stability—with job

satisfaction and job performance: A meta-analysis. *Journal of Applied Psychology* 86(1): 80–92.

7. Hass RW, Katz-Buonincontro J, Reiter-Palmon R. 2018. The creative self and creative thinking: An exploration of predictive effects using Bayes factor analyses. *Psychology of Aesthetics, Creativity, and the Arts* (May): 1–13.

8. Karwowski M, Beghetto RA. 2018. Creative behavior as agentic action. *Psychology of Aesthetics, Creativity, and the Arts* (July): 1–14.

9. Liu Z, Riggio RE, Day DV, Zheng C, Dai S, Bian Y. 2019. Leader development begins at home: Overparenting harms adolescent leader emergence. *Journal of Applied Psychology*, advance online.

10. van Ingen DJ, Freiheit SR, Steinfeldt JA, et al. 2015. Helicopter parenting: The effect of an overbearing caregiving style on peer attachment and self-efficacy. *Journal of College Counseling* 18(1): 7–20.

11. Schiffrin H, Liss M, Miles-McLean H, Geary K, Erchull M, Tashner T. 2014. Helping or hovering? The effects of helicopter parenting on college students' well-being. *Journal of Child and Family Studies* 23(3): 548–57.

12. Reed K, Duncan JM, Lucier-Greer M, Fixelle C, Ferraro AJ. 2016. Helicopter parenting and emerging adult self-efficacy: Implications for mental and physical health. *Journal of Child and Family Studies* 25(10): 3136–49.

13. Miller CC, Bromwich JE. 2019. The unstoppable snowplow parent (Style Desk). *New York Times*, March 17, ST1.

14. Breckenridge LM. 2017. Curbing the "helicopter commander": Overcoming risk aversion and fostering disciplined initiative in the U.S. Army. *Military Review* 97(4): 14–21.

15. Lorinkova NM, Pearsall MJ, Sims Jr HP. 2013. Examining the differential longitudinal performance of directive versus empowering leadership in teams. *Academy of Management Journal* 56(2): 573–96.

16. Maynard MT, Luciano MM, D'Innocenzo L, Mathieu JE, Dean MD. 2014. Modeling time-lagged reciprocal psychological empowerment–performance relationships. *Journal of Applied Psychology* 99(6): 1244–53.

17. Seibert SE, Wang G, Courtright SH. 2011. Antecedents and consequences of psychological and team empowerment in organizations: A meta-analytic review. *Journal of Applied Psychology* 96(5): 981–1003.

18. Raub S, Liao H. 2012. Doing the right thing without being told: Joint effects of initiative climate and general self-efficacy on employee proactive customer service performance. *Journal of Applied Psychology* 97(3): 651–67.

19. Brewer N, Wells GL. 2006. The confidence-accuracy relationship in eyewitness identification: Effects of lineup instructions, foil similarity, and target-absent base rates. *Journal of Experimental Psychology: Applied* 12(1): 11–30.

20. Moore DA, Healy PJ. 2008. The trouble with overconfidence. *Psychological Review* 115(2): 502–17.

21. Greenberg S, Stephens-Davidowitz S. 2019. You underestimate yourself (op-ed). *New York Times*, April 7.

22. Van Zant AB, Moore DA. 2013. Avoiding the pitfalls of overconfidence while benefiting from the advantages of confidence. *California Management Review* 55(2): 5–23.

23. ohnson DDP, Fowler JH. 2011. The evolution of overconfidence. *Nature* 477(7364): 317–20.

24. Jones N. 2002. The underdog might win the day. *New Scientist*, August 3, 22.

25. Charness G, Rustichini A, de Ven Jv. 2011. Self-Confidence and strategic deterrence. *Tinbergen Institute Discussion Papers*.

26. Elizabeth H. 2017. Alaska's 40 years of oil riches almost never was. *National Public Radio*.

27. Whyte G, Saks AM. 2007. The effects of self-efficacy on behavior in escalation situations. *Human Performance* 20(1): 23–42.

28. Brosseau-Liard PE, Poulin-Dubois D. 2014. Sensitivity to confidence cues increases during the second year of life. *Infancy* 19(5): 461–75.

29. Tenney ER, Small JE, Kondrad RL, Jaswal VK, Spellman BA. 2011. Accuracy, confidence, and calibration: How young children and adults assess credibility. *Developmental Psychology* 47(4): 1065–77.

30. Kominsky JF, Langthorne P, Keil FC. 2016. The better part of not knowing: Virtuous ignorance. *Developmental Psychology* 52(1): 31–45.

31. Vergauwe J, Wille B, Hofmans J, Kaiser RB, De Fruyt F. 2017. Too much charisma can make leaders look less effective. *Harvard Business Review Digital Articles*, 2–6.

32. Vergauwe J, Wille B, Hofmans J, Kaiser RB, De Fruyt F. 2018. The double-edged sword of leader charisma: Understanding the curvilinear relationship between charismatic personality and leader effectiveness. *Journal of Personality and Social Psychology* 114(1): 110–30.

33. Howell JM, Avolio BJ. 1992. The ethics of charismatic leadership: Submission or liberation? *Executive* 6(2): 43–54.

34. Stajkovic AD, Lee D, Nyberg AJ. 2009. Collective efficacy, group potency, and group performance: Meta-analyses of their relationships, and test of a mediation model. *Journal of Applied Psychology* 94(3): 814–28.

35. Gully SM, Joshi A, Incalcaterra KA, Beaubien JM. 2002. A meta-analysis of team-efficacy, potency, and performance: Interdependence and level of analysis as moderators of observed relationships. *Journal of Applied Psychology* 87(5): 819–32.

36. Fransen K, Haslam SA, Steffens NK, Vanbeselaere N, De Cuyper B, Boen F. 2015. Believing in "us": Exploring leaders' capacity to enhance team confidence and performance by building a sense of shared social identity. *Journal of Experimental Psychology: Applied* 21(1): 89–100.

37. Jong Ad, Ruyter Kd, Wetzels M. 2006. Linking employee confidence to performance: A study of self-managing service teams. *Journal of the Academy of Marketing Science* 34(4): 576–87.

38. Karau SJ, Williams KD. 1993. Social loafing: A meta-analytic review and theoretical integration. *Journal of Personality and Social Psychology* 65(4): 681–706.

39. Osborn KA, Irwin BC, Skogsberg NJ, Feltz DL. 2012. The Köhler effect: Motivation gains and losses in real sports groups. *Sport, Exercise, and Performance Psychology* 1(4): 22–53.

CHAPTER 12: GROWTH

1. Arnold J, Clark M. 2016. Running the penultimate lap of the race: A multimethod analysis of growth, generativity, career orientation, and personality amongst men in mid/late career. *Journal of Occupational and Organizational Psychology* 89(2): 308–29.

2. Yan Q, Bligh MC, Kohles JC. 2014. Absence makes the errors go longer: How leaders inhibit learning from errors. *Zeitschrift für Psychologie* 222(4): 233–45.

3. Heslin PA, VandeWalle D. 2008. Managers' implicit assumptions about personnel. *Current Directions in Psychological Science* 17(3): 219–23.

4. Dweck CS. 2012. Mindsets and human nature: Promoting change in the Middle East, the schoolyard, the racial divide, and willpower. *American Psychologist* 67(8): 614–22.

5. Silvia PJ, Beaty RE, Nusbaum EC, Eddington KM, Levin-Aspenson H, Kwapil TR. 2014. Everyday creativity in daily life: An experience-sampling study of "little c" creativity. *Psychology of Aesthetics, Creativity, and the Arts* 8(2): 183–88.

6. du Plock S. 2017. Everyday therapy: Putting the wonderment back into our daily lives. *Existential Analysis: Journal of the Society for Existential Analysis* 28(1): 93–105.

7. Kaufman JC. 2018. Finding meaning with creativity in the past, present, and future. *Perspectives on Psychological Science* 13(6): 734–49.

8. Stoll JD. 2019. A KitchenAid recipe for a tight job market: Companies discover investment in workers as a way to keep churn low. *Wall Street Journal*, February 2, B5.

9. Huang X, Iun J. 2006. The impact of subordinate-supervisor similarity in growth-need strength on work outcomes: The mediating role of perceived similarity. *Journal of Organizational Behavior* 27(8): 1121–48.

10. Wolters CA. 2004. Advancing achievement goal theory: Using goal structures and goal orientations to predict students' motivation, cognition, and achievement. *Journal of Educational Psychology* 96(2): 236–50.

11. Bakker AB, van Woerkom M. 2018. Strengths use in organizations: A positive approach of occupational health. *Canadian Psychology/Psychologie canadienne* 59(1): 38–46.

12. Douglass R, Duffy R. 2015. Strengths use and life satisfaction: A moderated mediation approach. *Journal of Happiness Studies* 16(3): 619–32.

13. Gladwell M. 2008. *Outliers: The Story of Success.* Boston: Little, Brown.

14. Ullén F, Hambrick DZ, Mosing MA. 2016. Rethinking expertise: A multifactorial gene-environment interaction model of expert performance. *Psychological Bulletin* 142(4): 427–46.

15. Eskreis-Winkler L, Shulman EP, Young V, Tsukayama E, Brunwasser SM, Duckworth AL. 2016. Using wise interventions to motivate deliberate practice. *Journal of Personality and Social Psychology* 111(5): 728–44.

16. Lisman J, Sternberg EJ. 2013. Habit and nonhabit systems for unconscious and conscious behavior: Implications for multitasking. *Journal of Cognitive Neuroscience* 25(2): 273–83.

17. Wood W, Neal DT. 2007. A new look at habits and the habit-goal interface. *Psychological Review* 114(4): 843–63.

18. Graybiel AM, Smith KS. 2014. Good habits, bad habits. *Scientific American* 310(6): 38–43.

19. Neal DT, Wood W, Quinn JM. 2006. Habits: A repeat performance. *Current Directions in Psychological Science* 15(4): 198–202.

20. Wink P, Staudinger UM. 2016. Wisdom and psychosocial functioning in later life. *Journal of Personality* 84(3): 306–18.

21. Le TN. 2011. Life satisfaction, openness value, self-transcendence, and wisdom. *Journal of Happiness Studies* 12(2): 171–82.

22. Flitter E. 2018. Bank fires a broker long accused of abuse. *New York Times,* April 3, B3.

INDEX

Affordable Care Act, 79

agency, company stories about, and perception of company commitment, 26

Alaska, oil exploration in, 162–163

Arkadium: awards for excellence at, 112; company profile, 185; culture of gratitude in, 64; displays of values and goals at, 144; employee development programs, 157; feedback culture at, 143–144; performance evaluations at, 122; and positive feedback, emphasis on, 144; sabbaticals offered by, 170

art: on campuses of best companies, 150–151; and objective self-awareness, 150, 151

arts and crafts by employees: companies encouraging, 171; and stimulation of creativity, 171–172

Asch, Solomon, 96

authentic self, expression of: companies encouraging, 127–129; positive effects of, 129

autonomy: benefits of, 134; companies supporting, 85; definition of, 5, 126; freedom to be authentic self, 127–129; and job satisfaction, 130; and meaning in work, 115–116; and people-centric human resources departments, 13; as practice of best companies, 136–137; and sense of ownership, 130–134; support for, in companies with learning environments, 172, 181; as universal human need, 5

autonomy of teams, 134–137; alternative names for, 135; best uses of, 135; and practical utility, ensuring of, 136

bad behavior: power differentials and, 52–53; proliferation in uncontrolled company culture, 51–52

BAF. *See* Big Ass Fans

Bagnoli, C., 36

BambooHR: autonomy allowed to employees, 85; company profile, 185–186; core values of, 55–56; and culture of respect, 16, 18; egalitarian work spaces at, 84; and employee growth, support for, 174; empowerment of workforce at, 158; life skills classes for employees, 56; overtime work, discouragement of, 84–85; panda mascot of, 84; policy on nonjudgmental discussion of mistakes, 27–28; quality of life as central goal of, 55, 69; support for employee time off, 86–87

Basic Family Budget Calculator, 77

basic needs, and calculation of poverty line, 76–79

Basic Needs Budget Calculator, 77

Bell Labs, 136

belonging: and atonement for rejected behaviors, 95; criteria for, 92; definition of, 5; and happiness, 91; need for, and pressure to conform, 95–96; negative effects of exclusion, 94–95; psychological benefits of, 91, 93; as universal human need, 5, 92; US decline in, 91; value of, 105

belonging, employees' sense of: activities for developing, 92–94; counterproductiveness of superficial exercises in, 92; good companies' awareness of importance, 92;